HARDPRESS.NET
HOME OF HARD-TO-FIND BOOKS

An Essay on Mr. Pope's Odyssey
by Joseph Spence

Address:
HardPress
8345 NW 66TH ST #2561
MIAMI FL 33166-2626
USA
Email: info@hardpress.net

AN ESSAY ON Pope's *ODYSSEY*:

IN WHICH
Some particular *Beauties* and *Blemishes* of that Work are consider'd.

——— ——— Each finding, like a friend,
Something to blame, and something to commend.
Pope's Miscel. Vol. I.

Le choix des grans mots *donne aux choses une espece d' ame & de vie; les* beaux mots *sont la lumiere propre et naturelle de nos pensées: mais un discours* tout simple *exprimera quelquefois mieux la chose, que toute la pompe & tout l' ornement.* Boileau.

Printed for *James* and *J. Knapton*, R. *Knaplock*, *W.* and *J. Innys*, *J. Wyatt*, *D. Midwinter*, Booksellers in St. *Paul*'s Church-Yard, *LONDON*: And *S. Wilmot*, Bookseller in *OXFORD*. 1726.

Price One Shilling and Six-Pence.

THE

PREFACE.

THERE is no Person more Odious than the Man who makes himself greatly Eminent. It is a sort of tacit Reproach on the rest of the Species: and every one feels his own meanness the more sensibly, when he looks toward those exalted Genius's, who have gain'd a Superiority over the rest of mankind. This may make it obvious to imagine, that the following Dialogues are partly design'd as Invectives; and produc'd chiefly from that Blind-side in Self-love, which makes Men willing to derogate from every one, who has *merit* enough, to provoke; and *fame* enough, to make others think themselves lessen'd by the overgrowth of his Character.

Tho' this reasoning be exceedingly true in general, it ought to be consider'd ſider'd, at the ſame time, that any diſlike to the Eminence of others naturally ariſes, only among ſuch perſons, as are got into the ſame paths of Fame. The Gentlemen of the Sword cannot bear to have others riſe over their head; the Men of Genius look maliciouſly on a prevailing Poet: But *Pope*, I preſume, never envied *Marlborough* the Battle of *Blenheim*, any more than that Hero envied him his Tranſlation of the *Iliad*.

'Tis for this Reaſon I might almoſt ſay, that I *cannot* envy Mr. *Pope*. So far at leaſt I am unbiaſs'd; I can hear the Applauſes, which are given that Great Man; I can admire the Paſſages, which contribute to the deſerving them; but I cannot be uneaſy at thoſe, or detract from theſe, out of any prejudices ariſing from this Paſſion. Give me leave to ſay farther, that in reading that Work of his, which occaſion'd this Eſſay, no one cou'd be more delighted, than I was, in ſeveral parts of it. Many Beauties I ſaw in it; and I imagin'd I ſaw ſome

Faults:

Faults : In ſome particular Converſations on this Head, I have found my ſelf indifferent in the Caſe : and now I have here flung the Thoughts on both together, I hope, with ſome degree of Impartiality. But if ſome things ſhou'd be blamed without ſufficient Reaſon, or others commended too highly, and in a manner diſproportion'd to what they deſerve, I ſubmit each to the many better judges, who may happen to meet with theſe ſheets. I ask pardon for any Errors in them : I beg to be ſet right.

Prefaces, I think, are the only places in which a Man may be allow'd to talk freely of that worſt of ſubjects, *Himſelf* : I hope no body will deny one the uſe of ſo *aukward a Privilege;* and ſhall therefore go on without any farther Apologies.

To many it may perhaps ſeem arrogant to find fault at all with ſo diſtinguiſh'd and ſo noble a Poet as Mr. *Pope*. Indeed here are ſome things propoſed as faulty from his Tranſlation ; but they are only propoſed: the

World is to judge of them. Where I have been miſtaken in any of theſe Points, it is not for want of a due deference to the merits of this Writer; but from the ſhortneſs of my own ſight. On the contrary, if any ſuch Criticiſms happen ſometimes to be right, the Eminence of the Poet will be ſo far from being a reaſon againſt them, that it makes any true Cautions the more proper, and in ſome ſenſe perfectly neceſſary.

Beſides: The learned World, as I take it, have ever allow'd a Liberty of thinking and of ſpeaking one's ſentiments. That *ſerene Republick* knows none of the diſtance and diſtinctions which cuſtom has introduced into all others. There is a decent familiarity to be admitted between the Greateſt and the Meaneſt Perſon in it. This has often raiſed a Thought in me, which has ſomething wild and agreeable in it, when indulged to any degree: 'Tis in Relation to the peculiar happineſs of Men of Letters; in that they can ſit down in their cloſets

and

and converſe with the greateſt Writers of every Age, or of any Nation; and that in as much freedom and intimacy, as their neareſt Friends cou'd ever uſe toward any of them, when living. What an illuſtrious Aſſembly is there on thoſe Shelves? The Courts of *Auguſtus*, *Lewis* the Fourteenth, or *Charles* the Second, never beheld ſuch a frequency of great Genius's, as ſtand round a Man in his own private Study. How large an Happineſs is it for a Perſon to have it in his Power to ſay at any time, That he is going to ſpend the Afternoon with the moſt agreeable and moſt improving Company, he will chuſe out of all Ages? If he is in a gay Humour, perhaps with *Horace* and *Anacreon*, and L[d] *Dorſet*; or if more ſolid, either with *Plato*, Mr. *Locke*, or Sir *Iſaac Newton*.

'Tis this eaſe of acceſs, 'tis the liberty ariſing from it, which conſtitutes and preſerves the felicity of the *Republick* of Letters. The meaner ſort, which compoſe it, are all Free-

voters;

voters; and may ſpeak their real Opinion without reſerve: at the ſame time the Characters too, even of the greateſt and firſt Men in it, muſt be form'd and eſtabliſh'd on this openneſs of Judging, and that freedom of Obſervation.

But waving whatever has been ſaid of this Liberty in the Learned World, moſt people will be apt to help one to an Excuſe of another kind: for moſt, I think, are very ready to agree, that Mr. *Pope* is only the Maſter-hand in this Tranſlation; and that he has been obliged with the aſſiſtance of ſome other Gentlemen in ſeveral parts of it. Tho', I believe, I am acquainted with this affair more than many who ſpeak of it with a great deal of Confidence and Aſſurance, any mention of it in the Piece is purpoſely avoided. Mr. *Pope* has recommended the whole with his Name; He gives the finiſhing ſtroke to every thing: and the Dialogues ſpeak of him, as if he were really the Author of the whole. It

wou'd

wou'd have been a confuſed thing, and often not practicable, to have ſpoken at every turn to the right Perſon. This has occaſion'd ſeveral applauſes of the Poet, which may ſeem too high for a ſtranger: But as I have ſince had the greateſt reaſon to be perſwaded, that Mr. *Pope* is not the ſole Tranſlator; I have at the ſame time equal reaſon to think, that the other Gentlemen engaged are perſons of eſtabliſh'd Characters in the Poetick World. —After this, perhaps, thoſe Compliments may ſtill be allow'd to ſtand, as they are: I hope they are never wrought too high for Mr. *Pope* himſelf; and I believe they may generally be ſpoken very juſtly of his *Seconds* in the Work.

One word more, and I have done. As to the manner of theſe Dialogues; 'Tis the old *Platonick* way, which *Cicero* brought from *Greece*, and uſed ſo happily in the *Latin* Tongue. It has had its Succeſſes too among the Moderns: *Fontenelle* will always be read with the greateſt Pleaſure, where he he has follow'd it; That Writer is peculiarly happy in all his Dialogues, of whatever ſort; and, in general, may be ſaid *to talk as well with Pen and Ink,* as any Man in the World. Mr. *Dryden* and Mr. *Addiſon* have recommended it among us by their Example. Indeed the method it ſelf is more capable of variety, and (which makes it particularly proper for the preſent Caſe) it hath ſomething of Action and Reality in it. Beſides that the common way among us of merely keeping up a Diſcourſe between two blind Names, is perhaps not very Commendable: the Perſons of the Dialogue in ſuch Caſes are generally like thoſe Actors, who have no Character in the Play; and who only come in *to talk* upon the Stage. They have no more diſtinction, no other marks by which you may know one from another, than the two *Capital Letters*, which uſually ſtand for them. It is much otherwiſe, and and much better, among the Perſons introduced by the Writers in the other method:

method: their Great Names I uſe only to authorize this *manner* of Dialogue, as that is all which I can pretend to imitate in them.

As I ought to beg pardon of the Reader, for troubling him with ſo long a Preface; I ſhall at the ſame time take the opportunity of begging Pardon of *Antiphaus* and *Philypſus*, (the two Gentlemen who are diſguiſed under the Perſons of theſe Dialogues) for giving to the World, what was chiefly their Thoughts, in a manner ſo much inferiour to what either of them might have done themſelves. I wiſh I might have leave to mention their real Names in this place: That would add a weight to every thing they ſay. Tho' indeed the Sentiments of thoſe Gentlemen, were they fully repreſented, would not want the luſtre of any Authorities to ſet them off; except that of the the Reaſonableneſs with which they both *think* and *ſpeak*; and for both which they have made themſelves ſo remarkable in the World.

AN

An ESSAY &c.

EVENING the FIRST.

ANTIPHAUS manag'd his Affairs so as to get this Winter sooner than usual to the Country-seat of his Friend *Philypsus*. It is there that he passes his time, when ever he can clear himself from the hurry of Business, in a retirement every way agreeable; and in a full enjoyment of those Pleasures, which attend on a particular Friendship, in an open and improving Conversation. The Conversation there does not run in the present polite way of *saying and saying nothing*; when alone, they usually fall into some Points of Learning; and as both of them are particularly fond of Poetry, their Disputes turn more frequently on that Subject, than any other. Indeed their differing in Sentiment can scarce be call'd *Disputes*; for whenever their Thoughts do not meet, each of them shews a diffidence in his own Opinion, and a willingness to submit to the Judgment of his Friend.

It is by this means that they fall into each others Sentiments, more than cou'd well be expected from Men of so different a Turn. The enlarged Genius of *Philypsus* always led him to dwell upon the most beautified Parts of a Poem with the greatest Pleasure; while *Antiphaüs*, who has a very clear Head, and has given much into a strict way of thinking, is taken most with just Descriptions, and plain natural Ideas: The one was so possest with the Pleasure which he felt from fine Thoughts and warm Expressions, that He did not take a full Satisfaction in low Beauty, and simple Representations of Nature; the other, on the contrary, had such an aversion to *glitterings* and *elevation*, that he was distasted at any the least appearance of either. If the latter was prejudiced for the Ancients, from the Purity and Justness, which we find in most of their Works; *Philypsus* had his *foible* too, and

was

was ſometimes caught by the Flouriſh and Colouring of the Moderns. In a word, if *Philypſus* wou'd ſometimes contemn a Point as low and mean, tho' in reality proper enough, and naturally expreſs'd; *Antiphaus*, in his turn, might happen now and then to blame a Paſſage which requir'd a good degree of Ornament, as being too glaring and artificial.

Among ſeveral other Topicks, one Evening, they happen'd to fall into a diſcourſe on Mr. *Pope*'s new Tranſlation of the *Odyſſey*. As they both found Beauties in that Piece agreeable to their particular Taſtes, they had read it over with a great deal of Pleaſure: however *Philypſus* was the Perſon who admired it the moſt. "There are ſome Lines, ſays he to *Antiphaus* (pointing to the *Odyſſey* which lay before them) there are ſome Favourites of mine in that Poem, which you muſt not look upon with your uſual ſeverity: Prithee *Antiphaus*, be more ſenſible to the Flame and Spirit of a Writer, who is evidently Our preſent *Laureate in Genius*, and the moſt enliven'd Tranſlator of the Age. "I will very readily allow what you ſay of that Great Man, return'd *Antiphaus*; and ſhall always pay a deference to your more lively taſte of the Fine and Sublime in Poetry; but you muſt give me leave to diſſent from you in ſome Particulars: if I do not agree with your Sentiments, in relation to ſeveral Lines and Paſſages of that Tranſlation, 'tis perhaps becauſe I fall ſo much ſhort of you, in your *inward ſenſe* of the high and elevated Beauties of Language. As I cannot imagine that to be the reaſon, ſays *Philypſus*, I beg to hear thoſe Particulars you talk'd of; I am perſwaded, ſeveral of the Paſſages, which I have obſerv'd you to be leſs taken with in reading the Tranſlation, will upon a cloſer view appear to be really Beauties; to tell you the truth, I long to make a Convert of you; and beg you wou'd be full and large in communicating whatever Remarks you have made on this Performance. The Evenings are long; we have ſufficient time upon our Hands; and I know not how we can paſs it away more agreeably.

Antiphaus paus'd for ſome time, and ſeem'd to be taken up in recollecting his Thoughts on this Point: at laſt taking a Tablet out of his Pocket, "Since you "deſire it (ſays he) I will ſhew you what "Obſervations I made as I went over the "Work; they are the Thoughts which "ſtruck me *en paſſant*, and many of them "will perhaps appear little and trifling.

You

You will allow me, I believe, in the first place, That Lines very good in themselves, may be bad when consider'd as a Translation. The aim of a Translator is to give us the *Spirit* of the Original; and where the Original is just, the very *manner* is to be observ'd. By the Manner, I would not intend the express words, or the meer turn of a Period; but that the Imitation ought to be easy, simple, and unadorn'd, wherever the first Writer uses either of those Styles with Judgment. You are well acquainted with that plain humble manner of *Homer*, which is more particularly kept up by him in the *Odyssey:* And as much as I admire several parts in this Translation, I cannot but think there are places in it, which differ from the Manner of *Homer*, without sufficient reason for a Change. The Poet, in several parts of that Work, seems to me to have let fall some Lines that are forc'd; some of too much flourish, and ornament; and a few, even swelling, and unnatural; where the Original is with good reason plain, and natural, and unadorn'd.

Where we admire the Simplicity of *Homer* with Justice, we cannot avoid blaming the want of it in his Translator. Mr. *Pope* intimates in one of his (*a*) Notes,

(*a*) B. 14. 1.

That no Reproach has ever fall'n upon *Homer*, in relation to his ſinking too Low, or being too Familiar; That as to theſe Particulars he preſerves an Univerſal Juſtneſs: and that there is not any one place in his Poem, which can be juſtly cenſur'd upon this account. If ſo, a Tranſlator of *Homer* has no occaſion for raiſing any thing, beyond what it is in the Original; If he follows his Maſter it is ſufficient: All additional Flouriſh and Glitterings, where we ſhould meet with the plain and the familiar, are at beſt ſo many beautiful Excreſcencies.

There is one Caſe, which ſeems more particularly to lead Mr. *Pope* into a glaring Stile: 'tis almoſt ever to be found in his Deſcriptions of *Day*, of *Light*, and of the *Morning*. 'Tis true, theſe are ſubjects which in themſelves may require ſome brightneſs in the language; but there is a great difference between giving one Light, and dazling ones Eyes. Beſide the conformity to the Original, there is another certain and eaſy way of judging, whether the Brightning in theſe or any other Points, be proper or not: that Light, we may be ſure, falls in a wrong manner, or an undue proportion, which does not make the thing more viſible.

There

There are of theſe Deſcriptions, *Philypſus*, which ſeem both to refine too much upon the Original, and to err according to this Rule. Did you ever obſerve thoſe lines on one of the moſt agreeable Images in the World, The break of Day? they are in the beginning of the third Book: If you will give me leave, I will read them to you.

The *ſacred* Sun, above the Waters rais'd,
Thro' Heaven's *eternal, brazen Portals blaz'd*;
And wide o'er Earth diffus'd his *cheating* Ray,
To Gods and Men, *to give the golden Day*.

Several of theſe Expreſſions ſeemed to me at firſt ſight to take from the Nature and Simplicity of the Deſcription; and when I turn'd to the Greek, I found thoſe very Expreſſions to have no Foundation there. 'Tis the ſame Caſe in the following Lines:

(*a*) Soon as the Morn, in *orient Purple dreſt*,
Unbarr'd the Portal of the roſeate Eaſt &c.
(*b*) — When the Morning-Star with early Ray
Flam'd in the front of Heaven, &c. ———

You will find theſe ſhort Sketches in *Homer* to be much more ſimple and natu-

(*a*) Tranſlat. Book 4, V. 411. Orig. ℣ 306.
(*b*) B. 13, 112. ℣ 93.

ral:

ral: I leave it to your Judgment, whether they appear better with theſe Colourings, or not. To add one Inſtance more of the ſame thing. Is it more proper for *Circe* to tell *Ulyſſes*, That he ſhould ſtay that Night with her, and *ſet ſail the next Morning?* or to hear her giving him leave, to

(a)Spread his broad Sails, and *plough the liquid way*,
Soon as the Morn *unveils her Saffron Ray*.

I muſt own, ſays *Philypſus*, this would have been more fit for the Deſcription of a Voyage, than for a Speech: in a Place too, where we only find Orders given for ſetting Sail at ſuch a time.

To me, proceeded *Antiphaus*, Mr. *Popé* ſeems to Beautify too much in ſeveral other Points, beſide thoſe Topicks we have been talking of: as where he calls the Nobles of *Phœacia*, (b) *A radiant Band* of Noblemen; and where he introduces *Helen* with (c) *a Gale of rich Perfume breathing before her*. If *Homer* mentions *Cups of ſolid Gold*; in Mr. *Pope*,

(d) The Gold gives *luſtre* to the *purple* Draught:
(e)And in the *dazling* Goblet *laughs* the Wine.

(a) B. 12, 35. μ' 24.—ἅμα δ' ἠοῖ φαινομένηφι Πλεύσεσθ'———

(b) B. 6, 306. ζ' 257. (c) B. 4, 158. δ' 121.

(d) B. 1, 188. α' 142. (e) B. 3, 601. γ' 472.

You

You cannot but obſerve, by the way, that the Original here is deſigned to ſignify the *real* intrinſick Value; while only the *outſide* and more glittering Circumſtances are what the *Engliſh* dwells upon entirely: but to go on. ——— The Horns of a Bullock are in this new Language, (*a*) *Budding Honours*; and thoſe of a Ram (if I am not much miſtaken) (*b*) *tranſlucent Creſcents*. *Pallas* is well known to have had *Blue Eyes* given her by the Ancients; now it is

(*c*) Celeſtial Azure brightning in her Eyes.

This heightning of things, by a ſevere Critick might be thought blameable; and indeed whenever it interferes, where the Paſſions ought to be touch'd, it certainly is ſo in an higher degree. The Reader is delighted when, after a melancholly Scene, he ſees *Penelope* reviv'd by a Meſſage from the Gods; and (*d*) ſecretly enjoying the Satisfaction of her Soul: but what Paſſion, what Idea has he, when inſtead of this he is told of her (*d*) *Hearts dilating and glowing with florid Joy?* ——— Paint to him that unhappy

(*a*) B. 3, 493. γ' 384. (*b*) B. 4, 107. δ' 85. (*c*) B. 1, 408. δ' 314. (*d*) B. 4, 1096. δ' 840.

Princeſs

Princeſs in her Diſtreſs, retiring *ſilently*, and crying herſelf to Sleep; only ſhew the Circumſtances, and the Reader muſt be moved: Does her Behaviour and her Sufferings ſtrike him ſo forcibly, when he finds it embelliſh'd into

(a) ——*Echoing Grief*, and *Silver-ſtreaming Eyes*?

But however theſe Paſſages may ſeem to be weaken'd by the finery and luxuriance of the Language, this certainly is not ſo much the fault of *Pope*, as of the Age: We give much into an airy way: If a Verſe runs off ſmooth, 'tis no matter for depth or clearneſs; and as the Ancients valued Thoughts more than Sound, we ſeem to be taken with Sounds more than Thought. To ſpeak out, we are got into an idle manner of Verſifying; and if Mr. *Pope* ſometimes falls into it, we are not ſo much to blame him for thoſe Particulars, as to wonder, that he does not do it more frequently, in ſo general a debauch of Taſte among us.

Hold (interrupted *Philypſus*) if You go on at this rate, You will ſeem only to be got into the old Cant of running down our own Times: I do not believe, but that I cou'd name ſome Poet among us,

(a) B. 1, 462. & 363.

to

to anſwer any of thoſe who flouriſh'd in the *Auguſtan* Age. As to the preſent Point, we rarely hear of any ſuch thing as *Tranſlation* among them: In *Satyr*, we have the great Names of *Rocheſter*, *Dryden*, and *Oldham*: (not to mention the new kind of Satyr, introduc'd among us by *Butler*.) In *Critical Poems*, there are (You know) two or three very good, beſide that incomparable Piece by Mr. *Pope*, all to weigh againſt poor *Horace*. As for *miſcellaneous* Subjects; think of *Cowley*, *Pope*, *Waller* and *Pryor*, to mention no more of them. In the *Epick*, *Milton* may diſpute the Laurel with either *Virgil*, or *Homer*; and in *Dramatick* Pieces, of either kind, we have Writers that indiſputably exceed any of the Ancients.

Antiphaus was not inclin'd to enter into a diſpute of this nature. "I was only ſpeaking, ſays he, of our preſent Taſte in Poetry, and the prevailing manner of thoſe writers who are now upon the Stage. As to this, *Philypſus*, give me leave to ſay, that the language of our Writers, and the practice of the World, is much infected with the *Fineſſe*. I think 'tis Mr. *Locke* obſerves, *that the humours of a People, may be learnt from their uſage of words.* This ſymptom of the diſeaſe is very ſtrong in the preſent Caſe: thus to ſay that a verſe

is

is *bien tourné* is the highest commendation among the French Criticks: in general, the *Beau Monde* is the only name now, for what was call'd by a very different one formerly; as a *fine* Scholar, *polite* Literature, and the *Belles Lettres* are the leading expressions, when we would speak of Learning in the best sense. And I appeal to you, who are so well acquainted with all our Poets, whether their practise, in particular, does not fall more and more into the *Finesses*, we have been complaining of. We may partly judge of this from some Lines in the Best of them, the Writer whose Works lye before us: I was just going to give you a few more instances of it, from the *Odyssey*.

Is there any Figure so much abus'd by the Moderns, as what they call the *Antithesis*? they run it into a down right playing upon Words. *Cowley*'s Poetry cou'd not *live* without it: *Dryden* uses it almost perpetually, in his Translation of *Virgil*; and was ridicul'd, You know, on that head by the late Duke of *Buckingham*. I have observ'd with pleasure, that Mr. *Pope*, in his Translation, very much avoids this little beauty, which the other affected so excessively; yet I have a place before me, where one of this kind has slipt from his Pen: It runs thus. (He

is

is speaking of a Stranger's Arrival at the Court of *Penelope*, disorder'd so much by the riot of the Suitors.)

——When, to taste her hospitable board,
Some Guest arrives, with rumours of her Lord;
(*a*) And these *indulge their want*, and *those their woe*;
And *here the tears*, *and there the goblets flow*.

Pardon me, says *Philypsus*, there you do not seem to do the Translator Justice; the Figure is countenanc'd by *Homer* himself: You see here is an *Antithesis* in the Original. "That (answer'd *Antiphaus*) seems rather to be a Contrast, to set the riot of the Suitors in a stronger light: But call it what you please, it is only single there, whereas you see it multiplied, and worn to Rags in the Translation. This over-doing a Point is observable in many other Cases, as much as in the former; and in some, is carried on to a degree which borders upon the *Forc'd*, and *Unnatural*.

Telemachus, bursting into Tears at the Name of his Father, endeavours to hide his Sorrow from *Menelaus*, who was then talking with him. *Homer* says only, that (*b*) *Menelaus observ'd him*;

(*a*) B. 14, 426. ξ', 376. (*b*) B. 4, 154. δ, 116. ——, νόησε δέ μιν Μενέλαος.

which words Mr. *Pope* draws out into this Couplet:

> The Conscious Monarch pierc'd the coy disguise,
> And view'd his filial love with vast surprize.

For an humble natural Description of a Tripod (or Caldron) set upon the Fire, I wou'd recommend you to the following lines:

> The Flames *climb* round it with a *fierce embrace*;
> (*a*) The fuming Waters *bubble o'er the Blaze.*

But above all, in my Opinion, are these on a Person tired and quite spent:

> —— *Lost in lassitude lay all the Man,*
> (*b*) Depriv'd of Voice, of Motion, and of Breath;
> *The Soul scarce waking, in the Arms of Death.*

Or these:

> (*c*) Ye Gods! since this *worn frame refection knew,*
> What scenes have I survey'd of dreadful view?

Wou'd you Imagine, that all which countenances this in the Original, is a Passage in *Ulysses*'s Speech after his Ship-

---

(*a*) B. 8, 474. θ', 437. Γάστρην μὲν τρίποδος πῦρ ἄμφεπε, θέρμετο δ' ὕδωρ. (*b*) B. 5. 585 ε', 456. (*c*) B. 6. 262. ζ', 220. —— δηρὸν ἀπὸ χροός) ἐστιν ἀλοιφή.

wreck,

wreck, in which he intimates, *That he had not bath'd for a considerable time?*

I find it so, (says *Philypsus*) and own the Lines to be somewhat forc'd and unnatural; indeed those you have repeated seem generally to draw too near to that Character. But I cannot conceive by what means they found so harsh to me at present: when I read the Piece, there was scarce a Line of them which gave me any offence. —— Yes; it must be by your tearing them from the Body of the work, that they now seem not so agreeable. Really, *Antiphaus*, this is not fair usage of an Author; You rob them of their Order and Connection; and 'tis thence that they perfectly lose the Beauty, which they had in the Whole. Very true, reply'd *Antiphaus*; the warmth of Reading, the thread of the Story, and a general tunableness in the Verse, will carry a Man on strangely; and may sometimes cheat him into a false Pleasure. But then it is for this very reason, that I shou'd think, the justest method of forming a judgment on Particulars is, to consider them apart. However, let us try it for once in a more entire Passage, than any of the former. Let me see; The place I have dipt upon, is where *Minerva* tells *Ulysses* that she will transform him into the figure of an Old Man; that he may view the posture of his Affairs unsuspected and unknown: The Lines in *Homer* may be thus read into English.

Οδ. ν', 397, to 403.

"I will make you (says that Goddess
"to the Hero) entirely unknown to all
"Men; the beauty and smoothness of
"your Skin shall be taken away, your
"Limbs bent, and the Hair of your Head
"turn'd grey. I will then fling a Garb
"over you that shall make you frightful
"and odious to those that see you. All
"that flame and life in your Eyes shall
"be lost; I will so far deform them that
"you shall look contemptible to all the
"Suitors, to your own *Penelope*, and to
"your Son, whom You left yet an In-
"fant in your Palace.

You know that Mr. *Pope*, in comparing some Passages in the Prophesies of *Isaiah* with the famous Eclogue of *Virgil*, turns the latter into Prose; If we follow that Example in the present case, his Translation of these Lines runs thus:

Od. 13. V. 453, to 464.

It fits thee at present, to wear a dark disguise, and walk secret, unknown to the Eyes of Mortals; For this my Hand shall wither every Beauty, and every elegance of of Form and Face, *Spread* a bark of Wrinkles *over thy ſmooth Skin, turn* the auburn honours of thy Head *hoar, disfigure with coarſe attire every Limb, and extinguiſh all the Fire in thy Eyes; add all the decays of Life, and all the wants of it, eſtrange thee from thy Own, thy Son and thy Wife;* every ſight *ſhall turn from the loath'd object, and the blind ſuitors* ſcorn their deſtruction.

Give me leave to go out of my way a little, to try the ſame Experiment on a ſingle Paſſage from the *Iliad*, which is flouriſh'd, and ſet off in an extraordinary manner. It is in the Nineteenth Book, where we have a poetical account of a fine Breed of Horſes; The Original runs thus:

Ἰλ. ύ, 221. 225.

"Three Thouſand Mares graz'd theſe
" Meads, with their young Foals run-
" ning by them; *Boreas* was enamour'd
" of them as they fed there, and turn-
" ing himſelf into the ſhape of a fine
" black Horſe, accompliſh'd his deſires:
" Of this breed, were twelve of the Colts.

Mr. *Pope*'s Tranſlation, (only allowing equivalent Expreſſions to blind the Rhimes) runs thus:

Iliad, B. 20. V. 262. 270.

His ſpacious Paſtures bred three Thouſand Mares, and three Thouſand *Foals fed beside* their Mothers: *Boreas enamour'd of the* sprightly train, *conceal'd his* Godhead in the Locks of Hair *that flow'd over his Shoulders*; *he* neigh'd *to his* Loves with dissembled Voice, *and* cours'd the dapple Beauties *o'er the Meadow*: *Twelve others of* unrival'd sort *sprung hence*, swift as their Mother *Mares* and Father *Wind*.

This, if over-wrought, is the more blameable, because the matter is carried very far even in the Original, and so is the less capable of being stretch'd any farther. Mr. *Pope*, in his note upon the Place observes, *That Homer has the happiness of making the least Circumstance considerable*; *and that the plainest matter* shines *in his dress of Poetry*. It is true, it shines sufficiently in that. Some brightning is necessary in Poetry: but an excess of it, *Philypsus*, may dazle, or may blind our Eyes; it can never assist, or delight them.

By comparing these Passages, You will see that which I intend; the difference of Manner in the Ancient and Modern Poetry: In the latter we find Expressions added, which seem to be added for beauties, and which in reality perhaps only turn the Plainness and Strength of the Original, into the *Fine* and the *Artificial*.

Upon

Upon *Philypsus*'s acknowledging that he thought the Point too much labour'd, and the Translation unequal; Yes, says *Antiphaus*, the Translator himself seems to be sensible of it in the present Case; for soon after, when the former Passage is repeated in the (*a*) Original, he gives an entirely new (*b*) Turn to it; And I believe, upon hearing the Lines, you will be of opinion that (excepting a word or two) it is render'd with a better grace and with more Justice, than we find in the former.

She spake, then touch'd him with her powerful [Wand:
The Skin shrunk up, and wither'd at her Hand:
A swift Old-Age o'er all his Members spread,
A sudden Frost was sprinkled on his Head.
Nor longer in the heavy Eye-ball shin'd
The glance Divine, forth beaming from the Mind;
His Robe with Spots indelible besmear,
In Rags dishonest flutters with the Air.

Mr. *Pope* without question is happy in a great share of Judgment, as well as Vivacity and Spirit in Writing: but it is next to impossible, in so long a Translation, especially as it is in *Rhime*, not to give sometimes into Sound and Ornament; when to crown all, the Vogue of the World goes so strong for both. Do not ask, whether I should desire to see

(*a*) v', 430. (*b*) B. 13, 497.

both

both of them banisht out of Poetry; far from it: Expressive Sounds are of use in the most natural, and Variety in the management of them, is necessary to keep up Attention in the Reader: That, and Ornament, is what sets Poetry above Prose. All I wou'd say is this, that Sound is not sufficient where we might expect Sense; and that in *humble* Passages, in *natural* Descriptions, or in moving most of the *Passions*, additional ornaments are so many blemishes. Dressing up the expressiveness of *Homer*, in such fineries, is much the same as if one shou'd throw a very gay modern dress over the *Hercules* of *Farnese*, or any of the most Nervous Statues of the Ancients.

But You will allow Ornament, where the subject will bear it, and where the Original leads the Way?--In a translation (answer'd *Antiphaus*) it is proper perhaps, only in the latter Case; but allowing it in both, it shou'd never be over-wrought in either. Too much Finery is always Affectation: and I wish our Writers at present were not so generally given *to elevate and surprize, and all that,* as Mr. *Bayes* calls it.

The running into this excess so much, is what has unsinew'd our Poetry. 'Tis with Poetry, as it is in Buildings; the being

being vaſtly Studious of Ornament does not only take away from the Strength of the Work, but is a ſure token of a vitiated taſte in the Deſigner.

You are always blaming the Modern Refinements, ſays *Philypſus*; but will you not allow that this taſte of the Age is a ſufficient juſtification at leaſt of Mr. *Pope*, in thoſe caſes where he complies with it? —We muſt *write* ſo as to pleaſe the World, and *ſpeak* ſo as to be moſt eaſily underſtood: Cuſtom will often wear away the propriety of things of this Nature; and as for the propriety of language, that depends upon it entirely. I allow, to uſe your own thought, that a profuſion of Lace and Embroidery wou'd be a diſguiſe upon an Old Hero; but they are ſo far from being improper, that they are becoming on the Heroes of our Age.——

They may become the Heroes of our Age (replied *Antiphaus* ſmiling) perhaps on a far different account: there is another Character now wove into and blended with that of a Soldier, to which theſe things are very agreeable: How many are there of theſe Heroes, as you call them, whoſe Courage reaches no farther than their Sword-knot, and whoſe Conduct is taken up wholly in their Dreſs? But conſider a Man barely as a Soldier; think

think of him in the midſt of ſome warm Action, and theſe little Ideas of him will diſappear:- Then it is *that* poſture, *that* preſſing on the foe, *that* graſping of his Sword, *that* fierceneſs in his Eyes, *that* ſerenity and *that* eagerneſs on his countenance, which ſtrike us wholly, and take up all our attention. Yes, *Philypſus*, if you view a real modern Hero in a true light, thoſe fineries do not ſet well upon him: and I think, I never ſaw any thing more truly ridiculous, than the Piece we were laughing at the other Day, in your Picture-Gallery. —-Good Heaven! The Duke of *Marlbrough* in the heat of an Engagement, with a full-bottom'd Wigg, very carefully ſpread over his Shoulders!

But to return to the preſent taſte in Poetry.——If this Corruption of the Age cou'd excuſe a Writer for what he compoſes now, muſt it be carried down as far as *Homer's* Days? muſt his Heroes love, and talk, and fight *a-la-mode?* muſt his ſtrong, ſententious lines, be ſet to the new polite airs of *Handel* and *Bononcini?* Yet, were what you wou'd alledge of any force, it wou'd carry the matter thus far; and the whole *Iliad* and *Odyſſey* ought to be enervated down to the preſent taſte. No, whatever may be allow'd to any of the proper genuine productions of this Age,

Age, it ought not to make an inrode upon all others: let *Homer's energy* and *pathos* be violated as little as is possible; Nature ought to rule in his Works, and those of the Antients: as ornament, and surprize, and elevation, have in their turn the Empire of the Modern World.

You see I beg into shew the old heat, that this subject (I think) always betrays me into.——I beg pardon, *Philypsus*; and will attend more to what I am about for the future.—I shou'd have given you some instances of this *Elevation* from the translation before us. *A-propos*, What a glaring description of a Sword have we in the Eighth *Odyssey*?

——Whose blade of Brass *displays*
A ruddy gleam; whose hilt *a Silver blaze*;
(a) Whose ivory sheath *inwrought* with *curious pride*,
Adds *graceful terror to the wearer's side*.

Homer says, that *Hermione* was *as beautiful as Venus*; this is low and humble in comparison of Mr. *Pope's Hermione*,

(b) On whom *a radiant Pomp of Graces* wait,
Resembling *Venus* in *attractive state*.

Where a prodigy is sent to the *Ithacensians* in Council, *Homer* says that *they*

(a) B. 8, 437. V. 403. (b) B. 4, 19. V. 14.

were

were ſtruck at the ſight of it, and revolv'd in their Minds what it might preſage to them: this Mr. *Pope* renders after the following manner,

> (*a*) The wondring rivals gaze with cares oppreſt,
> And chilling horrors freeze in every Breaſt.

How mean is it, and how much like proſe, to tell us, that *Penelope heard the mirth of the Suitors?* to elevate this ſufficiently, You muſt ſay

> *(b) The ſhrilling Airs the vaulted Roof rebounds,*
> *Reflecting to the Queen the Silver Sounds.*

This falſe way of *animating* Poetry, as no doubt many will be pleas'd to call it, grows particularly prejudicial and abſurd in any caſe, where the *Paſſions* are to be raiſ'd in the Reader, or deſcrib'd in the Perſons of the Poem. Where we wou'd move Pity, in particular, nothing is (*c*) *more odious than a ſhew of Eloquence.* Nature has provided a Sympathy in our Souls; She has put a biaſs into our Temper, that inclines us forcibly to Compaſ-

(*a*) B. 2, 183. β' 156. (*b*) B. 4, 425. δ' 338.
(*c*) Odi reum cui eſſe diſerto vacet. *Quintil.* Lib. 11. c. 1.

ſion;

sion; and we shou'd (*a*) leave her to her own work in such points, without any of the impertinent assistances of Art.

The lines You have just repeated, interrupted *Philypsus*, are such as I cannot admire: but I think you carry the point too far against Art in general. Is there not the greatest Art required in moving the passions? why then have *Cicero*, and all the Criticks of old, given us so numerous rules in this Case? Yes, reply'd *Antiphaus*, great Art, or rather a great Genius, is very necessary toward any excellence this way. But what I have said was intended not so much against the *Use* of Art, as the *Appearances* of it. 'Tis the greatest of Arts, to conceal the Art you use; and to have it very evident, is the greatest of Blemishes. The Criticks, and *Cicero* in particular, speak with the greatest plainness against any thing of that kind. Where the passions are to be touch'd, apparent art is apparent fraud; so that here particular care should be taken, that nothing be over-wrought.

'Tis on this account, that when You compare the following lines to the Ori-

(*a*) Quicquid meris adjicietur affectibus, omnes eorum diluet vires, & miserationem securitate laxabit. *Quintil.* Instit. L. 11. c. 1.

ginal,

ginal, You will not, I dare say, be over fond of them:

The *Soul of Friendship to my hope is lost,*
(a) *Fated to wander from his natal coast.*
He said: *chill horrors* shook my *shivering Soul,*
(b) *Rack'd with Convulsive pangs in dust I roll.*

And that entire passage of *Penelope.*

Rolling Convulsive on the Floor, is seen
The piteous object of a prostrate Queen.
Words, to her dumb Complaint a pause supplies,
And breath, to waste in unavailing Cries:
Around their Sovereign wept the *menial Fair,*
(c) To whom she thus *address'd her deep despair,* &c.

I wish this false elevation and profusion of Ornament does not carry Mr. *Pope*, in some few Cases, into down right *Fustian.* (d) *A Man's being lost in Lassitude*, and a *Soul scarce waking, in the Arms of Death*, look'd very much that way. Do You remember where he talks of (e) *Princes on Princes roll'd*, and (f) *Gods being heap'd on Gods?* Or how in another place we are told, that

(g) ———— ——*The Pharian Isle*
Fronts the deep Roar of disemboguing Nile?

You know the Character of some of Sir *John Falstaff*'s Attendants, in the *Merry*

(a) B. 4, 248. Λ', 182. (b) B. 4. 726. Λ', 539.
(c) B. 4, 957. Λ' 721. (d) See p. 14.
(e) B, 11, 151. (f) Obs. 27. on B. 11, Ver. 383.
(g) B. 4, 480.

Wives

Wives of Windsor; a sort of Men, who are industrious in talking hard Words; and whose *Humour*, is to be *unintelligible*. One wou'd almost Imagine, the humble Account of shutting a Door, in the end of the First *Odyssey*, to be copied from those illustrious Originals:

——————————The Door *reclos'd*;
The Bolt, *Obedient* to the silken Cord,
(*a*) To the *strong Staple's inmost depth restor'd*,
Secur'd the Valves.——

I own (says *Philypsus*) I cannot but give up those lines to you, and several of the other You mention'd before. The first lines, when You repeated them, I took tobe the very worst, You could pick out of the *Odyssey*: But I know not how it comes about, You rise gradually in your demands upon me; and are got insensibly from lines in that piece, which were forc'd and too much beautified, to things unnatural, and shocking. When I thought of making a Convert of You to an entire admiration of Mr. *Pope*, I fancy, I was much mistaken; at this rate, you will turn the Tables upon me: and to tell You the truth, I cannot but confess, that

(*a*) B. 1, 555. *a*, 441.—Θύρην ἐπέρυσσε κορώνῃ Ἀργυρέῃ.——

the Poet has, in ſome Caſes, fallen into each of the faults You mention.

In ſome Caſes doubtleſs (reply'd *Antiphaus*) that Gentleman is not to be commended: I take his Tranſlation to be as good, as any Tranſlation of *Homer*, into *Engliſh*, and in *Rhime*, cou'd be expected to be; In all probability, we might ſafely add, that no other Writers of the Age cou'd, in the whole, have perform'd ſuch a task ſo well. But a perfect Piece of this kind cannot be expected: If *Homer* himſelf is allow'd to Sleep a little, his Tranſlator certainly may Nod ſometimes.———

One thing I obſerv'd (interrupted *Philypſus*) in the lines you have repeated; that the faultineſs of ſeveral of them was owing to an Exceſs in one of the greateſt Beauties of Poetry, I mean, the *Metaphors* too frequent in them. I obſerv'd the ſame (ſays *Antiphaus*) as I was collecting theſe little Remarks: it occaſion'd my uſing a particular Paper for that ſingle point: If it did not grow ſo late, I wou'd ſhew it to You; but——No, let us have it now, cry'd *Philypſus*: I never knew any thing of yours too long, and if it be that Paper in your Hand, I ſhou'd think it much too ſhort; were it not for my concern for the Poet, and the deſire

I

I have of finding as few Faults in his Writings as poſſible.

Metaphor, ſays *Philypſus*, is certainly the moſt univerſal enlivener of Poetry. At the ſame time that it adds to the dignity of Verſe, it gives it an agreeable variety; together with a power of Painting out all its Images, in the boldeſt and ſtrongeſt manner in the World. 'Tis this which animates thoſe objects, which muſt otherwiſe be ſtill and unaffecting: it flings every thing into Motion, Life, and Action: By this the Arrow is *eager* and on the Wing, by this the Sword *thirſts* for Blood, and the Spear *rages* in the Hands of the Warriour. *Metaphor* raiſes each ſubject out of the heavy narrative way: it creates new Beings; it repreſents the paſſions of Men, and even meer *Names*, as animated and imbodied; and ſhews them in the poſture and attitudes of Agents. Thus when the Battles are going to join, You ſee *Rage ſtalk* amidſt the Combatants; pointing with one *Hand* to the Enemy, and in the other, ſhaking the *Torch of War*. By this, the Valleys and Mountains *rejoice*, when *Peace* once more *ſpreads* her downy Wings, and *Plenty* deſcends from Heaven upon the *happy* climate. 'Tis *Metaphor* which makes the Woods and Caves *anſwer* to the voice of the Poet, and the murmuring Stream *compassionate* his complaints: 'Tis this which makes the *Nile know Cæsar*; and *the Sea*, its present *Monarch*.

If Mr. *Pope* manages this powerful Figure frequently to the best advantage, sometimes he happens not to be so happy in the use of it. The force of *Metaphor* is to make things strong, clear, and sensible: any confusion destroys the very end of it; and yet a little inaccuracy may occasion gross errors this way. Sometimes what is just with the *Figurative*, may disagree with the *Proper*: sometimes again, an idea which might stand with the *proper* expression, will be inconsistent with the *figurative*. A misapplication either way is very obvious, and yet it gives a jar to the Ideas, and makes the sense of a line to be perplexed and in confusion.

It sounds but oddly to talk of a Person, and of his Picture, without any manner of distinction: To say, that *the piece, drawn by Sir Godfrey Kneller for Mr. Pope, is an excellent Poet and Writes with the greatest Command imaginable*; Or, that *Mr. Pope is a very good piece, and his face very well colour'd, tho' he is but just recover'd from a fit of Sickness*; either of them wou'd carry a mixt incoherent sense with

them:

them: This I take to be partly the Case in the following Lines,

(a) Now from my *fond embrace* by Tempests torn,
Our other *Column of the State* is born;
Nor took a *kind adieu.*——
(b) They *sweep* Neptunes smooth *Face.*
(c) Declining, with his *sloping Wheels*
Down *sunk* the *Sun.*——

To say *the God of Light was driving his Car, down the Steep of Heaven* (as Mr. *Pope* somewhere expresses it) is metaphorical; To say *the Sun is setting*, is proper: but shou'd one say, *The Sun is setting with sloping Wheels*, This would be neither Metaphorical, nor Proper; nor cou'd it raise any thing in the Mind, but a confusion of Ideas.

Again:

(d) As some lone Mountain's monstrous growth he stood,
Crown'd with rough thickets and a nodding wood.

Again:

(e) Hear me, Oh *Neptune!* thou whose *Arms* are *hurl'd*
From Shore to Shore, and *gird* the solid World.

I think, *Neptune* has the luck of it; for 'tis the same Deity, that in another

(a) B 4, 962. Δ', 727. Παῖδ' ἀγαπητὸν——
(b) B. 9, 210. Ι, 180. Πολλὰ ἅλα πόντον ἐρετμοῖσι.
(c) B. 2, 437. Β, 388. Δύσετο Ἠέλιος.
(d) B. 9, 224. Ι, 192.——ῥίον ὑλήεντι
(e) B. 9, 618. Ι, 528. Κλῦθι, Ποσειδάων γαιήοχε——

place

place makes juſt ſuch a Figure, as I have ſeen him in ſome *Mortlock-Hangings*:

(*a*) The raging Monarch ſhook his *azure Head*,
And thus in ſecret to his Soul he ſaid. &c
(*b*) This ſaid, his *Sea-green Steeds* divide the Foam.

Such confuſions of the *Metaphor* and the *Proper* have a great reſemblance to that abſurdity (of mixing *Fable* and *Reality* together) which appears ſo groſly in Mr. *Dryden's Hind and Panther*; and which was the very thing, that provoked Lord *Halifax* to ridicule that Piece, with ſuch infinite humour and good ſenſe. The Noble Author's Words on that ſubject, may give a Side-light to what I mean in the preſent Caſe. Speaking of the Ancient Fabuliſts, " They wrote (ſays he (*c*) " in Signs, and ſpoke in Parables: all " their Fables carry a double meaning: " The Story is one and entire; The Cha- " racters the ſame throughout; not bro- " ken, or chang'd, and always conforma- " ble to the nature of the Creatures they " introduce. They never tell you that " *the Dog*, which *ſnapt* at a ſhadow, loſt " his *Troop of Horſe*; that wou'd be un- " intelligible.——This is his (*Dryden's*)

(*a*) B. 5, 365. 6, 285. (*b*) B. 5, 480. 6, 380.

(*c*) Preface to the *Hind and Panther Tranſvers'd.*

new

"new way of telling a Story, and con-
"founding the *Moral* and the *Fable* to-
"gether. After instancing from the *Hind and Panther*, he goes on thus. "What
"relation has the *Hind* to our *Saviour?*
"or what notion have we of a *Panther's*
"*Bible?* if you say, he means the *Church*,
"how does the *Church feed on Lawns, or*
"*range in the Forest?* Let it be always a
"Church, or always the Cloven-footed
"Beast, for we cannot bear his shifting
"the Scene every Line.

I had almost forgot to tell You, that upon consulting the Original there was no *Metaphor* at all to be found, for either of the Lines, I last repeated from the *Odyssey*. We have now *Metaphors* perpetually; the Translator is vastly fond of them. I need not say that an Excess this way is very blameable; You know the Criticks speak against it in a high strain, and one of them goes so far as to say, that this (*a*) *Figure, when frequent, obscures the Piece, and fatigues the Reader: when continual, 'tis no longer a Poem, 'tis all Allegory and Enigma.*

As a false Mixture of the proper and the figurative confuses the sense; The

(*a*) Frequens (*Metaphoræ usus*) & obscurat, & tædio complet: continuus vero in allegoriam & ænigma exit. *Quintil.* Instit. L. 8. c. 6.

joining

joining *Metaphors* together, which do not agree, makes it still more dark and perplexed. These are like (what they call) *Medley-Pieces*; a huddled kind of Pictures, which shew a Variety of Objects, flung together without any order or design: As that in the beginning of *Horace's Art of Poetry*, they join the Limbs of one Creature to the Body of another; and confuse all the properties and circumstances of an Action.

If the Poet be not very careful he may by these means tye not only things improper, but even contrarieties, together. Do not the following Lines border on this? to me the *Metaphors* in them seem to be improperly united.

From *Elatreus*'s strong Arm the *Discus* flies,
And *Sings with unmatch'd Force* along the Skies:
And *Laodame whirls high*, with dreadful sway,
(a) *The Gloves of Death.*——

At the same Time, nothing can be more *Proper* and *Narrative* than the Original in that place. *Again:*

(b) From his Eyes *pour'd down* the *tender Dew.*

(a) B. 8, 140. θ', 130.
Δίσκῳ δ' αὖ πάντων προφερέστατος ἦεν Ἐλατρεύς,
Πὺξ δ' αὖ Λαοδάμας——

(b) B. 11, 486. λ', 390.
——Θαλερὸν κατὰ δάκρυον εἴβων.

But

(a) But *Antichus* unable to controul,
Spoke *loud* the *languish* of his yearning Soul.

In these the Action is describ'd in words, that import a *violence*; while the Act to be express'd, is plainly something *still* and *gentle*.

Nothing is more known in relation to the *Metaphor*, than that rule of *Cicero's*; (b) *That it shou'd be so modest, as to seem to have been* handed *into the place of the proper Word, not to have forced its Way thither: it shou'd fall into it in a free,* voluntary *manner*. Otherwise it will make the sense dark and intricate; and that absolutely destroys all the use of it: for as *Metaphor* shou'd be the (b) *greatest Light and Ornament of Language, Obscurity is the most absurd thing, and the most to be avoided in Metaphor*.

If so, I wou'd ask whether it be very natural to talk of (c) *the Womb of a Vessel?* What congruity is there? What Idea have You of the *Forehead* of *Night*, of a *Star*, or of the *Heavens*? yet in the Tran-

(a) B. 4. 788. & 286.

(b) Verecunda debet esse Translatio, ut deducta esse in alienum locum, non irruisse; atque ut precario, non vi venisse videatur. —— Est hoc magnum ornamentum orationis, in quo obscuritas fugiend. est. *Cicero* de Oratore. Lib. 3.

(c) B. 2, 439.

flation

ſlation we meet with *Metaphors* of this kind: and tho' it may be tolerable to talk of *the* (*a*) *Front of Heaven*; the other two, (*b*) *The blazing Forehead of a Star*, and (*c*) *the Matron Brow of Night*, are ſcarce to be born with. For my part, I ſhou'd not have expected theſe Expreſſions from Mr. *Pope*: They rather put me in mind of another Gentleman, who in a Poem of his ſpeaking of the Church of *England*, ſays that

(*d*) Divinely bright her *Frontlet-Stars* appear'd,
While up towards Heaven her raviſh'd Eyes ſhe
[rear'd.

I deſire you would give me your Sentiments on another paſſage: what do you think of the Images in the following Line?

They cuff, they tear, their Cheeks, and Necks they
[*rend.*

Do You remember whom 'tis ſpoken of? Really, ſays *Philypſus*, I cannot well determine, whether it is ſpoken of *Men*, or of a couple of *Beaſts* fighting. —Of neither, anſwer'd *Antiphaus*: 'tis uſed of *Eagles* in the (*e*) *Odyſſey*; and in the (*f*) *Iliad*, of a couple of *Vultures*.

(*a*) B 13, 113. (*b*) B. 5, 352. (*c*) B. 1, 534. (*d*) *Tate*'s Mauſolæum. (*e*) B. 2, 179. (*f*) *Iliad* 16, 524.

There's

There is an Obſervation ariſing from this, which ought to be conſider'd, in transferring *Metaphors*: it may be ſaid, that the word *Cheeks* in this Verſe, is juſtified by the Original. Cuſtom, *Philypſus*, is the great Rule of Words: and what is eaſy in one Language, will not bear in another; becauſe uſage may have ſoften'd in one, what in the other is yet harſh and unwarrantable. This is evident from the very Word in debate. Thus we uſe *Cheeks* in Engliſh of ſome Creatures beſide Men; the Term is ſo far familiarized, and ſounds very well: Yet to talk of the Cheeks of a *Pheaſant*, or the Cheeks of a *Vulture*, will by no means ſound the ſofter for it's prevailing in thoſe other particulars.

However, this is agreed on all hands; that a *Metaphor* is not to be uſed, unleſs it gives a greater light, and makes the thing more ſenſible to us. Are the Borrow'd terms, in this Caſe, *more* expreſſive than the Native? Nay, do they give you *as clear* Ideas, as the Native would? Do they give you as clear, where the Poet talks of (*a*) *aſſwaging Thirſt with a generous Vintage*, or of *Polypheme*'s doing the ſame thing with a (*b*) *Milky deluge*? What do

(*a*) B. 6, 298. (*b*) B. 9, 353.

you think of an (*a*) *Ozier-fringed Bank*, of a *Voice* (juſt heard) (*b*) *wounding the Ear*, or of the Seas being call'd *the* (*c*) *howling deſart of the Main*? Mr. *Pope* (*d*) *queſtions whether the nodding of a Mountain be a natural Image*; ſhou'd not You be apt to think too, that *a Mountain* (*e*) *ſhaking the Foreſts on his ſides*, is fitter for an Earthquake, than a *Metaphor*? What ſort of Idea have You of a (*f*) *well-fought Wall*, or a (*g*) *thrice-ear'd Field*? in a Word, have You any Idea at all, when he tells us of *Jove's* (*h*) *rearing a Tempeſt*, or of *the* (*i*) *whiſtling Winds waking the Sky*?

Philypſus conſulted his own Mind all along as theſe points were offer'd; and endeavour'd very fairly to diſcover, whether the Images were as clear and evident, as they ought to be: He knew that the great uſe and (*k*) *beauty of Metaphor, was to give Light and Perſpicuity to a deſcription*; to cloath Words (as he us'd to ſay) with Subſtance; and to make *Language viſible*: But as, upon this View, he cou'd not anſwer fully what had been

(*a*) B. 14, 533. (*b*) B. 5, 515. (*c*) B. 4, 748. (*d*) B. 14, 510, Notes. (*e*) B. 13, 400. (*f*) B. 5, 395. (*g*) B. 5, 159. (*h*) B. 5, 391. (*i*) B. 3, 213.

(*k*) Modus nullus eſt *florentior*; nec qui plus luminis afferat Orationi. *Cicero* de Oratore, Lib. 3.

pro-

produc'd, he was willing to evade it as much as he cou'd. These Instances, says he (turning to *Antiphaus*) tho' few for so large a Piece, when laid together, are apt to incline ones judgment to the prejudice of the Translator: it will not be fair to look only on the worst side of him; We owe it to Justice, and to the Excellencies of that great Man, to give one Evening to his Beauties, as well as this to his Defects.---Be so good then (interrupted *Antiphaus*) as to undertake that part for the next: You know me so well I need not assure you, that I shall be as much pleas'd with hearing the Beauties, as I am uneasy in repeating the Faults of this Writer.

After some other discourse, *Antiphaus*, going for his own apartment, and reflecting upon what had pass'd between him and his friend, took occasion to observe; "How impossible almost it is for "the greatest Genius not to fail sometimes, in an undertaking of this Nature: and how unavoidable it will be "for the Reader, (in a Poem generally "well wrote) not to be led away from "observing those faults, by the vast Power of Ornament, the easy Fluency of "the Verse, and his Engagements to "the Beauties of a favourite Piece.

The best qualified (added he) *will thus err, when ever they* write *for Fame; and the most judicious will be thus deceiv'd, when they* read *for Pleasure.*

An

An ESSAY &c.

Evening the Second.

BETWEEN company and busineſs, it was ſome time before *Philypſus* and *Antiphaus* cou'd get an Evening to themſelves; the latter had waited for it with ſome impatience; and did not fail, pretty early in it, to remind *Philypſus* of his promiſe. I long, ſays he, to ſee your Remarks: ſuch a method of viewing a Poem, is ſomething like the way of our favourite *Vertot* in writing Hiſtory: we have the material Parts of it, without paſſing thro' the dead Lines, which go toward the Narrative; or the leſs ſignificant Paſſages, which are to fill up the Chain of Events. You muſt not expect any great Matters, anſwer'd *Philypſus*: Tho' I have had longer time than we talk'd of at firſt, it has been ſufficient only for collecting ſome of the ſcatter'd Beauties of this excellent Tranſlation.

Some of the Lines which you repeated the former Evening, ſhew'd that the Greatneſs of his Genius, had led Mr. *Pope* ſometimes into an Exceſs: if things can be too much beautified, that fault does certainly belong to him. In a few lines, I confeſs, he diſcovers a greater love of Ornament, than is becoming. This is the fountain of all the ſeveral Peccadillo's which you obſerv'd from his writings; whatever there is to be found in them either too *glaring*, or *forc'd*, or *figurative*, or too much *elevated*, may fairly be accounted for this way. You, Sir, produc'd ſome Paſſages, as I remember, under each of theſe Characters: But how pardonable is it, for ſo exalted a Genius, to run ſometimes into an exceſs of Ornament? And how admirable for ſuch, to excell often in the juſt, handſome, natural *Manner*? As Mr. *Pope*, in the former, may poſſibly want ſome favourable Allowances; He muſt certainly command the higheſt Eſteem in the latter.

Is not almoſt the entire (*a*) *Epiſode* of

(*a*) B. 4, 493. to Verſe, 776.

Me-

Menelaus and *Proteus* particularly juſt, and beautiful? What can have a greater ſhare of Nature, without any exceſſes, than the Adventure with (*a*) *Nauſicaa*? How juſtly are the Paſſions preſerv'd in (*b*) *The Deſcent into Hell*; and before, in all the Speeches (*c*) of *Circe* and *Calypſo*?

Tho' theſe Paſſages are generally of too great a length to bear repeating in a ſingle Evening, you will indulge me with the reading ſome of the moſt finiſh'd Parts of them.

The whole *Epiſode* is particularly well wrote; but the things chiefly to be admir'd in it are, the *Metamorphoſis* of *Proteus*;——His Speech on the unhappy Curioſity of Men; — the account immediately after, of the Deaths of *Ajax* and *Agamemnon*; and, above all that enliven'd Concluſion, in Relation to *Elyſium*, and, the future Happineſs of *Menelaus*. You remember the various Transformations of *Proteus*; and, I believe, will allow them to be exceedingly well expreſs'd:

A Lion now, he curls a ſurgy mane;
Sudden, our bands a ſpotted Pard reſtrain;
Then arm'd with tusks, and lightning in his eyes,
A Boar's obſcener ſhape the God belies:
On ſpiry volumes there a Dragon rides;
Here, from our ſtrict embrace a Stream he glides:

(*a*) B. 6. (*b*) B. 11. (*c*) Books 5, and 10.

Here

And last, sublime his stately growth he rears
(*a*) A Tree, and well-dissembled foliage wears.

The Lines are extremely good, says *Antyphaus*; but I had a Thought came into my Head, that possess'd me, all the time, you were reading them: I cou'd not forbear thinking, what an happy Contrivance it wou'd be in the Managers of the *Old House*, to bring this Deity upon the Stage, in the same manner, that he appears in these Verses. Such a Performance wou'd set their Character in the most eminent Light: They wou'd infallibly get the start of their ingenious Rivals; and poor *Doctor Faustus*, and his *Dragon*, wou'd no longer be the highest Entertainment of the *Beaux Esprits* of this Age.

I am got into another Part of the Poem (says *Philypsus*) which might serve, in some measure, to arm their Rivals of *Lincolns-Inn-Fields*, against so formidable an Undertaking. There are Passages in the *Descent into Hell*, capable of furnishing out a great deal of the *Wonderful*, and *Surprizing*, in this way. But to return: can any thing be more Pathetick, than this whole Book? especially, the lat-

(*a*) B. 4, 615. to 622.

ter part, when *the Heroes* come to make their Appearance. Tho' I am always loſt in the Variety of Beauties, which we find in it; I muſt ſingle out the Speech of *Agamemnon*, and read (at leaſt) the Concluſion of it to you:

When War has thunder'd with its loudeſt Storms,
Death thou haſt ſeen in all her ghaſtly Forms;
In duel met her, on the liſted Ground,
When hand to hand they wound return for wound:
But never have thy Eyes aſtoniſh'd view'd
So vile a deed, ſo dire a Scene of Blood.
Ev'n in the flow of joy, when now the bowl
Glows in our Veins, and opens ev'ry Soul,
We groan, we faint; with Blood the dome is dy'd,
And o'er the pavement floats the dreadful tyde—
Her breaſt all gore, with lamentable cries,
The bleeding innocent *Caſſandra* dies!
Then, tho' pale death froze cold in ev'ry vein,
(*a*) My Sword I ſtrive to wield, ——but ſtrive in [vain.

Surely nothing in Nature can be conceived of greater Strength and Emotion, than this Circumſtance. We ſee the Hero weltring on the Floor, all cover'd with Blood, and in the laſt agonies of Death. It was then, that he heard the Cries and Shrieks of the Daughter of *Priam*, purſued by the Traytors, and ſtab'd to the Heart by the barbarous

(*a*) B. 11, 528. λ', 423.

Cly-

Clytemnestra: expiring as he was, he endeavours to raise up his Arm, and at last gets his Hand upon the hilt of his Sword; which he had strength only to grasp, with a look full of Rage, Compassion, and Revenge. Methinks, *Antiphaus*, I see him now expired, and dropt upon the Floor: but tho' expired, there is still that Rage and Passion in his Countenance; he still grasps his Sword, and seems to threaten the Traytors and the Adulteress with his looks.

I know nothing finer (says *Antiphaus*) than these last Efforts of dying Heroes. They affect the Soul wonderfully: And the weakness of their Body, which will not permit their acting at such times, in my Opinion sets off their Courage, and their Desire of Action, in the strongest Light imaginable. There is nothing unnatural in this; tho' indeed it follows Nature to its last Pitch: The best Historians, as well as the first Poets, make use of such Circumstances very finely; and I remember Instances of it (*a*) in *Livy* and (*b*) *Sallust*, that carry this

(*a*) Etiam quos vires sanguisque desereret, ut intra vallum hostium *caderent*, nitebantur. *Liv.* vol. 3. p. 145. per *Hearne*.

(*b*) Catilina vero longe a suis inter hostium cadavera repertus est, paullulum etiam spirans, ferociamque animi quam habuerat vivus, in vultu retinens. *Sall. Bell. Cat.* juxta finem.

Matter

Matter as far as (a) *Virgil* or *Homer.* But ſome Moderns, as uſual, ſtretch it ſo immoderately, that they go beyond nature; and the Moment it is ſo, it muſt be ridiculous. How often have we laugh'd at thoſe Rants of *Taſſo*, and *Arioſto*? It wou'd be very well if their Heroes only *threaten'd in Death*, but they muſt *die (b) away, without being at all the Weaker*: ſome of them (in the heat of Battle, you may be ſure) *forget that they are (c) kill'd*, and ſo *keep on fighting*: like *Strada's Soldiers*, who after *they are cut in Two, (d) ſurvive themſelves; and fight on with that half of their Bodies, that is left them; to revenge the other, which was knock'd on the Head, an hour or two before.*

Such things as thoſe (anſwer'd *Philypſus*) are not *Blemiſhes* in a piece; they are downright *falſities*; meer *outrages* againſt Truth, as well as common Senſe. Nothing can be invented more ridiculous: they are like the *incomprehenſible Lies* of Sir *John Falſtaff*; and put one in mind of his *fighting with* Blount, *an hour by* Shrews-

(a) G. 4, 526. Æn. 9, 444.

(b) Minacciava morendo, e non languia. *Taſ.*

(c) Il pover' huomo, che non ſen' era accorto Andava combattendo, ed era morto. *Arioſt.*

(d) Dimidiato corpore pugnabant ſibi *ſuperſtites*, ac *peremptæ* partis ultores. *Strad.* Dec. 2. Lib. 2.

bury

bury *Clock*, after that Gentleman had been kill'd before very heartily by *Prince Henry*.

On the contrary; *Homer* is as great a friend to Truth and Nature, as he is to Poetry: He knows how to raiſe, every thing, as far as it will bear; he has always a Command of whatever is proper to be ſaid; and, which is yet greater, always underſtands when he has ſaid enough.

But we forget our ſelves, *Antiphaus*: this Digreſſion has carried us ſo far, that if we do not ſoon go on with this Speech of *Agamemnon*'s which occaſion'd it, we ſhall not know where it left off: After that pathetick account of his Death and the barbarity of his Queen, he proceeds:

Nor did my traitreſs Wife theſe Eye-lids cloſe
Or decently in Death my Limbs compoſe.
O Woman, Woman! when to ill thy Mind
Is bent, all Hell contains no fouler Fiend.
And ſuch was mine! who baſely plung'd her ſword
Thro' the fond Boſom, where ſhe reign'd ador'd!
Alas! I hop'd, the toils of War o'ercome,
To meet ſoft quiet and repoſe at home;
Deluſive hope!——O Wife, thy deeds diſgrace,
The perjur'd Sex, and blacken all the race;
And ſhou'd poſterity one virtuous find,
(*a*) Name *Clytemneſtra*, they will curſe the kind.

(*a*) B. 11, 540. λ', 433.

The

The turn of Expreſſion in this, is much more lively and paſſionate, than the language of *Homer* himſelf. As you cannot value any delays, where we meet with ſuch Improvements; I am ſure you will give me leave to read you the Speech of *Ulyſſes* juſt after: That I mean, in which he gives *Achilles* an account of his Son *Pyrrhus*'s behaviour in the War.

——Hear with pleas'd Attention the renown,
The wars and wiſdom of thy gallant Son:
With me from *Scyros* to the Field of Fame,
Radiant in Arms the blooming Heroe came.
When *Greece* aſſembled all her Hundred States,
To ripen Counſels, and decide Debates,
Heavens! how he charm'd us with a flow of ſenſe,
And won the heart with manly Eloquence!
He firſt was ſeen of all the Peers to riſe,
(a) The third in wiſdom, where they all were [wiſe.——

Give me leave (ſays *Antiphaus*, interrupting him)——that very Verſe I have formerly taken notice of; the Tranſlator ſeems to me to have uſed an unneceſſary Caution in it: He is tender of making *Ulyſſes* commend himſelf *by Name*, where *Homer* does it with the greateſt bluntneſs.——

I know it, ſays *Philypſus*; but that I ſhould have put to the account of his

(a) B. 11, 626. λ', 511.

Improvements on this Speech. Cou'd any thing have been more groſs, than to have imitated that line in its own *coarſe, ruſtick* Dialect? Is it not better on all Hands for ſuch a Sentiment to be *imply'd*, than to be *expreſs'd?*

Cuſtom and Prejudice (anſwered *Antiphaus*) have now render'd it unpolite, and even ſhocking, for a Man almoſt in any Caſe to commend himſelf: But it was not thus anciently. It is certain, that it was not thus in the times of thoſe Heroes, whom *Homer* deſcribes; and *Homer* therefore acts with Propriety, in making *Ulyſſes* ſay, that *Neſtor and Himſelf were the wiſeſt of all the Grecians.* Now, is the Tranſlator in this Caſe to follow his Author, or not? Is he to preſerve *the Manners* of the Ancients in the characters of his Heroes? or is he to modernize them, and to make *Ulyſſes* and *Achilles* appear the moſt accompliſh'd, fineſt Gentlemen in the World?

That will be carrying the Matter too far, replied *Philypſus*; I ſpeak it only as to this particular; and I own I am yet to be convinc'd, that this Humour of commending themſelves, was really ſo prevalent among the Ancients. Perhaps this is one of the Places where *Homer nods*: it might be a ſlip of haſte or inattention.——

No,

No, interrupted *Antiphaus*, nothing can be more certain, than the freedom and honesty of Speech us'd among the Ancients, in this particular; not only before *Homer*, but very long after his time.——If *Homer's Ulysses* here calls himself the wisest of the *Grecians*, his *Achilles* does not stick at calling himself *the Best and most Valiant of them*; and that too, in a Council of all the *Princes*: *Virgil* has given us his Approbation of both the one and the other, in making *Æneas* talk frequently of his own piety and valour. I cou'd tire you with Quotations of this kind: *Socrates*, in *Plato*, is always brought in to his advantage; and yet there he does just the same thing with *Ulysses* in the present case: he himself quotes the Oracle, which pronounc'd him to be *the Wisest of Men. Xenophon* represents *Cyrus*, upon his Death-bed, as taking notice of the greatest Beauty of his own Character, his Humanity; in a Piece which, every one knows, was designed for the Character of a *perfect Prince.* In a word, whole Treatises have been wrote of this very thing, and in this very strain. *Cæsar*, and the great *Jewish* writer of his own Life, frequently commend themselves: the greatest Critick, as well as the greatest Orator, among the *Romans*, who ſo often reckons *Modeſty* among the things which are moſt neceſſary toward rendering a Man great in his Profeſſion; how open and frequent is he in praiſing himſelf, and in ſetting his own Merit in a true Light? But what puts this beyond diſpute (and ſhews at the ſame time, that a juſt Commendation of one ſelf, may by very conſiſtent with the *greateſt Modeſty*) is to be found in the *ſacred Writings*, in which *Moſes* ſays of himſelf, *that he was the Meekeſt Man upon Earth.*

Thus free were the Ancients in commending themſelves; and not to conſider here, whether we, or they were in the right; (whether their *Behaviour* may not be thought to have had more of *Veracity* in it; and our Method to have been grounded, in a great degree, on a *falſe Eſtimate* of things: however that be) I think enough has been ſaid, to ſhew that *Homer* was not *drowſy*, when he wrote this line; and that *Ulyſſes* might uſe it, without any thing of a vitious Arrogance.

To confeſs the Truth (ſays *Philypſus*) I was really ignorant in this point of the Uſage of the Ancients, and had modelled their *Manners* too much by our own. I now ſee my error; and think the Tran-

ſlator

ſlator might have ſpared the excuſe, which he (*a*) makes for this Indecency in *Ulyſſes* behaviour: 'tis plain, it wou'd not have been ſo improper, before a People, leſs noted for Vain-glory, than the *Phæacians*. I thank you, *Antiphaus*, for this new Light; and ſhall go on with the Heroe's Character of *Pyrrhus*, without thinking him ſo aſſuming, as he formerly appear'd to have been. After placing the Son of *Achilles* next to *Neſtor* and *Himſelf* in Wiſdom, he proceeds to give an account of his Courage; and in that, ſets him above all the *Grecians*, without Exception.

But when to try the fortune of the day
Hoſt mov'd tow'rd hoſt in terrible array,
Before the van, impatient for the fight,
With martial port he ſtrode, and ſtern delight.—
When *Ilion* in the horſe receiv'd her doom,
And unſeen armies ambuſh'd in its womb;
Greece gave her latent warriors to my care,
'Twas mine on *Troy* to pour the impriſon'd war:
Then, when the boldeſt boſom beat with fear,
When the ſtern eyes of Heroes dropp'd a tear;
Fierce in his look his ardent valour glow'd,
Fluſh'd in his Cheek, or ſally'd in his Blood;
Indignant in the dark receſs he ſtands,
Pants for the battle, and the war demands;
His voice breath'd death; and with a martial air
(*b*) He graſp'd his Sword and ſhook his glittering [Spear,

(*a*) Note on Ver. 626, B. 11. (*b*) B. 11, 650. λ', 531.

How well is the earnest Spirit of a young Heroe described throughout this whole Passage? How does the impetuousness of his Soul appear, in these previous Actions of the warrior? Had one the poetical Liberty of making comparisons, I shou'd not stick at saying, that this has a great resemblance to that admirable description of a *War-horse*, in the most finisht Poem in the World.

——(*a*) *Tum, siqua sonum procul arma dedere;*
Stare loco nescit, *micat auribus, & tremit artus,*
Collectumque premens volvit sub naribus ignem.

I am apt to believe, that Mr. *Pope* had this behaviour of *Pyrrhus* in his Eye, when he gave those lively Strokes in the entrance of his *Ode for Musick*. We see the Heroes there in the same Postures, when animated by the martial strains of *Orpheus*.

(*b*) Each chief his sevenfold shield display'd,
And half unsheath'd the shining blade;
And Seas, and Rocks, and Skies resound
To arms, to arms, to arms!

By the sudden flow of their Spirits, and the rapidity of their Imagination, they prevent the War: They shew a

(*a*) *Virgils* Georgicks. 3, 83. (*b*) Stanza. 3.

noble

noble forgetfulneſs of the Place and Circumſtances of things about them, and think themſelves already engaging with the abſent Enemy.

There is one Speech more of thoſe I mention'd at firſt, which I cannot forbear repeating to you; tho' I am ſenſible, that I have been too long upon this Head already. It is that of *Circe* to *Ulyſſes*, in the *tenth Odyſſey*:

Then wav'd the wand, and then the word was [given:
Hence to thy fellows! (dreadful ſhe began)
Go, be a Beaſt!——I heard and yet was Man.
Then ſudden whirling like a waving Flame
My beamy faulchion, I aſſault the Dame:
Struck with unuſual fear, ſhe trembling cries,
She faints, ſhe falls; ſhe lifts her weeping eyes.

What art thou? ſay! from whence, from [whom you came?
O more than human! tell thy race, thy name.
Amazing ſtrength theſe poiſons to ſuſtain!
Not mortal thou, nor mortal is thy Brain.
Or art thou he? the Man to come (foretold
By *Hermes* powerful with the Wand of Gold)
The Man from *Troy*, who wander'd Ocean round,
The Man, for Wiſdom's various Arts renown'd:
(*a*) *Ulyſſes*?——Oh! thy threatning fury ceaſe. ---

What ſtarts? what terror, and amazement? What paſſionate breaks are there in theſe lines? How ſolemn is the

(*a*) B. 10, 395. κ', 330.

begin-

beginning? how emphatical the account of the action? and how lively the surprize and confusion of the Inchantress, upon finding the inefficacy of her Charms? Nature here appears in every Word that she says; if the Disappointment is great and shocking, the lines too are all impetuous and abrupt: if the passions strong and various, the Expressions in the Translation are instant and pressing, and the stile often chang'd: How great and swift is the Alteration, from an imperious cruel Tyrant, to a poor weak helpless Woman? And how is it equal'd by that judicious shifting of the scene in this piece? There the change is as sudden and immediate; and nothing can be greater than the fall from the haughtiness of

Go, be a Beast! ———

to the meanness of the line, just after,

She faints, she falls; she lifts her weeping Eyes.

You cannot but observe farther, my *Antiphaus*, that the lines in this description, are every where improv'd with those Figures, which the Ancient *Criticks* have always look'd upon as the most proper to express an hurry of Passion. The *Transposition*, the *Omission* of Words, the pressing use of *Exclaiming* and *Inter-*

rogation,

rogation, and the general *Inconnection* which runs through it, are all apply'd in the most natural and poetical Manner. There is a Note of the Translator on a Passage not long before this, which gives us in one view several excellent Observations of this kind, and which no doubt he had in his Eye here; for the rules of it are exactly follow'd in the present case. This Poet is the best Commentator on himself; give me leave therefore just to look back for his (*a*) Note on the Speech of *Eurylocus*; that you may see how exactly those Observations tally with his performance here, in every particular Article.

" We have here (says he) a very lively
" picture of a Person in a great fright :—
" the very manner of speaking, repre-
" sents the disorder of the speaker; he is
" in too great an Emotion to introduce
" his Speech by any Preface, he breaks
" at once into it, without preparation,
" as if he could not soon enough deliver
" his thoughts. ——— *Again* :

" There is nothing, which gives more
" life to a Discourse, than the taking
" away (*b*) the Connections and Con-
" junctions; when the discourse is not

(*a*) Note on B. 10, Ver. 295. (*b*) from *Longinus* de Subl. c, 17.

bound

"bound together and embarafs'd, it "walks and flides along of it felf. *Pe-* "*riods* thus cut off, and yet pronounc'd "with Precipitation, are figns of a lively "Sorrow; which at the fame time hin- "ders, yet forces him to fpeak.——
Again (in a like cafe)

"He fpeaks fhort, and in broken and "interrupted Periods, which excellently "reprefent the agony of his thoughts. --- "Afterwards we fee he breaks out into "Interrogations, which, as (*a*) *Longinus* "obferves, give great motion, ftrength, "and action to Difcourfe. If the Poet had "proceeded fimply, the Expreffion had "not been equal to the occafion; but "by thefe fhort Queftions, he gives "ftrength to it, and fhews the diforder "of the fpeaker, by the fudden ftarts "and vehemence of the Periods.

All thefe animated Figures, all thofe Arts of expreffing the Paffions, are beautifully wove into this fingle piece of Poetry: But there is one peculiar Excellence in it yet behind, which I admire beyond all the reft. It is a power almoft unknown even to Poetry before, and the Criticks have not as yet found out any Name for it. The extraordinary Beauty

(*a*) De *Subl.* c, 17.

I mean, is that *Insight* which the Poet gives his Readers into *Circe's Mind*: We look into her Soul, and see the Ideas pass there in Train. At first she is ignorant, then dubious, and at last discovers gradually in her Thoughts the Character, and very Name of the Heroe. *Circe*, skill'd as she was in all the arts of Magick, is limited in her Knowledge and Discovery of things: and in the present Discovery of the Person of *Ulysses*, her Mind acts with Tumult and Rapidity, but at the same time with a series and gradual Collection of Truths, at first unknown. Every one may perceive the Tumult, and the *successive Enlightnings* of her Mind. We are led into a full View of the shifting of her thoughts; and behold the various openings of them in her Soul.

What art thou? say! from whence, from whom [you came.
Or art thou He? *the Man to come* foretold ——
The Man, from Troy? ————
The Man, for *wisdom's* various arts renown'd,
Ulysses? ———— ————

I never read any thing which sets the actings of another's Mind so distinctly to the view. *Circe's* very Thoughts are made visible to us; they are set full in our Eyes; and we see the different degrees

grees, as it were of Light, breaking in upon her Soul.——'Tis a moſt charming piece of Poetry! and upon turning it every way, and conſidering all its ſeveral perfections, I believe one might venture to pronounce it, the moſt finiſht Piece, the moſt *compleat Beauty* in the whole Tranſlation.

Theſe are the productions of a Sublime Genius, and ſpeak an uncommon Spirit, together with a firm extenſive Judgment, and an exact Senſe of things. But you *Antiphaus* chiefly complain of this Writer for his Refinements and Elevation: there is too much of the *Enflure* (as the *French* call it) in his Works; and you cannot bear with ſuch a profuſion of Glitter and Embroidery in the Language. I do not deny, that the Paſſages you repeated, are generally blameable on theſe accounts; but beg leave to produce ſome inſtances, which may ſhew the Tranſlator, to be a maſter in the juſt and proper ſtile; as the former convince us of his Excellence in the poliſh'd, and enliven'd, and pathetick.

How humble are the lines in particular, (*a*) where *Ulyſſes* meets with *Minerva* in *Ithaca*, and how rural the (*b*)

(*a*) B. 13. (*b*) B. 14.

Scene

(*a*) Scene between him and *Eumæus* in that Iſland? So far, that for my own Part I muſt confeſs, I ſhou'd be more apt to imagine, that Mr. *Pope* on theſe Occaſions ſinks now and then into *Lowneſſes*, beneath the dignity of the Epick; than that he ſoars too high, or uſes any falſe Elevation.

As for the juſt and chaſte *Manner* of expreſſing things, it is very frequent in theſe Paſſages: There is a place juſt come into my Head, in which this very way of ſpeaking is deſcrib'd; the lines are cloſe and expreſſive; and, according to Mr. *Pope*'s Method in his *incomparable Eſſay*, are themſelves the beſt example of the thing they treat of; they are (*b*) in the Eighth Book:

With partial hands, the Gods their gifts diſpenſe;
Some greatly think, ſome ſpeak with manly ſenſe.
Here Heaven an elegance of form denies,
But Wiſdom the defect of form ſupplies:
This Man with energy of thought controuls,
And ſteals with modeſt violence our Souls;
He ſpeaks reſerv'dly, but he ſpeaks with force,
Nor can one word be chang'd but for a worſe.

The Concluſion of *Tireſias*'s Speech to *Ulyſſes* (proceeded *Philypſus*) I dare anſwer for it, you will think excellent in this way:

(*a*) B. 14. (*b*) Verſe, 185. & 170.

——— Peaceful ſhalt thou end thy bliſsful days,
And ſteal thy ſelf from life, by ſlow decays:
Unknown to pain, in age reſign thy breath,
When late ſtern *Neptune* points the ſhaft with death;
To the dark grave retiring as to Reſt,
(a) Thy people bleſſing, by thy people bleſt.

By this we ſee, how Mr. *Pope* can enliven any thing of this kind with the greateſt Juſtice and Beauty: Such (to mention but one more) is that ſingle Paſſage, as I take it, in all *Homer*'s Works, which deſcribes the Regions of the Bleſt. The Lines are very beautiful in the Original; and the Tranſlation has expreſs'd all the beauties of it, in a lively proper fluency of Verſe:

Elyſium ſhall be thine; the bliſsful plains
Of utmoſt Earth, where *Rhadamanthus* reigns:
Joys ever-young, unmix'd with pain or fear,
Fill the wide circle of th' Eternal Year.
Stern Winter ſmiles on that auſpicious clime;
The Fields are florid with unfading prime:
From the bleak pole no Winds inclement blow,
Mould the round Hail, or flake the fleecy Snow:
But from the breezy deep, the bleſt inhale
The fragrant murmurs of the Weſtern gale.
This grace peculiar will the Gods afford
(a) To thee, the Son of *Jove*, and beauteous *Helen*'s [Lord.

What can be more Juſt and Beautiful? The Thought proper and *adequate*; the

(a) B. 4, 776. &c, 564 to 569.

Words

Words *glowing;* and the Language *alive:* To me, the Verſes themſelves ſeem to run on with joy, and pleaſure. The delightful Softneſs of thoſe lines in *Homer*

> Ἀλλ' αἰεὶ ζεφύροιο λιγυπνείοντας ἀήτας
> Ὠκεανὸς ἀνίησιν, ἀναψύχειν ἀνθρώπους

is diffus'd thro' the whole Deſcription by Mr. *Pope* ; and the latter has the advantage of the Original, in concluding with a full elaſtick line, that carries a Spring with it, inſtead of the heavineſs of——Καί σφιν γαμβρὸς Διός ἐσσι.

I entirely agree with you (ſays *Antiphaus)* as to the turn of the Lines ; 'Tis very fine and vigorous: but methinks even in theſe, what anſwers the two particular Greek Verſes you have repeated, are too much flouriſh'd, and more remarkable for their Sound, than for any other Idea they may give the Mind. The Senſe ſeems to be almoſt overlaid by the *Fineſſe* of them.

I ſhall not ſtand with you for that Couplet, anſwer'd *Philypſus* : what I chiefly admire is the general flow of the lines in the whole Paſſage.

This manner of writing, *Antiphaus*, is very aſſiſtant in expreſſing the nature of the Subject : and indeed, tho' Mr. *Pope* does ſometimes go too far in the Florid and Artificial, we may ſay in general,

F 2 that

that he is a very *natural* Writer. His Imagination is lively, his Colours ſtrong, and his Hand maſterly in moſt of his ſtrokes. We ſhou'd loſe our ſelves in endeavouring to obſerve all that variety of Beauties of this kind, which are to be found in his Tranſlation: one Point I have particularly admir'd in it; The Poet's peculiar Air, and Happineſs in drawing Landſcapes; eſpecially hanging Woods, Slopes, and Precipices: Thus,

——High *Ithaca* o'er-looks the Floods,
(*a*) Brown with o'er-arching Shades, and pendent [Woods.

What Reader will be ſo unconcern'd, and ſo little taken with this Proſpect, as *Ulyſſes* is repreſented to be in another Part of the Poem? For 'tis the ſame place, that we have a deſcription of afterwards, when we are told, *That he*

——Deep-muſing, o'er the Mountains ſtray'd,
Thro' mazy thickets of the woodland ſhade,
And cavern'd ways, the ſhaggy coaſt along,
(*b*) With cliffs, and nodding foreſts over-hung.

In *Ulyſſes*'s firſt adventures on *Phæacia*, we are led on *ſucceſſively*, thro' ſeveral very beautiful Deſcriptions. Firſt we

(*a*) B. 3, 96. *y*' 81. (*b*) B. 14, 4.

have

have a (*a*) rocky Coaſt, excellently pictur'd in two lines only: thence we are carried into a (*b*) thick dark Wood, for that Night. The next Morning, we have a (*c*) View of the City; The firſt things which offer to the Eye are the Caſtle, and the Senate-houſe, riſing above the other Buildings; at a diſtance, acroſs the great Road, appears the Port with the Ships at Anchor, and their Sails fluttering in the Air: on the Shore, juſt by the Temple of *Neptune*, you ſee the *Phæacians* buſied in the Dock, all in their ſeveral Employments. After this View, you paſs thro' a (*d*) delicious Range of Groves, and Meadow-ground, up to the Walls; while on this ſide, (*e*) appear the Gardens all in bloom; and the Vineyards of *Alcinous* cloſe the Scene on the other.

There can be nothing better imag'd, and more natural, than theſe Deſcriptions are in Mr. *Pope*'s Tranſlation: they exceed even the Original it ſelf.

I beg leave to repeat another Deſcription to you, which lies not ſo diffus'd as the former; 'tis one ſingle View of *Ca-*

(*a*) B. 5, 520, 521. ε, 402. (*b*) B. 5, 613, to 622. ε, 480. (*c*) B. 6, 310, to 320. ζ', 262, 269. (*d*) B. 6, 350. ζ', 291. (*e*) B. 6, 355. ζ', 293.

lypso's Grotto; and what an exact and beautiful Draught of it does it give us?

—————A various Sylvan scene
Appears around, and groves of living green;
Poplars and Alders ever quivering play'd,
And nodding Cypress form'd a fragrant shade;
On whose high branches, waving with the storm,
The Birds of broadest wing their mansion form,
(The Chough, the Sea-mew, the loquacious Crow)
And scream aloft, and skim the deeps below.
Depending Vines the shelving Cavern screen,
With purple clusters blushing thro' the green:
Four limpid fountains from the Cliff distill,
And every fountain pours a sev'ral rill,
(*a*) In mazy windings wandring down the Hill.

Nothing can be more beautiful to the Eye, than these Landscapes are in the Poem: they make every thing present to us; and agreeably deceive us into an Imagination, that we (*b*) *actually See, what we only Hear:* As the Poet may improve all his Circumstances at pleasure, what the Criticks have observ'd in this Case, is not so extravagant, as one wou'd imagine; we really see things more fully and with greater delight in the Poem, than we shou'd in the reality; The Picture improves upon Nature: and we might look

(*a*) B. 5, 92. & 71.
(*b*) Τὰ ἀκουόμενα ὄψει ποιεῖ. *Longin.* περὶ Ὕψους.

on

on the Proſpect it ſelf with (*a*) *leſs pleaſure, than we hear it deſcrib'd.*

Whoever is ſhock'd at this, may be pleas'd to conſider *the Cave of the Nymphs*, in the Thirteenth Book: That alone may ſerve to ſhew, how largely Circumſtances may be added, in deſcribing the works of Nature; or in drawing poetical Proſpects.

Mr. *Pope* ſhews an excellent Hand in ſeveral other Places; as in the firſt View of *Circe*'s Palace at a diſtance, and conſtantly in the appearance of Land off at Sea.

Ulyſſes gives us an account of the former at his landing upon the Iſland of that Goddeſs.

(*b*) From the high Point I mark'd in diſtant view
A ſtream of curling Smoke aſcending blue,
And ſpiry tops, the tufted Trees above,
Of *Circe*'s Palace boſom'd in the Grove.

The other is very frequent: take a Deſcription or two of it, that come into my Mind at preſent.

(*c*) Like diſtant Clouds the Mariner deſcries,
Fair *Ithaca*'s emerging Hills ariſe.

(*a*) Κρεῖττον γάρ ἐστιν ἀκουσθῆναι λεγόμενον, ἢ ὀφθῆναι γινόμενον. *Dionyſius Hal.* Περὶ Συνθέσεως. γ'.
(*b*) B. 10, 173. κ', 150. (*c*) B. 13, 115, ν', 95.

Again;

Again;

(a) The distant Land appear'd ——— ———
Then swell'd to sight *Phæacia*'s dusky coast,
And woody Mountains half in vapours lost;
That lay before him, indistinct and vast,
Like a broad Shield amid the watry waste.

Nothing hath furnish'd *Homer* (as well as *Virgil*) with such a variety of natural Images, as this Element; and in nothing has Mr. *Pope* more finely copied his Original. But all these Beautiful Pictures, are only Pictures of *still Life*; this Gentleman's Excellency reaches farther; he is as masterly in all his Motions, and Actions; he can teach his Pencil to express Ideas yet in the Mind; and to paint out the Passions of the Soul.

Sometimes we have all the *Imagery* in Motion: If a Ship is to set sail, the Canvas swells to the Eye, the Streamers float in the Air, and the Sailors are all full of Noise and Business: (b) We see the Vessel move on, and here the rushing sound of the Water.

——— ——— The attending train
Load the tall bark, and launch into the main.
The Prince and Goddess to the stern ascend;
(c) To the strong stroke at once the rowers bend
Full from the West she bids fresh breezes blow;
The sable billows foam and roar below. ——— ———

(a) B. 5, 356, &, 279. (b) B. 2, 459. & 419.

What

With speed the Mast they rear, with speed unbind
The spacious sheet, and stretch it to the Wind.
High o'er the roaring Waves the spreading Sails
Bow the tall Mast, and swell before the gales;
The crooked keel the parting surge divides,
And to the stern retreating roll the tides.

At another time, you behold the Rowers, drawing (a) *the Oar to their broad Breasts*; and the different attitudes of them, as they (b) *bend*, or (c) *stretch* to the stroke.

(d) At once they bend and strike their equal oars,
And leave the sinking hills and less'ning shores.

This Idea of the Land seeming to sink and recede, is very beautifully added, in another Place, where we have the Description of a Person driving, very swiftly, in a Chariot: I believe you will hear the entire Passage with Pleasure, as it is all very Just and Natural:

With hasty hand the ruling reins he drew:
He lash'd the coursers, and the coursers flew.
Beneath the bounding yoke alike they held
Their equal pace, and smoak'd along the field.
The Tow'rs of *Pylos* sink, its views decay,
Fields after fields fly back, till close of Day;
(e) Then sunk the Sun, and darken'd all the way.

(a) B. 12, 183. μ', 147. (b) B. 12. 216. (c) B. 12. 265. (d) B. 13, 94, ν', 78. (e) B. 3, 618. γ', 435.

Again;

Again;

Along the waving fields their way they hold,
(*a*) The fields receding as the Chariot roll'd.

Give me leave (interpos'd *Antiphaus*) to obſerve one thing, by the way. Mr. *Pope* (poſſibly, to make this the more ſenſible to us at preſent) deviates a little from the Truth; and chuſes rather to ſhew the *Poet*, than the *Antiquary*. As I take it, the Horſes in the Chariots of the Ancients were not *beneath the Yoke*. Do not their Medals, and all the Pictures of them repreſent it otherwiſe? And does not the Verſe, here in the Original, ſhew its Poſition in reſpect of the Horſes, very particularly and diſtinctly?

However, this is a ſlip of a ſmall Nature: and had the thing been expreſs'd in exact Conformity to the *Grecian* faſhion in this particular, it might not have ſtruck the Reader ſo ſtrongly, as it does now, by its Agreement with the preſent Idea of the ſame thing.

I am not concern'd, ſays *Philypſus*, either in defending, or giving up that particular: I only inſtance this Paſſage, in general, for its expreſſiveneſs of ſuch an Action; and of the Ideas, ariſing in

(*a*) B. 3, 628. γ', 495.

the

the Mind upon it: As to that *End*, I believe it will hold very well. The Deſcription and Sentiment is very Natural, (reply'd *Antiphaus*) I beg you to go on without obſerving any little breaks for the future, which may be occaſion'd by ſuch Circumſtances, as do not affect the chief Aim and Deſign of a Quotation.

If the *Poet*, proceeded *Philypſus*, can paint out the *Ideas* in the Mind with ſo much Juſtice, as he appears to do by this inſtance; and more particularly by another mention'd before (of the ſucceſſive *openings* and *unfolding* of an unknown Truth, in the Mind of *Circe*) we ſhall find him to have been equally Happy in expreſſing the *Paſſions* of the Soul. Something of this has been mention'd already, and almoſt an infinite variety of Beauties of the ſame kind might be added. They abound every where in the Tranſlation, and are generally well touched. But there is the Deſcription of one Paſſion in particular, which is perſerv'd throughout the whole Piece: It is *Ulyſſes* his Love for his Country. Give me leave to repeat ſome of the firſt, and laſt Paſſages, in which it is expreſt. How ſtrongly does *Minerva* repreſent this, even in the very entrance of the Poem? She ſays the Hero

Hero is detain'd from *Ithaca*, by a Goddess (nothing human cou'd have forced him into so tedious an absence: by a Goddess)

> Who sooths to dear delight his anxious mind —
> Successless all her soft caresses prove,
> To banish from his breast his Country's love;
> To see the *Smoke* from his lov'd palace rise,
> While the dear Isle in *distant* prospect lies,
> (a) With what *contentment wou'd he close his eyes?*

The first Appearance of the Hero is most excellently imagined. *Calypso* has just receiv'd orders to detain *Ulysses* no longer from his Country; she finds him sitting alone upon the Rocks, the Tears trickling down his Cheeks, and his Eyes fixt upon the Sea. It was thus that he pass'd his Hours, in the Island of that Goddess: He constantly,

> In slumber wore the heavy Night away;
> On Rocks and Shores consum'd the tedious Da
> There sate all desolate, and sigh'd alone,
> With echoing sorrows made the mountains groan,
> And roll'd his eyes o'er all the restless main,
> (b) Till dim'd with rising grief, they stream'd again.

Pardon me, says *Antiphaus*; even here (tho' the Passion be strongly set out; yet) the Language of the two Passages, which you repeated last, is not entirely

(a) B. 1, 77. d, 59. (b) B. 5, 204. 6, 154.

free

free from the old Fault: the *Enſlure* is ſtill diſcernible. That *ſoothing an anxious Mind to dear delight*, falls ſhort of the plainneſs, and energy of the Original: ——To make the *Mountains groan with echoing Sorrow*, is yet more over-wrought. —And *the ſtreaming again of his Eyes*, is not exactly right in the Tranſlation, which does not mention, his *weeping before*; at the ſame time, that it varies from the Original, which ſays that he *never ceas'd from weeping*.

We meet with another Image of this (reply'd *Philypſus*) in the Evening before *Ulyſſes* ſets ſail for *Ithaca*; which, I believe, you will allow to be better expreſs'd. He was then in ſo delightful a Place, as the Court of *Alcinous*. They had a multitude of Diverſions there: the *Phæacians* were the happieſt People in the World; Races and Entertainments, Mirth, Wine, and Muſick were the chief Buſineſs of their Lives. *Ulyſſes* appears among them with a quite different face: he looks like a Creature of an higher Make, of an Order above them; and his Mind is taken up with farther Views, and other Deſires.

All, but *Ulyſſes*, heard with fixt delight:
He ſate, and ey'd the Sun, and wiſh'd the Night;

Slow ſeem'd the Sun to move, the hours to roll,
(a) His native Home deep-imag'd in his Soul.

We are continually put in mind of this fondneſs of the Hero for his Country: and in the laſt Caſe, it is particularly fixt upon the Reader by a very expreſſive (b) Simile. We may imagine the ardency of *Ulyſſes's* Love for his *Ithaca*, his own *proper* Country, when we conſider his Affection for his Country-men, the *Grecians* in general. Upon an occaſional revival in his Thoughts of the Deſtructions and Miſery they underwent before *Troy*, the Hero's Diſſimulation (great as it was) is overcome; his Paſſion breaks through every reſtraint: we immediately ſee him all in Tears. This tenderneſs of his, is painted in another Simile, the moſt pathetick that can be conceiv'd, and the moſt expreſſive of his Affection for his Country-men.

——— ——— *Ulyſſes's* griefs renew;
Tears bath his cheeks, and tears the ground bedew:
As ſome fond Matron views in mortal fight
Her Husband falling in his Country's right;
Frantick thro' claſhing Swords ſhe runs, ſhe flies,
As ghaſtly pale he groans, and faints, and dies;
Cloſe to his Breaſt ſhe grovels on the ground,
And bathes with floods of tears the gaping wound;

(a) B. 13, 38. v, 30. (b) See Mr. *Pope's* Note on the Place.

She

She cries, ſhe ſhrieks : the fierce inſulting foe
Relentleſs mocks her violence of woe,
To chains condemn'd as wildly ſhe deplores,
(*a*) A widow, and a ſlave on foreign ſhores.

It wou'd be endleſs to repeat every thing of this Nature; There are a Thouſand sketches of it in the *Odyſſey*. 'Tis ſufficient at preſent to obſerve, that Mr. *Pope* generally gives them to us in very lively Colours; and excells almoſt every where in the *Pathetick*. 'Tis certain (ſays *Antiphaus*) that he has an excellent Hand; his Images, which you have ſet before me, are as ſtrong as any of the Works of the Pencil. They are ſo, anſwered *Philypſus*; and, on that account, you will Pardon me for borrowing ſo many Metaphors from Painting in this Caſe; 'Tis unavoidable. The deſigns of Painting and Poetry are ſo united, that to me the Poet and the Painter ſeem ſcarcely to differ in any thing, except the *Mean* they make uſe of, to arrive at one and the ſame end. Both are to expreſs Nature: but the Materials of the one are Words, and Sound; of the other, Figure and Colours. *Poetry* can paint more particularly, more largely, and with greater coherence: *Painting* is

(*a*) B. 8, 580. 8, 530.

the more concife, and emphatical. If *This* may excell in fhewing one View diftinctly, *That* can fhew feveral in fucceffion, without any manner of Confufion. Any figure in *Painting* is confin'd to one Attitude; but *Poetry* can give as great a variety of Motion and Poftures, as the reality it felf. What feems a Paradox of Art in either, is their Power of expreffing two *oppofite Paffions* in the fame face. Of this fort (among a Multitude of like inftances) is the Mother of *Lewis* the Thirteenth, in the Gallery of *Luxembourg*; and every Piece in that fine Epifode, which concludes the fixth *Iliad*. In that *Picture*, the Queens Face ftrongly expreffes the Pain and Anguifh of her Condition, mix'd with a regard toward her Son, full of the greateft Pleafure and Complacence. In the *Poem* we have the greater variety, and each piece is perfectly juft and finifh'd. *Hector* fhews a fiercenefs for the War, and a tendernefs that inclines him to ftay for a laft interview; little *Aftyanax* has a Fondnefs and a Terror in his Eyes, at the fight of his Father; while *Andromache's* Face is all foften'd into a tender Smile; and at the fame time, wet with the Tears, that fall for her *Hector*.

I remember (ſays *Antiphaus*) it was to you that I was oblig'd for the firſt Obſervation, I ever met with, on theſe *Double Paſſions.* I have ſince read ſeveral things, (in the *Æneid*, as well as in the Works of *Homer*) with a pleaſure perfectly new, on account of the light, you then gave me, into this particular: And out of a Thouſand Places, that I have obſerv'd it in ſince, I know none ſo beautiful as that of *Achæmenides* in *Virgil*; which you mention'd to me, the firſt time we ever talk'd of this Subject.

That you know (reply'd *Philypſus*) to have been always my Favourite: I have read it over in *Dryden* ſo frequently, that I believe I can now repeat you his Tranſlation of it:

——From the Woods there bolts, before our ſight,
Somewhat betwixt a Mortal and a Spright;
So thin, ſo ghaſtly meager, and ſo wan,
So bare of Fleſh, he ſcarce reſembled Man:
This thing, all tatter'd, ſeem'd from far t'implore
Our pious Aid and pointed to the Shore;
We look behind; then view his ſhaggy Beard;
His cloaths were tagg'd with thorns, and filth his limbs beſmear'd:
The reſt in mein, in habit, and in face
Appear'd a *Greek*; and ſuch indeed he was;
He caſt on us from far a frightful view,
Whom ſoon for *Trojans* and for foes he knew;
Stood ſtill, and paus'd; then, all at once, began
To ſtretch his Limbs, and trembled as he ran;

Soon as approach'd, upon his knees he falls,
And thus with tears and sighs for pity calls:
" Now by the Pow'rs above, and what we share
" From Natures common gift, this vital Air,
" (*a*) O *Trojans*, take me hence.———

'Tis but too evident (continu'd *Philypsus*) that Mr. *Dryden* falls as much short of (*b*) *Virgil* in the chief turn, that relates to our present purpose; as *Virgil* has exceeded that (*c*) Passage in the *Iliad*, which seems to have given him the hint for drawing this admirable Image.

This Distraction of *Achæmenides* between several Passions at once, puts me in mind of the dubiousness and shifting of thoughts, which is illustrated by *Homer* by a very apt and expressive Simile; than which (says Mr. *Pope*) " There (*d*) " is scarce any thing, in the whole com- " pass of Nature, that can more exactly " represent the State of an irresolute " mind, wavering between two different " Designs; sometimes inclining to the " one,

(*a*) Dryd. Transl. Æn. 3, 788. (*b*) Æn. 3, 592.
——— Subito è sylvis macie confecta supremà,
Ignoti nova forma viri, miserandaque cultu
Procedit, supplexque manus ad litora tendit ———
——— Ubi Dardanios habitus & Troia vidit
Arma procul; paullum aspectu conterritus *hæsit*,
Continuitque gradum: mox *sese ad litora præceps*
Cum fletu precibusque *tulit*. ———
(*c*) Ιλ', κ', 358. (*d*) Note on Il. 14, 21.

"one, ſometimes to the other, and then "moving to that Point to which its Re-"ſolution is at laſt determin'd:

As when old Ocean's ſilent ſurface Sleeps,
The Waves juſt heaving on the purple Deeps;
While yet th' expected Tempeſt hangs on high,
Weighs down the cloud, and blackens in the sky,
The maſs of waters will no wind obey:
Jove ſends one guſt, and bids them roll away.
While wavering counſels thus his mind engage,
Fluctuates in doubtful thought the *Pylian* ſage;
To join the hoſt, or to the General haſte
(*a*) Debating long, he fixes on the laſt.

There is ſomething of this *Mélange of Paſſions*, (and thoſe too, the moſt beautiful in this Caſe, I mean of oppoſite *Paſſions*) in that line of *Milton*, where he ſays that Death

Grin'd horrible a ghaſtly ſmile ——

One wou'd almoſt be perſwaded, that *Homer* is the *dernier Reſſort* of all the fineſt Thoughts in Poetry; for this likewiſe is copied from him, tho' it fails very much (as to the Point in hand) both of the Original, and of Mr. *Pope*'s Tranſlation of it.——*Juno* makes a very mutinous Speech in an aſſembly of the Deities: The Infection took, as much as ſhe cou'd deſire: and that ſucceſs,

(*a*) Iliad 14, 30.

provok'd

provok'd and inflamed as she was, forced her to be somewhat pleased, in spite of her self: Upon this she shews a sort of (*a*) uneasy satisfaction, and such a Smile, as *Ovid* (*b*) gives to his *Envy* in the *Metamorphosis*.

To see the gath'ring grudge in every breast,
Smiles on her lips a spleenful joy exprest;
While on her wrinkled front, and eye-brow bent,
(*c*) Sate stedfast care and lowring discontent.

This struggle of Passions has been imitated by some Moderns: The first of the *French* Writers in Tragedy has a fine Occasion for it in the Wife of one of the *Horatij*; she was Sister at the same time to the *Curiatij*; so that you may imagine, how she must be distracted between the Interest of the two Cities, and that eminent contest which so particularly involv'd the two Families: She is introduc'd upon that Occasion, speaking to this purpose (*d*):

(*a*) Il. *b*, 103.

(*b*) Risus abest; nisi quem visi movere dolores. B. 2, 778. (*c*) *Pope*'s Iliad, B. 15, 113.

(*d*) Albeost j'ay commencè de respirer le jour,
Albe, mon cher pais, & mon premier amour,
Lors qu' entre-nous & toy je voi la guerre ouverte,
Je crains nostre victoire autant que nostre perte.
[*Corneille*.

Albe

Alba! my dearest Country! Why cou'd fate
Mark out no other foe for *Rome*, but *Alba*?
From our Defeat what Terror must I feel?
And yet —— I dread our Victory. ——

There are many things in *Virgil's* fourth *Æneid*, which might be produc'd on this Occasion: but 'tis more to our present Subject to consider that part of the *Odyssey*, from which some of its finest strokes are borrow'd. *Calypso*, when she acquaints our Hero with the design of his departure from her Island; upon his doubting her sincerity, swears very solemnly, that her Resolutions are real: the next moment, she falls into a Speech full of Insinuations and Arguments to detain him: both these speeches may rather be said to be *enliven'd* and *improv'd*, than to be *well translated* by Mr. *Pope*; this only wou'd be too narrow a Commendation of them: ---The first runs thus:

How prone to doubt, how cautious are the wise?
But hear, Oh Earth, and hear, Ye sacred Skies!
And thou, Oh *Styx*! whose formidable floods
Glide thro' the shades, and bind th' attesting Gods;
No form'd design, no meditated end
Lurks in the counsel of thy faithful friend;
Kind the perswasion, and sincere my aim;
The same my practise, were my fate the same.
Heaven has not curst me with a heart of steel,
(*a*) But giv'n the sense to pity and to feel.

(*a*) B. 5, 246. 6, 191.

One

One wou'd think now that the Goddeſs was to do nothing but to adviſe about his Voyage, and the Conveniencies for it: but her Paſſions immediately veer about; and the very next Page, the very next time ſhe ſpeaks, is all in a ſtrain entirely oppoſite to what ſhe has been ſaying in this:

Ulyſſes! (with a ſigh ſhe thus began)
O ſprung from Gods! in wiſdom more than Man!
Is then thy home the paſſion of thy heart?
Thus wilt thou leave me? are we thus to part?
Farewel! and ever joyful may'ſt thou be;
Nor break the tranſport with one thought of me.
But ah *Ulyſſes!* wert thou giv'n to know
What fate yet dooms thee, yet, to undergo,
(*a*)Thy heart might ſettle in this ſcene of eaſe &c.

I muſt not forget here, that the fineſt of the modern *Italian* Poets has expreſs'd this *Mélange*, on an occaſion which is attended with ſuch a Circumſtance, as exceeds any of the other: The particular in which he ſhews it, ſhews at the ſame time the *ſwiftneſs* of the intervening paſſion; and expreſſes the ſtrongeſt of any how immediately one flow of Spirits ſucceeds upon a former and quite contrary emotion. *Armida*, deſerted by her *Rinaldo*, breaths nothing but fury and re-

(*a*) B. 5, 265. 6, 208.

venge;

venge; ſhe purſues him in the heat of the battle; forgetful of her former paſſion, ſhe aims an arrow at his heart: but ſee, while it is yet in its flight, how the paſſions vary on her face! her rage and fury ſoften into tenderneſs and apprehenſions of his danger! in an inſtant her Love is too ſtrong for her Reſentment: in an inſtant, ſhe dreads leaſt her Deſign ſhou'd be effectual, and longs to be diſappointed in her aim:

(a)Swift flies the ſhaft: as ſwiftly flies her pray'r,
That all its vehemence be ſpent in air.

How finely are the Paſſions blended in this piece? the Tranſition from the extremity of fury to an exceſs of love, is manag'd in ſuch a manner, as to be wholly inſenſible: as when two Colours are loſt in the Shades of each other, the Eye is agreeably deceived; and we are delighted with the delicacy of their Union, tho' unable to diſcover where one commences, or the other ends.

In this particular there is not any thing that can equal Poetry, or bear to be compared with it, except its ſiſter-art of Painting; that might copy every

(a) Lo ſtral *volo*; ma *con lo ſtrale* un voto
Subito uſci, che vada il colpo a voto. *Taſſo.*

instance

instance, I have mention'd here: And certainly what makes so beautiful a Figure in the finest Poets, might deserve the imitation of the best Painters. Was not the *Dolon* and *Calypso* of *Homer* worthy the hand of a *Zeuxis* or *Parrhasius*, a *Protogenes* or *Apelles?* Wou'd not the *Aruns* or *Achæmenides* of *Virgil* have been a fine design even for *Raphael* and *Angelo* to have work'd upon? If our *Shakespear* can give us the struggle of Passions in the Breast of *Coriolanus*, *Thornhill* might trace the same, and speak them as well with his Pencil: And if *Corneille* expresses the contrary desires of the sister of the *Curiatij*, his Country-man *Le Brun* might have had a much finer Subject in the various Passions of the *Sabines*, rushing in amidst the two contending Armies; to prevent those fatal Consequences, in which the Victory of either party must necessarily involve them.

But what I have often thought of as the finest Subject of this kind, either for Poetry or Painting, is the first *Brutus* on the Judicial seat; just before the act of giving Sentence on his *own Sons*, for their treachery to the *Common-wealth*. What a noble strife was there between natural Affection, and the Love of one's Country? between Duty, and Desire; be-

between common Humanity, and the Spirit (perhaps the Pride) of a *Roman?* What a fine Groupe of Figures wou'd the Suppliants for the Criminals compose in such a Piece? On one side of the Tribunal, the *Wife* of the Judge and *Mother* of the Offenders; and all the Relations divided in the same manner, between a desire of moving Pity, and an abhorrence of the very Crime, for the Pardon of which they wou'd intercede: The People of *Rome*, on the other side, with looks full of mixt Passions; some struck with Pity amidst all their severity, some almost condemning and yet approving at the same time, the rigid justice of the Father; while others commiserate the Youth of the Sons, and seem incens'd at the *unnatural impartiality* of the Judge.

'Tis a Misfortune, that *Virgil*'s Hand was withheld from launching farther, (*a*)where he has touch'd upon this Subject: but it wou'd be well made up to us, if any eminent Person, in the other Art, wou'd undertake it: It might certainly make a finisht Piece: and Painting in this particular wou'd have the advantage of Poetry; as it could express this *Mélange* of passions directly, and wou'd strike the mind with them in their proper Union, all at once: whereas, when taken from

(*a*) Æn 6. 821.

the *Poetical Picture*, the combination is not ſo eaſy; and we ſcarce ever conceive it, ſo cloſely as we ought.

Were you to give me full ſcope, I ſhou'd carry the reſemblance between theſe Arts much farther than it has ever yet been carried: There is ſcarce a *Figure* or *Manner* in Poetry which I ſhou'd not imagine to have its tally in the Schools of the Painters: I cou'd find it even in the very next point, which comes in my way, in the *Emphatical*. Natural Deſcriptions, as they are Pictures which take in the various Circumſtances of a place or action, give us generally ſeveral Groupes of finiſht Figures: This, on the contrary, is a way of expreſſing Nature in Poetry, not unlike Out-lines and Sketches in Painting: and as the lines in Sketches are *fewer*, but the more *diſtinct*; this muſt be always *conciſe*, and very *expreſſive*.

There are ſeveral maſterly ſtrokes of the *Emphatical* kind in the *Odyſſey*: Such is that Speech of *Telemachus*, where he ſays

Prepar'd I ſtand. He was but born to try
(*a*) The *lot* of Man: *To ſuffer, and to die.*

Such is *Circe*'s whole ſpeech (*b*) which

(*a*) B. 3, 119. γ', 96, 95. (*b*) B. 10, 387, to 392.

I

I repeated to you before, on account of its *Pathos*. Such, in an high degree, is the first rencounter of the Hero with that Goddess,

Hence to thy Fellows (Dreadful she began)
(*a*) Go, be a Beast.——I heard; and yet was Man.

This *Manner* is necessary in all *Sententious* passages, and *moral* reflections; 'tis often strong in expressing the *passions*: and peculiarly useful in the *Sublime*. Take an instance of each, from Mr. *Pope*.

(*b*)——Pyrates and conquerors, of harden'd mind,
The foes of peace, and scourges of mankind,
To whom offending Men are made a prey,
When *Jove* in vengeance gives a land away;
Ev'n these, when of their ill-got spoils possess'd,
Find sure tormentors in the guilty breast:
Some voice of God close whispering from within,
"Wretch! this is Villany, and this is Sin."

The reflection upon seeing *Agamemnon* in *Ades*, is of this kind.

(*c*) Now all *Atrides* is an empty shade!

Just after *Atrides* speaks thus passionately in the account of his own Death, by the treachery of *Ægisthus*:

(*a*) B. 10, 382. κ', 321. (*b*) B. 14, 110. ξ', 88.
(*c*) B. 11, 490. λ', 392.

(a) But not with me the direful Murther ends;
These, These expir'd!——Their crime, they were my friends.

In the *Sublime*, nothing can be higher than the language of his Gods, *Neptune* and *Jupiter*:

(b) If such thy Will——We will it, *Jove* replies,

This latter is that short full way of Expression, so frequent in (c) *Virgil* and (d) *Homer*, copied perhaps by both from the admired Example of it in (e) *Moses*, and grown since into an (f) *Axiom* among the Criticks. It is the more to be commended in Mr. *Pope*, because the turn, he gives the Line, is perfectly his own: Indeed in every one of these instances, as I take it, the Chief of their strength and emphasis, is owing to the Improvements in the Translation.

Antiphaus cou'd scarce imagine, that these were all clear improvements upon *Homer*: He immediately consulted the passages in the Original; and was surpriz'd to find, how far they fell short of the Translation; especially, in the lines

(a) B. 11, 512. λ', 412. (b) B. 13, 177. ν', 154. (c) Naviget. Æn. 4, 237. (d) Ἀπόπεμπε. Οδ. ξ', 146. (e) The great *Fiat*. (f) Πᾶς ὁ δεσπότης δούλῳ μονοσύλλαβος. *Dem. Phal.* ζ'.

that

that anſwer *Circe's threat*, and the *complaint of Agamemnon.* I am pleas'd (ſays he) beyond meaſure, in conſulting theſe parts of the Poem, to ſee how much ſtrength and force there is added to them; have you not obſerv'd more inſtances of this kind? impart them to me, good *Philypſus*: 'Tis no matter for method or regularity; Give them to me immediately. ——Had I time (anſwer'd *Philypſus*) I cou'd find out ſeveral other places which have all their proper improvements; at preſent, I ſhall refer you to the beginning of *Menelaus* his ſpeech to *Telemachus* in the Fourth *Odyſſey*, *Neſtor's* (*a*) in the Third; and in the Tenth, the ſpeeches between *Ulyſſes* and *Circe.* --- I was going to point out ſome paſſages in the (*b*) *Deſcent into Hell:* but 'tis difficult to ſingle out particular beauties from that book; The whole of it is ſo excellently Tranſlated, and (I believe I may ſay) ſo generally improv'd.

The mentioning *Circe* juſt now, puts me in mind of another paſſage: 'Tis where *Homer* deſcribes the Metamorphoſis of the companions of *Ulyſſes.* They had (ſays he) the Shape and the Voice of

(*a*) V. 125, γ', 103. (*b*) Book 11.

Beasts, (*a*) *but their Mind remain'd firm and unalter'd* : this Mr. *Pope* improves into the following lines.

(*b*) Still curst with sense, their mind remains alone,
And their own voice affrights them when they groan.

The addition here is very Natural, and full of Beauty ; in such changes, particularities of this kind strike us very much : *Virgil* touches them on this Occasion (*c*) with his usual happiness ; and (*d*) *Ovid*, who has shown a particular talent for such subjects, has left us the very same thought with this of Mr. *Pope*.

I remember that Mr. *Pope* appear'd to me, upon my first reading his Translation, to have improv'd much upon the Original in his *Poetical Repetitions* of the same word, the Figure in which he is most frequent. Thus is it us'd in the following lines :

A Scene, where if a God shou'd cast his sight,
(*e*) A God might gaze, and wander with delight.

(*a*) κ', 240. Αὐτὰρ νοῦς ἦν ἔμπεδος ὡς τὸ πάρος περ.
(*b*) B. 10, 281.
(*c*) ——— ——— Quamvis collo timuisset aratrum,
Et sæpe in lævi quæsisset cornua fronte. *Ecl.* 6, 51.
(*d*) ——— ———Conata queri, mugitus edidit ore,
Pertimuitque sonos, *propriaque exterrita voce est.*
Met. 1, 638. (*e*) B. 5, 96. &, 73.

Never

(a) Never, *Never* wicked man was wise.
(b) Here, or in *Pyle*.——In *Pyle* or here, your foe.

And in these other very Pathetical,

[rolls the Main,
(c) Then stay, my Child!——Storms beat, and
Oh beat those Storms, and roll the Seas in vain!

'Tis yet more beautiful, when the Repetition holds farther; as in this Passage:

(d) Transported with the song, the listning train
Again with loud applause demand the strain:
Again Ulysses veil'd his pensive head,
Again unman'd, a show'r of Sorrow shed.

This sometimes gives an additional solemnity, and rises stronger and stronger each Line:

Celestial as thou art, yet stand deny'd:
Or swear that oath, by which the Gods are ty'd,
Swear, in thy soul no latent frauds remain,
(e) *Swear*, by the vow which never can be vain.

This is sometimes carried yet farther; and in *Virgil* particularly there is a fine Instance of this sort of Repetition (f) being doubled.

(a) B. 2, 320. β', 282. (b) B. 2, 356. β', 316.
(c) B. 2, 415. β', 370. (d) B. 8, 90. ϑ', 92.
(e) B. 10, 410. κ', 343. μέγαν ὅρκον ὄμοσσαι.
(f) Sævus amor docuit natorum sanguine *matrem*
Commaculare manus; *Crudelis* tu quoque, mater:
Crudelis mater magis, an puer improbus ille?
Improbus ille puer; crudelis tu quoque, mater.
Ecl. 8. v. 50.

But

But in nothing is this figure more beautiful, than in the (a) *Siren's Song*: That Piece of antient Musick, is greatly enliven'd in the Translation; the whole flows on in a peculiar Harmony, and the Chorus is very happily added in the Conclusion of it:

Celestial musick warbles from their tongue,
And *thus* the sweet deluders tune the song.
O stay, oh Pride of Greece! Ulysses, *stay*!
O cease thy course, and listen to our lay!
Blest is the Man ordain'd our voice to hear,
The song instructs the soul, and charms the ear.
Approach! thy soul shall into raptures rise!
Approach! and learn new wisdom from the wise.
We know whate'er the Kings of mighty name
Atchiev'd at *Ilion* in the field of fame;
Whate'er beneath the sun's bright journey lies.
O stay, and learn new wisdom from the wise!

The peculiar justice and propriety of this, is the manner in which these Goddesses apply to *Ulysses*; (a) by offering him knowledge; a thing the most opposite to their own Complexion; and a motive, the most likely to obtain upon that Hero. Mr. *Pope* has shewn his taste, and his judgment, very much in improving so finely upon this Circumstance: but what runs through the whole, is that musical enliven'd turn of the Verses. This is

(a) B. 12. 220. μ', 184. (b) See *Pope's* Note on the Place.

the

the happineſs, which of all things I admire in this writer: either in proſe, or verſe, he has the fineſt flow that can be imagin'd. I have often heard a very good Critick ſay, That *whenever he is reading any Proſe of Mr.* Pope'*s, he cannot help thinking that he ſhould never have wrote any thing elſe: and whenever he reads his Verſes, he is angry with him, for loſing any time from them, for Proſe.* How often has the ſame Gentleman apply'd to this writer thoſe Lines in *Milton,* in which he ſpeaks of the firſt Poet, as well as the firſt of Men?

——— (a) Such prompt Eloquence
Flows from his lips: In Proſe or numerous Verſe
More tuneable, than needed Lute or Harp
To add more ſweetneſs. ———

Among ſo many excellencies, the repeating thoſe Lines, which make the Chorus of this *Song of the Sirens* is not the leaſt beautiful Circumſtance: there are a Multitude of other paſſages, which deſerve to be mention'd on account of the fine *Repetitions* in them: theſe are what fell into my thoughts at preſent; and you have them in the ſame ſcatter'd manner, that they appear there: But one method of Improvement in this Tranſlation, I took

(a) Paradiſe loſt. B. 5, 152.

par-

particular notice of, and in that, I can be a little more full and diſtinct.

Mr. *Pope* has a very great happineſs in *Transferring Beauties.* He often guides his Tranſlation of *Homer* by ſome fine thought, or good expreſſion in any other eminent writer; and this has been the occaſion of ſeveral improvements in that work.

Have you never obſerv'd how he introduces the Elegance of *Virgil,* into the Majeſty of *Homer?* There are two (*a*) ſpeeches of *Circe,* which have much of the air of that of *Proteus,* in the fourth *Georgick;* and that of the *Sybill's* in the ſixth *Æneid.* The ſpeech of (*b*) *Tireſias* is improv'd, from another of the *Sybill;* ſo alſo is the Prophetical ſpeech, in the (*c*) ſecond *Odyſſey.*

There are ſeveral Imitations (in a ſhorter compaſs) of natural Images, and the like, introduc'd into *Homer* from the ſame treaſury: Thus the following Lines

(*d*) Down-ſunk the Heavy beaſt.
(*e*) *Læſtrigonia's* gates ariſe diſtinct in air.
(*f*)——The ſhores like miſts ariſe.
(*g*) And all above is Sky and Ocean all around. &c.

(*a*) B. 10, 385. (*b*) B. 11, 130. Æn. 6, 87 &c.
(*c*) V. 203. (*d*) B. 14, 572. (*e*) B. 10, 93. Æn. 3, 206.
(*f*) B. 12, 201. (*g*) B. 12, 474. Æn. 3, 193.

Although

Although the Tranſlator adds theſe fine ſtrokes from other Hands, they are brought in ſo naturally, that they ſeem to ſpring out of *Homer*'s ſentiment: And if an Inſtance or two ſhou'd be found among them which may vary a little from the Original, it is only to add ſome appoſite Thought, that is not only finer, but at the ſame time perfectly agreeable to the Subject. In ſuch caſes a Tranſlator may demand the greater liberty of enlarging: as a *Flattering Reſemblance* is always allow'd to Painters. I like that very ingenious Friend of yours, who calls the *French* Tranſlation of *Tacitus*, *La belle Infidelle*: That piece, you know, tho' not very preciſe and conſtant to its Author, is the more beautiful, and the more engaging.

However 'tis ſeldom that Mr. *Pope* varies much in theſe additional Beauties; his Tranſlation is generally faithful, even where it improves upon *Homer*: And he keeps the chief mark ſteadily in his Eye, tho' at the ſame Time it admits the ſide glances of Light, from other objects. Thus you will ſcarce ever find him deviating from his Author in ſuch caſes: tho' this manner of improving him by imitation from others is vaſtly frequent; and often ſo plain, that one may trace it

thro'

thro' whole ſcenes together: In particular, I cou'd almoſt be poſitive that Mr. *Pope* read over the *Eclogues* of *Virgil*, before he ſet about that Part of the Story, which lies between *Ulyſſes* and *Eumæus*; and indeed I ſhould be apt to conjecture that he uſually read thoſe Paſtorals, before he ſat down to any rural Scene in this Piece: If I am miſtaken in this, 'tis the (*a*) reſemblance of their beauties, which has deceiv'd me.

Sometimes we find the *Diction* beautified by ſuch Reſemblances, or the Sentiment improv'd from other hands. From the (*b*) *Sacred Writings* frequently; from parallel places in (*c*) *Homer* himſelf: From *Ovid*, *Seneca*, *Horace*, &c. among the Ancients; And from (*d*) *Dryden*, *Addiſon*,

---

(*a*) From *Virgil* B. 14, 76. B. 5, 96. See alſo B 2, 26. Æn. 3, 627. B. 2, 55. B. 3, 126. B. 4, 509. B. 6, 197. B. 10, 569. B. 11, 433, 434. &c.
(*b*) *Scripture*. B. 1, 483. B. 3, 424 451. B. 4, 145. 438. B. 5, 288. B 6, 235. B. 10, 591. B. 11, 239. B. 14, 109. And frequently in other places.
(*c*) *Iliad*. B. 11, 415. Iλ', ς', 41. &c.
Ovid B. 4, 808. B. 10, 282. B. 13, 193. B. 14, 224.
Seneca. B 5, 573.
Horace. B. 10, 556, 557. B. 14, 519.
(*d*) *Dryden*. B. 5, 80. B. 11, 531. &c.
Addiſon. B. 4, 371. B. 11, 684.

Milton,

Milton, and ſeveral others of the moſt celebrated Moderns. In his *Speeches*, we meet with improvements from the Examples and Rules of the Orators of old; and many, from our own Dramatick pieces. It wou'd not be difficult, for a Man of a good Taſte, to diſcern the Air ſometimes of *Dryden*, ſometimes of (a) *Shakeſpear*, and at others of *Otway*, among the ſpeeches in the *Odyſſey*. I ſhall only point out to you thoſe of *Agamemnon*, which are ſo very pathetick, in the (b) Eleventh Book: You will eaſily ſee that they have a new manner, which exceedingly reſembles the hand of the moſt moving of all our Tragick Writers, ſince *Shakeſpear*.

Antiphaus, upon conſulting the paſſages, immediately perceiv'd the ſpirit of *Otway* in them; He then deſired *Philypſus* to direct him to the other imitations he had mention'd: at firſt he did not think they deſerv'd ſo much commendation; but when he came to Compare the original Lines from the *Odyſſey*, with thoſe of Mr. *Pope*, he was convinc'd of their

Milton. B. 11, 725. And frequently in other places.
(a) *Shakeſpear*. B. 9, 420. B. 10, 410. &c.
(b) See Book 11. V. 531. And 537. to 544.

beauty: It delighted him to ſee, what Foundation the Original gave for ſuch a turn, and yet how new that turn was in the Tranſlation; he found almoſt in every one of them ſome addition for the better, and ſcarce in any a deviation from the ſenſe of *Homer*: It was *Homer's* ſenſe, but the Expreſſion of it was improv'd. I thank you, (ſays he turning to *Philypſus*) I thank you for this clearer view you have given me of the beauties of this Tranſlation: beſide theſe laſt, how many things have you repeated to me that are extremely juſt, pure, cloſe, and *emphatical?* how many perfectly true, and *natural?* how many handſomly beautified, and *enliven'd?* what *Pictures* of Things? what *Deſcriptions* of Actions? and what beautiful Expreſſions, both of the *thoughts*, and of the *paſſions* of the ſoul? in a word, what *improvements*, in ſome ſtrokes, upon the greateſt Genius of the World?——Yes, added *Philypſus*, upon the greateſt Genius of the World, aſſiſted by the native uſe of the moſt Noble, and moſt Poetical of all Languages. Then were we to conſider the inconveniences on the other ſide; the general difficulties of Tranſlation, and the difficulty of this in particular: How hard is it for a Poet to keep up his ſpirit and flame in another's another's Work? and how natural to flag in repreſenting Thoughts not our own? To maintain the vigour of Language and the poetick warmth thorough ſo long a work, and to expreſs the Soul of *Homer*, what a Genius does it require? what Spirit wou'd not ſink under ſo large an undertaking? Yet does Mr. *Pope* hitherto ſuſtain his Character in an handſome equal manner: and we may ſafely promiſe ourſelves the ſame of the remaining part of this work: As he enter'd upon this ſtage with the greateſt expectations of all Men, I doubt not but he will leave it with an Univerſal *Plaudite*.

But however great and handſome his performance is in the whole, I own with you that it has its faults, the common marks of Humanity: Yes, my *Antiphaus*, you convinc'd me the former Evening, that it is unavoidable for the greateſt Genius not to fail ſometimes. For my part (ſays *Antiphaus*,) I ſhall make no Apologies for the freedoms with which I then us'd this excellent writer: Any thing of that kind might look odd to you from one, whoſe conſtant Sentiment you know to be this; *that* the kindeſt way of commending a writer, is to find fault with him now and then, at proper intervals. Does not this evince an Impartiality in your views, and add an air of Sincerity and Juſtice to thoſe Commendations, which you give him? Your Criticks, who extol a Man Univerſally, and will not be ſatisfied with any thing under a perfect Character, without any the leaſt defect, are a kind of *Romantick Criticks*; they are rather making an Hero, than deſcribing a Man: They give you a Picture of ſomething, which exiſts no where but in their own Minds: and a compleat Poet, according to their repreſentations of ſuch, will after all be only (what the Earl of *Mulgrave* calls it;)

A Faultleſs Monſter which the world ne'er ſaw.

Very true, ſays *Philypſus*; that ſort of Criticks fail as much on one hand, as our more Modern Criticks have exceeded uſually on the other: Indeed the former err on the good-natur'd ſide; yet both of them are very much to blame: For as it ſhews a *miſchievous* ſort of *Frenzy* to ſtart errors, where there are really none; ſo an Obſtinacy not to ſee faults, where they are very evident, requires either a good degree of *Ignorance*, or a moſt *inveterate Fondneſs*.

I am entirely of your opinion, ſays *Antiphaus*, and ſince I find you in ſuch a temper

temper for it, I cou'd almoſt offer to ſhew you ſome farther remarks on that ſide of the Queſtion,—Have you any other then? (ſays *Philypſus.*) A Few, anſwer'd *Antiphaus*; but I beg one Evening more on this Topick. At preſent I ſhall only add my wiſhes, that we may conſtantly uſe thisfair method, in reading all the celebrated Pieces, which come out among us: Let us keep up the true ballance; and not ſuffer ourſelves to be prejudic'd either by too great fondneſs, or too violent diſlike. This is the great Rule of Antient Criticiſm: *Always to keep our Hearts open to the beauties of a Poem; and never to ſhut our Eyes againſt the defects of it.*

An ESSAY &c.

Evening the Third.

ALMOST all the next day *Philypsus* was taken up in reflecting on what had been said at the close of their last meeting: he began to be not so uneasy, as usual, in thinking that the faults of a favourite Poet were to be lookt into that Evening; he did not value Mr. *Pope* less than formerly, but he was throughly convinc'd that there was not so much of severity in this Method, as he had once imagin'd. "No: (says he to himself) Let us view impartially, that we may rationally admire: Where before I was immediately in love with his Beauties and fond of the Work, I now feel

feel an equal Pleaſure and an equal Eſteem; but it is in a different manner: I now ſeem to ſee the cauſes that move me to be pleas'd with thoſe fine Paſſages, and feel a more juſt and manly Satisfaction in them: 'Tis true, the Soul is not hurried away with that vehemence of delight, as formerly; but the agreeable Senſe I now have from them, is both more refin'd, and more laſting. How much is this *rational* way of admiring to be prefer'd to the common, vulgar *paſſionate* one? This is as a flaſh of Lightning; but the other is like the Light of the Day: 'Tis a ſerene, diffus'd, ſteady light, which at the ſame time that it diſcovers all Objects to us, is it ſelf the moſt beautiful of any.

But then (continued he) how blind was I to the defects of this Poet. Has not *Antiphaus* ſhown me ſeveral, which before I had no ſenſe of, and which now appear evidently to be ſuch? Indeed that over-ſight was more excuſable in reading the Works of this celebrated Writer, than it wou'd have been in any other: Reaſon may well loſe ſomething of her Liberty, when ſhe is taken up with an Object every way ſo agreeable and engaging: However, for the future, I reſolve to keep my ſelf obſtinately from being

being over-pleas'd with any thing; and to read his, as all other the best Pieces, in spight of all their Beauty, by that Rule which *Antiphaus* has laid down.

With these Thoughts he open'd the Translation which lay on his desk; and was very busy in considering it, when Company came in, and interrupted him for that Night: The next Day he employ'd himself in the same manner; This sort of view was new to him, and of course the more agreeable: Sometimes he met with a line or two, that disgusted him a little; but much more frequently was he struck with the Beauties of the Poem; and those he enjoy'd with a full Delight, as he found that Delight to be rational and just. This search drew him on strangely; he did not know how to leave off: And tho' *Antiphaus* stay'd for the Evening before he wou'd disturb him, he found him still closely employ'd at it: "My *Philypsus*, (says he) I'm glad to see you engag'd thus in the *Odyssey*: What new light shall we have into the excellencies of this writer? Have not you been collecting other Beauties out of the Translation?——I have met with several other, reply'd *Philypsus*: So many indeed, that it wou'd be almost endless to collect them. But to tell you the Truth, my my business was quite contrary to what you imagine: I was upon a more difficult task; I was endeavouring to try what Faults I cou'd discover in it. That is by much the more difficult, says *Antiphaus*: The few Faults of that Piece are scarce discernible among such a superiour number of Beauties: How seldom do we perceive the disagreeableness of a single feature, in a Face that is very taking in the whole? Well; but have you been able to overcome this Difficulty? can you discover any thing farther of this kind in the *Odyssey?* Very little, answer'd *Philypsus*: There is but one point yet, that has afforded me any number of Instances; And that is a Fault, directly opposite to what you particularly insisted upon, in our first Conversation on this Subject.

It was then, you know, that we consider'd several Points in which Mr. *Pope* appears to Elevate and Flourish too much: Have you never observed, on the contrary, that there are a few *Lownesses* in his Writings; and that he sometimes sinks into a Diction, which borders on the *Mean* and *Vulgar?* I have, reply'd *Antiphaus*, in some few lines: but if you have made any remarks of that kind, I beg rather to see those of your observation. The

The two Friends were always ready to comply with the desires of each other: *Philypsus*, as usual, without prefacing or debating the matter, immediately shew'd him the following Lines.

(*a*) A Gallant leader and—*a man I lov'd.*

(*b*) The *old man* early rose, walk'd forth, and sate
On polish'd stone before his palace gate.

(*c*) Or has Hell's Queen an empty image sent,
That wretched I might even my joys lament.

(*d*) Struck at the word my very heart was dead.

(*e*) *Euryclea*, who great *Ops* thy lineage shar'd,
And watch'd all Night, all Day: a faithful guard.

(*f*) They led me to a good Man and a wise.
(*g*) And sure he will, for wisdom never lies.

In the note upon this line (says *Philypsus*) we have a couplet repeated from the *Iliad*, which I fear is of the same stamp.

(*h*) Who dares think one thing and another tell,
My soul detests him as the gates of Hell.

I must confess, says *Antiphaus*, that the Lines you have repeated, carry a mean air

---

(*a*) B. 10, 259. κ', 225. (*b*) B. 3, 523. γ', 405.
(*c*) B. 11, 258. λ', 212. (*d*) B. 10, 588 κ', 496.
(*e*) B. 2, 393. β', 345. (*f*) B. 14, 392. ξ', 359.
(*g*) B. 3, 25. γ', 20. (*h*) Iliad 9. 412. ι' 313.

with

with them; but possibly what looks like a fault, may really be a beauty in some of them.

Some subjects require a simplicity of stile: Beside Mr. *Pope* is to follow *Homer*; and shou'd *Homer* use an humble stile in these places, even to appearance improperly, yet one should be apt to look upon it, as a sufficient justification of his translator.

For my part (reply'd *Philypsus*) I have always thought, that there is a wide difference between an *humble* and a *mean* stile; but (not to urge any thing of that kind) in the greater part of the instances just repeated, I am certain, there is not a sufficient likeness between the manner of the Original and the Translation.

I shall only except the two last, which are indeed plain and proverbial in the *Greek*. There is a simplicity, as Mr. *Pope* tells us in his notes, a noble simplicity in the diction; and which, in my opinion, is not Equally kept up in the *English*: but those I shall not insist upon.

As for the rest, that mean close of the first of these Lines, is in *Homer* an (*a*) Handsome sentiment, deliver'd in a sound-

(*a*) ——— Πολίτης ὄρχαμος ἀνδρῶν,
Ος μοι κήδιστος ἑτάρων ἦν, κεδνότατός τε. κ', 225.

ing

ing verſe: and the meaneſt Expreſſion in the ſecond, (*a*) is poetical in the Original. The ſame will hold, in ſome degree, of the other Lines. As it happens Mr. *Pope* in his (*b*) Note upon one of them,

They led me to a good Man and a wiſe;

has given us this proſe tranſlation of the ſame words;

The Gods guided me to the habitation of a perſon of wiſdom:

Now it might be thought a rude queſtion, to ask whether is the more *poetical*, his *proſe* or *verſe* Tranſlation of this Line?

Indeed where *Homer* leads the way, the caſe is very different: I cannot ſay how far it might be juſtifiable, to blame a Tranſlator for following his Author: and it was for that very reaſon, that I ſhou'd not have taken any notice of the *delightful Hiſtory of the Coat and Cloak*, which is given us in one of the longeſt ſpeeches in the Fourteenth *Odyſſey*.

But we have ſeveral inſtances of *additional Lowneſſes:* I obſerv'd particularly that they were pretty frequent, when the Scene is in *Ithaca:* Thus;

(*a*) ——— Γερήνιος ἱππότα Νέστωρ, γ', 405.
(*b*) B. 14. Obſervation XVIII.

His

His task it was the wheaten loaves to lay,
(a) And from the banquet take the bowls away.

Again;

But if, to honour lost, 'tis still decreed
(b) For you my bowl shall flow, my flocks shall [bleed.

Again;

(c) Is this, returns the Prince, for mirth a time?
When lawless gluttons riot, mirth's a crime, &c.

The meanness here (interpos'd *Antiphaus*) is occasion'd by a just design; that of writing in a stile, agreeable to the simplicity of the subject: In several other places, it has a less excusable rise; I mean, the labour and difficulty of Rhime. The Poet's being in haste to get this drudgery off his Hands, sometimes draws him into the use of Expressions, which are flat and contemptible. Thus I believe, we may account for the Lownesses in these Couplets:

While with my single ship *adventurous I*,
(d) Go forth the manners of *yon Men to try*.
Mean-while the Gods the dome of *Vulcan throng*,
(e) *Apollo* comes, and *Neptune* comes *along*.
——— ——— When great *Alcides* rose,
(f) And *Euritus*, who *bad the Gods be foes*.

(a) B. 14, 507 ξ', 455. (b) B. 1, 482. α', 378.
(c) B. 2, 347. β', 310.
(d) B. 9, 202. ι, 174. (e) B. 8, 362. θ', 322.
(f) B. 8, 256. θ', 225.
Οἳ ῥα καὶ ἀθανάτοισιν ἐρίζεσκον περὶ τόξων.

You need only read over one ſingle paſſage, to gueſs how frequently the ſenſe may be leſſen'd and broke by this means; and how often we are put off with low, wretched words, merely for want of a more generous Rhime.

You remember the Speech of *Ulyſſes*, when ſhip-wrack'd in his voyage from *Calypſo*'s Iſland; 'tis transfer'd, you know, by *Virgil* into his ſtorm; and both are very ſtrong, and animated. This is the paſſage which I beg leave to read to you from Mr. *Pope*:

Happy! thrice happy! who in battle ſlain
Preſt in *Atrides*' cauſe the *Trojan* plain:
Oh! had I dy'd before *that well-fought wall*,
Had ſome diſtinguiſh'd day renown'd my fall;
(Such as was that, when ſhow'rs of jav'lins — *fled*
From conquering *Troy* around *Achilles* —— *dead*)
All *Greece* had paid my ſolemn fun'rals —— *then*,
And ſpread my glory with the ſons of men.
A ſhameful fate now hides my *hapleſs head*,
Un-wept, un-noted, and —— *for ever dead*.
A mighty wave, ruſh'd o'er him as he ſpoke,
The raft it cover'd, and the maſt it broke;
Swept from the deck, and from the rudder *torn*,
Far on the ſwelling ſurge the chief was *born*:
While by the howling tempeſt *rent in twain*,
Flew ſail and ſail-yards ratling o'er the main.
Long preſs'd he heav'd beneath the *weighty wave*,
Clog'd by the cumbrous veſt *Calypſo* gave:
At length emerging, from his *noſtrils wide*
And guſhing mouth, effus'd the briny tide. &c.

The meanneſs of this paſſage, in comparison either of the original *Greek*, or of *Virgil's* imitation of it (which the *English* Translator, I doubt not, had in his eye) appears to be in a great measure owing to a poverty of Rhime. It has given a low turn to the whole passage; and that *lowness* is still most evident in the *terminating* of the Lines.

There are a Thousand other things (resum'd *Philypsus*) which contribute to the meanness of stile; even a desire to avoid it, will occasion it: 'Tis not uncommonly seen that the straining to elevate a point, will make it really the more mean and ridiculous: as nothing shews the littleness of a dwarf, more than strutting.

One wou'd be apt to suspect this to be the case in the following verses:

(a) There figs Sky-dy'd, a purple hue disclose—
There *dangling pears* exalted scents unfold,
And *yellow apples ripen into gold.*

And in these other:

(b) Lur'd with the *vapour* of the fragrant feast
In rush'd the suitors with *voracious haste*

Sometimes one single word will lessen

(a) B. 11, 727. λ', 588. (b) B. 1, 190. α', 144.
Ες δ' ἦλθον μνηστῆρες ἀγήνορες.——

the ſentiment, and break in upon the dignity of verſe. Thus where the *Greek* call's *Memnon, The glorious Son of Aurora,* we find it in the Tranſlation only (*a*) *Swarthy Memnon.* This, by ſinking below the Original: it may be as faulty, to ſtick too cloſe to it. (*b*) *Hogherd and Cow-keeper,* (ſays Mr. *Pope* in one of his Notes) *are not to be uſed in our Poetry, tho' there are no finer words, than thoſe which anſwer them, in the* Greek *language:* for the ſame reaſon I ſhou'd think that the uſe of the word (*c*) *Sty*, which occurs ſo often in the Tenth Book, might be varied; and in the Sixth,

(*d*) The *Spindle*, glowing with the purple orb.

In general, what do you think (*e*) of *Scudding before the gales to Pylos?* of a (*f*) *ſore Soul?* and of (*g*) *Sacrificing throngs?* are not theſe Expreſſions to, low for verſe? and is it not too low and ruſtick even for proſe, to talk of *the* (*h*) ſwelling loins *of a Goddeſs,* or of *a Nymph's* (*i*) pacing *along the Sand?*

(*a*) B 4, 256. Ἠοῦς φαεινῆς ἀγλαὸς υἱός. δ', 188.
(*b*) B 14, Note 1. (*c*) B. 10, 277. 338. 459. &c.
(*d*) B. 6, 370. ζ', 306. (*e*) B. 3, 221. γ', 180.
(*f*) B. 3, 252. (*g*) B. 3, 17. γ', 12. (*h*) B. 5, 296.
(*i*) Ibid. 192.

Your

Your Inſtances, reply'd *Antiphaus*, ſufficiently ſhew, that (beſide the inconvenience of Rhime) Mr. *Pope* does ſometimes, without that wrong Biaſs, deviate into a meanneſs of Expreſſion: They are directly contrary to his uſual Spirit. There is a caſe (ſays *Philypſus*) juſt come into my Head, which ought not to be forgot; we may ſee by it, on the other hand, how much this Gentleman can improve upon expreſſions in the Original, beyond the other tranſlators of *Homer*. That venerable old Poet uſes a phraſe which, tho' I do not believe it to have been mean in his times, does moſt certainly ſound ſo in the preſent: In ſpeaking of a Perſon entirely loſt in melancholly, he ſays that he was continually (*a*) *eating up his own Mind*: So great a Man, as *Cicero*, has endeavour'd to give this in (*b*) *Latin*; but with that uſual unhappineſs, which attended him in all his Poetry. In another part of *Homer*, we have the ſame manner of Expreſſion; and it is as meanly tranſlated by ſeveral Hands. The Paſſage is a part of *Jupiter*'s Speech to *Juno*; in which, to ſet out the violence of her hatred to *Priam*

(*a*) Ὃν θυμὸν κατέδων. *Il.* ζ', 202.
(*b*) Ipſe ſuum cor edens. *Tuſc. Quæſt.* lib. 3.

and his family, the God ſays, that *ſhe wou'd* (*a*) *eat them, or ſwallow them up quick.* *Actius Labeo*, a wretched tho' a Court writer, tranſlated ſeveral Books of the *Iliad* into *Latin*; and if we may gueſs at the reſt, by the only Verſe left us of that Work (which, as it happens, anſwers this very Line) we have no great Reaſon to lament the loſs of it: This an old Scholiaſt has preſerv'd, for a taſte of the Performance:

> *Crudum manduces* Priamum, Priamique *piſinnos.*

Labeo, as Mr. *Pope* obſerves in his Note upon the (*b*) place, is equal'd by *Ogilby*;

> Both King and People thou woudſt eat alive:

As is *Ogilby* by *Hobbs*;

> And eat up *Priam* and his people all.

Such a general meanneſs in giving us this Expreſſion of the *Greek* Poet, muſt make us look upon Mr. *Pope* with the greater regard, if he can keep it from ſinking in *Engliſh*: This he has not only done, but gives it to us in an handſome poetical turn:

> Let *Priam* bleed! if yet thou thirſt for more,
> (*b*) Bleed all his ſons, and *Ilion* float with gore!

(*a*) Ὠμὸν βεβρώθοις Πρίαμον Πριάμοιό τε παῖδας. *Il.* Δ', 35. (*b*) *Il.* B. 4, 56.

This

This expreſſes the full ſentiment; and that, with an air of greatneſs, and majeſty in it: 'Tis now Language not unfit to be put into the mouth of *Jupiter*.

Antiphaus was extremely pleas'd to ſee ſo great a change in *Philypſus*; and that (ſuddain as it was) it had not affected him in the uſual manner. As Men generally run from one extreme to the other, he was afraid, that the making him ſenſible of the Faults of the Tranſlator, might give him ſome diſtaſte to his beauties: but as he found he was fall'n into the Indifferent juſt manner of Reading, he thought he might now ſafely go on with him farther in the ſame way. "The defect (ſays he) which you have prov'd in ſome particulars on Mr. *Pope*, is ſufficiently recompenc'd by his Flame and Spirit, and the general beauty of his diction: 'Tis from this Quarter that I am ſtill the moſt apprehenſive of Faults, in that Gentleman's compoſitions. Surely, ſays *Philypſus*, you have nothing more to produce on that head? Yes (reply'd *Antiphaus*) I have a word or two to add, to what we obſerv'd upon it, the other Night. There are a ſort of Verſes, very frequent in our modern writers, which run very ſmoothly off the Tongue; the ſtream is eaſy, but there is neither depth nor clearneſs

clearneſs in it: The truth of it is, they are undiſturb'd with Meaning; And their calmneſs is *as the calmneſs of the Night, which is* dark *withal.* If I might have leave, I ſhould call ſuch verſes as theſe, *Un-ideal Verſes*; and I fear there are ſome few of them to be met with in the *Odyſſey.*

Pray obſerve what an unthinking harmony there is in this couplet, which comes firſt into my Head;

(*a*) Soft he reclines along the murm'ring Seas,
Inhaling freſhneſs from the fanning breeze.

And what a Panegyrick in this?

——— Every Eye
(*b*) Gaz'd as before ſome brother of the sky.

I will read you but a few more:

(*c*) The Royal Palace to the Queen convey.

And

(*d*) ——Plan with all thy arts the ſcene of fate.

(*e*) Of deathful arts expert, his Lord employs
The miniſters of blood in dark ſurpriſe.

But among all of them, upon comparing the Original and the Tranſlation, this ſeems to be the *non-pareil*:

(*a*) B. 6, 284. ζ', 236. (*b*) B. 8, 18. Ἐθηεῦντο ἐσιδόντες. θ', 17. (*c*) B. 2, 378. β, 336. (*d*) B. 13, 442. ν', 386. (*e*) B. 4, 708.

Then

(a) Then warp my voyage on the Southern gales
O'er the warm *Lybian* wave to ſpread my ſails.

Mr. *Pope* has had a Critique on ſome Lines of his *Iliad*, which is chiefly taken up in diſcovering, or making *Falſe English* of them: If this can neither darken the Line, nor affect the Senſe conſiderably, it ſeems to me not to be of any concern in Compariſon of the former *fineſſes*. The antient Criticks were much kinder on this head: and 'tis hence that we owe many of our Figures in *Rhetorick*, to Peccadillo's againſt *Grammar*. I am the moſt unfit in the World to determine in this Caſe, becauſe I have alway found my ſelf as much averſe to the *Grammatical* ſort of Criticiſm, as I am fond of the *Poetical*: but I am apt to think, that there are not many faults of this kind juſtly chargeable on the *Odyſſey*. Of the few which I have by chance obſerv'd, the chief are to be met with in the cloſe of his verſes; Thus it occurrs, if I remember right, twice or thrice in that ſhort paſſage, which I repeated to you the other Evening, on the Transformation of *Ulyſſes*. This Rhime *Philypſus*, is a terrible Thing: it has ſpoil'd more Lines——Good *Antiphaus*

(a) B. 4. 104. δ', 85. Καὶ Λιϐύην.

(cry'd

(cry'd *Philypſus* haſtily) be not ſo invete-rate againſt Rhime: does not it ſoften and beautify verſe? and turn poetry into a ſort of muſick, to a good Ear?——I am not Univerſally an Enemy to Rhime, you know; (return'd *Antiphaus*) It does very well in *Odes* and *Sonnets* to *Armida*: But for any thing very ſolid or pathetick, ſurely 'tis an Ornament too comtempti-ble, as well as too much abus'd. The firſt Piece of *Latin* Rhime I know of, that famous *Stanza* of *Adrian*, does well enough; 'twas ſpoke out of pure Gaiety and good Humour: but to introduce it gravely into poetry, as it was the effect of a miſerable deprav'd taſte, ſo will the productions of thoſe Ages ſhew how hap-pily it ſucceeded. The *Runick* Lays (an-ſwer'd *Philypſus*) I do not pretend to ad-mire: but ſurely you will allow it to have ſucceeded better in our Language, than it did in the hands of that monkiſh Clan of Poets. 'Tis true (ſays *Antiphaus* ſmi-ling) we have not improv'd it yet into *middle Rhimes*, and ſome other of their ex-cellencies. Perhaps it wou'd have been happy too for our Poetry, if we had con-fin'd this *Muſick*, as you call it, to its proper ſubjects. How wretchedly does it ſound in ſome of our Tragedies? in ſuch, all the Actors to me ſeem rather to be *playing at Crambo* with one another, than endeavouring in the leaſt to affect the Audience. With all the violence that Mr. *Dryden* wrote in this cauſe, you ſee he was forc'd to recant at laſt; The only true reaſon of his perſiſting in it at all is, I believe, very obvious, tho' the laſt he wou'd have given us: It was then the Humour of the Age; *Dryden*, every one knows, wrote for Money; and his buſineſs was to pleaſe his Cuſtomers.

And now I have mentioned Mr. *Dryden*, it may be worth the enquiry, to conſider a little more particularly, what that writer has ſaid on this ſubject; as he muſt be allow'd, on all hands, to have been one of the niceſt Judges of Harmony, one of the greateſt Maſters of Verſification, and one of the beſt Poetical Criticks in general, that our Nation has ever produced.

In reading what he has given us, in different places, on this head, 'tis eaſy to ſee, that he very much obſerves a difference between *Rhime*, in the *genuine* ſenſe of the word, by which he always intends the true Harmony of Verſe; and *Rhime*, in the *loweſt* ſenſe; or that gingle, and playing with ſounds, in which the Moderns have exceeded all the other Ages of the World; and which indeed, ſince

ſince the laſt revival of Letters, has bad fair for the *Univerſal Monarchy* in Poetry.

Tho' *Dryden* underſtood Rhime in the firſt ſenſe, as well as moſt Writers, and yet generally ſtoop'd to the uſe of it in the other: Nevertheleſs I am inclined to believe, that he always ſaw thorough the Defects and Inconveniencies, not to ſay the Barbarity and Childiſhneſs, of it. Indeed one might be juſtified in ſaying even this; for *Dryden* himſelf follows *Voſſius* in calling it expreſly, (*a*) *A Childiſh ſort of verſe*; and ſays that ſome *Rhiming Hexameters*, which may be diſcover'd in *Homer*, were probably the remains of a *Barbarous Age*: "*Virgil* (adds "that writer) had them in ſuch abhor-"rence, that he would rather make a "falſe *Syntax*, that what we call a Rhime. "—The nicer Ears in *Auguſtus* his Court "cou'd not pardon him for a Line, in "which he had only dropt ſomething "like it: ſo that the principal Orna-"ment of Modern Poetry, was account-"ed *deformity*, by the *Latins*, and *Greeks*.

After obſerving that the *Greek* tongue falls naturally into *Iambicks*, and the *Latin* into *Heroick* verſe, he calls all our little arts of Rhiming, *Barbarities*: And

---

(*a*) Preface to *Virgil*'s Paſtorals, p. 95.

adds, that "As *Age* brings Men back "into the ſtate and infirmities of *Child-* "*hood*; upon the *fall* of their Empire, "the *Romans doted* into *Rhime*.

What you have now read to me (interpos'd *Philypſus*) ſhews ſufficiently, that Mr. *Dryden* cou'd give up an old Friend, and abuſe him heartily behind his back; That writer cou'd ſpeak the ſevereſt things of Rhime, when he was got into a vein of Proſe-writing: But the preſent ill treatment he gives to it, may perhaps be on ſome particular Occaſion; and in ſome Caſes, I cannot deny that Rhime may be a very improper Ornament.

No (return'd *Antiphaus*) he is here ſpeaking of Rhime in general, and on a general occaſion: If you wou'd know his ſentiments of Rhime, more particularly in relation to the preſent purpoſe, and its uſe in tranſlating an *Heroick Poem*; as it happens, there is a remarkable paſſage, wrote by him on this very occaſion: it was in his more advanc'd Judgment; and particularly, as he himſelf informs us, when he was in his great Climaterick. He is ſpeaking of *Hannibal Caro's* Tranſlation of the *Æneid*: "The performance, (*a*) ſays he, is very

(*a*) Dedication to his *Æneid*. p. 417.

" mean, tho' that Poet took the *advantage* " of writing in Blank-verſe, and freed " himſelf from the ſhackles of Modern " Rhime. I will not make a digreſſion " here (proceeds that Writer) tho' I am " ſtrangely tempted to it; but will only " ſay, that he who can write *well* in " Rhime, may write *better* in Blank-verſe. " Rhime is certainly a conſtraint even " to the *beſt* Poets, and thoſe who make " it with *moſt eaſe*:——What it adds to " *ſweetneſs*, it takes away from *ſenſe*; and " he who loſes the *leaſt* by it, may be " call'd a *Gainer*. It often makes us " *ſwerve* from an Author's meaning: as " if a mark be ſet up for an Archer at " a great diſtance, let him aim as exactly " as he can, the leaſt Wind will take his " Arrow, and divert it from the White.

Thus far Mr. *Dryden*. And his opinion weighs the more with me in this caſe; becauſe, if any thing, we might expect that he ſhou'd be prejudiced in favour of Rhime, but the reaſon of the thing, You ſee, prevailed over all other conſiderations: He goes ſo far as to condemn his own manner of Writing, rather than ſuffer ſuch a corruption to paſs without a ſevere Cenſure; and to that end, very generouſly gives up his Practice, to his Judgment.

Indeed

Indeed I know of but one argument (and that the meereſt *Circle* in the World) to ſupport the preſent practiſe of writing in rhime; we muſt *uſe* it, becauſe 'tis all the *faſhion*. We who were never ſo far infected, can laugh heartily at ſome of the *French*, for rhiming thoroughout their Comedies; yet Rhime in Tragedy was very becoming among us, in an Age, not the leaſt knowing and polite. Diſuſe has made us ſee the flatneſs and inconvenience of that Ornament; and nothing reads more inſipid, than the beſt Pieces left us in that way. Tell me *Philypſus*; why do we ſo much diſlike thoſe Beauties of their kind in our Age?

I believe, ſays *Philypſus*, 'tis as you obſerve. Now the taſte is alter'd, and the faſhion worn off; we can look back, and perceive with eaſe the prejudice of that beauty; where the End is to ſtir up the Soul, by true repreſentations of Nature: To *raiſe* (a) *Terror or Compaſſion, is the buſineſs of the tragick Poet*; and to endeavour to raiſe either with Rhime

---

(a) La Tragedie roulât ſur deux paſſions: Scavoir la terreur que doivent donner les ſuites funeſtes du vice; & la compaſſion, qu' inſpire la vertu perſecurée & patiente. Archiev. de *Cambray*. Sur l'Eloquence Dial. 1.

and all its Harmony, ſeems to me more proper for an *Italian* Opera, than an *Engliſh* Tragedy.

Very true, ſays *Antiphaus*; and do you not judge it as abſurd, where any other Paſſions are to be mov'd, as well as Terror and Compaſſion?—— Undoubtedly, reply'd *Philypſus*.——And is it not the buſineſs of the Epick, to awake the Soul? to raiſe in it an eſteem for Virtue, and an hatred to Vice? in a Word, to move the Paſſions, particularly thoſe very Paſſions you have mention'd? Why then is Rhime, which you diſallow in Tragedy, to be thought uſeful and commendable in the Epick?——As for moving the Paſſions (ſays *Philypſus*) Rhime, I allow you, is of no uſe in either; but it is a fine Ornament, which may be more proper in the one, than in the other: In Dramatick Pieces the Perſons ſhould be ſuppos'd to ſpeak extempore; but there can be no ſuch thing conceiv'd in an Epick Poem----I beg your Pardon (ſays *Antiphaus*) Tho' not ſo ſtrongly, yet this is often ſuppos'd in an Epick, as well as in Tragedy: Do you think that *Homer* is telling you a ſtory, or *Ulyſſes*, when we are got into *Phæacia*? In the 2*d Æneid*, have you not ſeveral intermediate Ideas, which agree not with a Reader, but a Spectator ?--Yes, Sir; in all active Poems, as well as Tragedy, The Author is to disappear, as much as possible: the greatest Art of them is to deceive us into an imagination, that we hear the very Persons speaking, and see them acting before us. *In ipsis Omnia sunt oculis.* Every Poem the nearer it comes to this, the more perfect it is. Consider too, how much of any good Epick piece is purely Dramatick: 'tis scarce to be imagin'd, for Instance, how small a number of Lines in the *Æneid* are properly *Virgil's*: they almost all belong to the Persons engag'd in the Poem; and where the Lines are spoke, we see the attitudes and behaviour of the particular Persons, and receive the words from their Mouth.

Much of what you urge is true; (answer'd *Philypsus*:) but yet you must allow, that Rhime sounds unnatural in Tragedy, and agreeable in pieces of the other kind. That is, as we were just saying, (reply'd *Antiphaus*) because in these 'tis at present all the Mode: let the fashion alter, and this beauty will look as false in one, as it has already in the other. This *Italian* Taste of your *Tasso's* and *Ariosto's* led away the first Poet of our Nation, who attempted any thing toward an Epick; and probably we ſhou'd to this Day have thought it the only proper for our Language, had it not happily been diſdain'd by the great Genius of *Milton*, who choſe rather to follow the true old *Roman* manner. It was *Milton* who flung off our Fetters; and we may venture to ſay in the prophetical manner of a very good Poet now living, *that* (a) *He* ſhall *for ever be honour'd as our deliverer from that bondage.* What a pity it is, he did not ſuffer us ſtill to continue in it, ſince we are ſo fond of our Chains? How happy wou'd it have been, to have given up the Nervouſneſs and Majeſty of his Poem, for *Pryor*'s Eaſe, or the Sweetneſs of *Waller*? I know not what they world may ſay to it; but, for my part, when I read in the Biſhop of *Sarum*'s Hiſtory, *That* Paradiſe Loſt *is a noble Piece* (b) *tho' the Author affected to write it in blank verſe*: it always puts me in mind of the Gentleman, in the monkiſh Ages of Poetry, who ſaid of *Virgil's* Æneid, that *it was really a very good Poem; and wanted nothing, but the* (c) *Sweets of Rhime, to make*

(a) Mr. *Watts*'s Horæ Lyr. Pref. p. 31. (b) Biſhop *Burnet*'s Hiſtory of his own Times. p. 163.
(b) See the *Spectator*. V. 1. Numb. 60.

it, the most perfect Work in its kind.

Well, (says *Philypsus*) I own, there is the greater majesty in Blank verse; but you will own too, that the other is the more beautiful. Yes, (reply'd *Antiphaus*) but for that very reason is Blank-verse undoubtedly the more proper for the *Epick*; as that is the most majestick kind of Poetry imaginable. And even as to the Sound, Those musical returns (if allow'd to be true Beauties) are more than ballanc'd by the *Dead Manner*, introduc'd with them into Poetry; What I mean, is that *perpetual likeness* in the cadence, and turn of the Periods: How frequently do they fall in several repeated Couplets, without any variety, or relief to the Ear? You will sometimes meet with a Rhime-Poem, all the Lines of which run off entirely with the same pauses; the stream always equal, and so level that you can scarce perceive it to move: What do you think of each Couplet, chiming on in the same stops and measure, with the most tedious uniformity of sound imaginable?---That is the fault of the Poet, not of the use of Rhime, says *Philypsus*: I could name you a Poem of this kind, which has almost as great a variety in the Periods, as any Piece in Blank-verse. Possibly you mean a a piece with Mr. *Oldisworth*'s Name to it, (says *Antiphaus*) which I have heard you commend particularly on that score. 'Tis true our Poets of late have endeavour'd to diversify the sound, as much as possible: We see great improvements of this kind, in the excellent Translator of *Vida*'s *Poeticks*; and several in the most nervous and vigorous of all our Translators, both in his *Manilius* and *Lucretius*: Mr. *Pope* seems to have thought of this much more frequently in his *Odyssey*, than in the former Translation of the *Iliad*; and gives us an admirable (*a*) Observation upon it, toward the conclusion of his last work. But after all, let our Poets manage the cadence and structure in Rhime-verse never so artfully, it will fall vastly short of Blank in these particulars; Indeed Rhime is a natural Enemy to them: it breaks and disturbs both the structure, and the cadence. The very sound of any periods the best contriv'd will convince one of this: when a person of a good Ear is reading them, you may observe, that he endeavours to drop the Rhime, and lose the gingle of it, as much as possible: and

(*a*) Od. B. 14; Observ. 2.

when

when the ſound of it is not ſufficiently kept under; you will find, that it ſpoils the continuance, and occaſions too great a break in the period.

You may ſee by what I have been ſaying, that this charge is not deſign'd againſt *ſingle Couplets*; The corruption in this reſpect evidently ceaſes, where there are no periods to be varied. To determine preciſely where it will grow prejudicial, wou'd be difficult, and is not very material: Tho' I know not but what it might be uneaſy to a very nice Ear, to have only four Lines together with regular Rhime: and poſſibly on this very account, the Stanza but of two Couplets has generally unequal Rhimes, (the Second Line anſwering the Fourth) and that of Three, varies in the laſt Couplet. However forc'd or delicate this obſervation may be thought, one thing I cou'd aſſert with ſome degree of Confidence: I dare ſay, any one of a good Ear, who reads only ten Lines of the beſt Rhime-Verſification, and an equal number of *Milton*'s true harmonious Verſes, upon this view; will find a nobler ſound, and that variety (which is neceſſary to the beauty of periods, and to the pleaſure of a Reader) much ſtronger and much fuller in the latter.

What

What has been ſaid of *Couplets*, may in a great Meaſure be ſaid of *Odes*, which conſiſt of proper *Stanzas*: As theſe come next to Couplets for ſhortneſs, they have ſcarce room, ſingly, for the tedious Uniformity, we have been complaining of: and unleſs the *Ode* be long, they do not produce it by their *Number*. There may be a variety too of ſingular uſe in this ſort of Poetry, where a perſon can run theſe *Stanzas* artfully into one another; if the interweaving of them be not ſo frequent and equal, as to bring in that very Satiety we wou'd avoid. Thus qualified Rhime is, at leaſt, very tolerable in *Odes*: And even in *Pindaricks*, the moſt extenſive and lofty of any, the prejudice of it is not ſo preſſing; There is ſo great a Liberty (I mean, in our modern *Pindaricks*) of varying the Numbers, and of fixing or deferring the Rhime at pleaſure. But above all, in ſingle Couplets, Rhime is moſt allowable; and in them indeed, I ſhould think, it deſerves the preference to Blank-verſe: it may pleaſe the Ear more, and cannot do that miſchief, for which it is chiefly to be avoided in all large Pieces, and all compoſitions of a nobler ſort. In this reſpect, it is with Poetry, as it is in Building: A Pile compos'd of Stones, cut juſt alike,

all

all equal and uniform; and diſposed alike, without any thing either great or beautiful in the whole; will yield to one of a good deſign, form'd of materials various and unequal, and perhaps ruder, or leſs exactly poliſh'd: At the ſame time, the particulars of which it is made taken ſingly, will evidently exceed the others. Thus we find, in a walk of Trees, that the two Oppoſites, when cut to anſwer each other, look better, than if they were in diſagreeing Figures; but a Wood, or a Garden full of Trees, all in one Figure, wou'd be rather diſpleaſing to the Eye than otherwiſe: In the two ſimilar Figures, we ſhould have a pleaſing *Uniformity*; but in this large repeated view of the ſame thing, we ſhou'd loſe that *Variety*, which a late very ingenious Writer has ſhewn to be inſeparable from the Idea of Beauty; and which the mind ſeems to require the more, as the number of Objects is encreas'd.

It is a known Rule in verſification, that the Second Rhime ought not to reſemble the ſound of thoſe in a preceding Couplet. When it is carried to the fartheſt, it will not bear beyond the Third Line; and even that is run generally into an *Alexandrine*, that in ſome degree the

the turn of the Period and the Numbers may be varied. Now why ſhou'd it not be as diſagreeable to have a perpetual uniformity of Periods, as a continued likeneſs of Rhime? The latter no Man in the World will allow to be proper: nay, it cou'd not be born with, only for three Couplets together.

But ſuppoſing Rhime a real beauty in Poems of an higher kind, which I am perſwaded it is not; (to ſpeak nothing of its uniform returns, and the havock which it makes in the Periods; nor even of the *diverſion* it gives the thoughts of the *Reader*, and its general diſſervice to pieces that ſhou'd be ſolid and pathetick: to omit all this) the ſingle reaſon which introduc'd this queſtion is, as I take it, ſufficient to determine it. If Rhime is exceedingly apt to miſlead a *Writer*, often to cramp, and ſometimes to ſpoil his ſentiments; its benefits, as being only benefits of Sound, will be far from ballancing thoſe inconveniences of ſo much ſuperiour a nature. This at leaſt is the Caſe with Rhime: it gives either an impertinent pleaſure, or an unneceſſary trouble to a writer; and at the ſame time, that it diſtracts his attention, it encreaſes his difficulties: in a word, 'tis a falſe bent put upon the thoughts of of thePoet; and, in the beſt, proves frequently a counter-biaſs too ſtrong for their good Senſe.

I own, it is with a ſtrange readineſs, that people fall generally into this taſte; it has almoſt *univerſal conſent* on its ſide: and the few Aſſerters of the Liberty of Verſe meet with little Praiſe, or even Countenance, from the World. How many Perſons would fly into unreaſonable Heats upon hearing half that I have ſaid to you? I ſhould beg the favour of any ſuch Perſon, who wou'd pleaſe to be diſobliged in it, to ask himſelf what argument there is for this practiſe, which has ſo generally obtain'd in the modern World: If he can find none, 'tis eaſy to bring the matter more home, and to ask farther, whether he thinks Rhime wou'd be proper in the *Odyſſey* or *Æneid*; and then, what ſingle reaſon can be aſſigned, why it ſhould be improper in a *Latin* or *Greek*, and not ſo in an *Engliſh Epick.* ——Yes, *Philypſus*, I am perſwaded it is nothing but uſe, which makes it ſupportable at preſent; and whenever the world recovers it ſelf from this *agreeable Stupor*, it will then appear as ridiculous to the Reader, as it has been inconvenient to the Poet. This I really imagine, that in future, and perhaps far diſtant Ages, the

Criticks, when they look back on any the best Poem of this ſort, (which may be deliver'd down to them from their Anceſtors) will be at a loſs to give any account of their Manner of Writing. When they read Mr. *Pope's Iliad* or *Odyſſey*, they will often applaud the greatneſs of his thoughts; and often admire the happineſs of his diction, as far as the preſent Language ſhall be preſerv'd to them. They will honour his remains, and when they look toward his Aſhes with veneration, "There (will they ſay) "lies the Great Man, who in ancient "Days, is ſaid to have ſhewn the nobleſt "Genius to Poetry in the World: what "beauties do we diſcover in him, thro' "all this ruſt of time, and ſo much ob-"ſolete language? He is every way to "be commended as far as any of our an-"cient Poets are; Only he fell into the "common fault of thoſe Ages; and al-"ways ſhews that trifling labour of "making the laſt ſyllable of every alter-"nate line, ſound like the cloſe of the "foregoing: Bating this inſignificant "taſte of thoſe times, how much is he to "be praiſed, and how much to be ad-"mired?

It

It wou'd have been much better, and much more for their honour, for Mr. *Dryden* in his time, or Mr. *Pope* in ours, to have broke thorough this tedious Slavery; and to have freed the World from a taste so irrational, and barbarous.---I own it to you; I have something of an Impatience in me to see this great Reformation in Poetry set on foot: I wish it cou'd be brought about in our Time: and if not, almost envy those, who in future Ages shall be so happy, as to see Men awake from this Lethargy of Verse: when all the Poets shall conspire to restore strength to their Sentiments, and nerves and variety to their Numbers: when the Writers shall throw aside all those idle Arts and Tricks, which we now play with Sounds; and *true Harmony* shall flourish, without incroaching upon *true Sense*.

(a) O might I live to hail the glorious day,
And sing loud *Peans* thro' the crowded way,
When in triumphant state the *British* Muse,
True to herself, shall *barbarous* aid refuse;
And in the *Roman* Majesty appear,
Which none know better, and none come so near!

(a) Conclusion of the *Earl* of *Roscommon*'s Essay on Translated Verse.

Philypsus began to be moved by what his friend had urg'd on this head: I confess (says he) You are a powerful adversary to Rhime; but you must allow one some time to get a thorough dislike of a thing, which has once been so agreeable. There are some allowances too to be made in the present case; I believe, no man is less embarass'd by the use of Rhime, than Mr. *Pope*; and his command in Writing will take off much of your objection at present: tho' I own your reasoning against this Fashion in general, to be very strong and forcible. However, this Writer has a peculiar happiness in it, and his Language flows with the greatest ease in the World: I believe you can scarce instance a verse, in the whole Work, which does not run off smooth and handsomely. 'Tis true (says *Antiphaus*) there are very few in it that are harsh, or any way faulty, either in Sound, or Composition: two or three which I remember of that kind are scarce worth repeating—Yes (interrupted *Philypsus*) if you have observ'd any such, let us have them. What do you think of this? says *Antiphaus*:

(a) And to the deaf Woods wailing breaths her [woes.

(a) B. 6, 138.

Or

Or of these ;

(*a*) Rich Tapestry, stiff with inwoven gold.

(*b*) By what strange fraud *Egysthus* wrought, relate,
(By force he cou'd not) such an hero's fate.

No bird of air, no dove of swiftest wing
Shuns the dire rocks : in vain she cuts the skies,
(*c*) The dire rocks meet, and crush her as she flies;

(*d*) I climb'd a cliff——
To learn if ought of *mortal* works appear,
Or chearful voice of *mortal* strike the ear.

(*e*) *Deem* not unjustly by my *doom* opprest, &c.

These Lines are somewhat faulty in the sound, or posture of the words : but I only mention them ; it wou'd be frivolous to make particular remarks on them : You may see, *Philypsus*, that my stock is quite out when I sink so low : my task this Evening was difficult enough to me ; and indeed 'tis not easy for any one to find many faults in a Piece, which comes from such excellent hands. Have you nothing farther to observe on it ? (says *Philypsus*) I think I have heard you speak formerly of some Contradictions——That particular I had forgot, says *Antiphaus*; there are indeed some *seeming Contrarieties* in this work : these are of two sorts ; one, in which the

(*a*) B. 4, 406. (*b*) B. 3, 311. (*c*) B. 12, 78. (*d*) B. 10, 172. (*e*) B. 1, 86.

Tranſlator is *contrary* to his Original: and the other, when the Tranſlation ſeems to have ſome little Circumſtances in it contradictory to one another.

Since you mention the thing, I believe I can recollect a paſſage or two, in which the ſenſe is preſs'd ſo far, or ſo much altered from what it was, that they ſeem directly oppoſite to the Original. When the *Grecian* Commanders were drawn into *Troy*, in the famous Wooden Horſe; the Enemy upon ſuſpicion of the deſign, us'd an artifice to make them *cry out* by ſurprize, if there were really any perſons conceal'd in it. *Homer* tells us, that all of them *ſat very ſilent*: only *Anticlus*, one of the Officers, was juſt *ready* to anſwer; when *Ulyſſes*, who ſat by him, *ſtopt his mouth by force*, prevented his making any noiſe, and ſo preſerv'd all their Lives. Inſtead of which the Tranſlation ſays, that this *Anticlus*,

(*a*) ——— Unable to controul,
Spoke loud the languiſh of his yerning ſoul.

In another place, where in *Homer* we hear of an Hero, falling in the defence of

---

(*a*) B. 4, 388. Δ', 287.

his

his Country, *under the Walls of his native City*; Mr. *Pope*, in drawing out the Circumſtances of it, ſpeaks as if it was (*a*) *on a foreign ſhore.* In the Second Book, we meet with three or four particulars of this kind.——There *Telemachus* deſires the ſuitors (as it is in *Homer*) to leave him, and be quiet; as in Mr. *Pope*, to (*b*) *riſe in his aid.*——There the ſame Prince is ſaid to *draw his hand* gently *out of that of Antinous*; inſtead of which the Tranſlation, I think, tells us that he *frown'd*; caught away his hand (*c*) *ſternly*; and *ſtrode away* in a paſſion. 'Tis the ſame Caſe with *Mentor* in the Council: he roſe to make a ſpeech to them, with (as the *Greek* ſignifies) a *wiſe* or *friendly* air; but in the *Engliſh*,

(*d*) *Stern* as he roſe he caſt his Eyes around
That *flaſh'd with rage*; and as he ſpoke, he *frown'd*.

These look like contrarieties between *Homer*, and his Tranſlator; there ſeem to be a few others, between paſſages in the Tranſlation it ſelf.

(*a*) B. 8, 580. θ', 524. —ἑῆς πρόσθεν πόλιος——
(*b*) B 2, 77. β', 70.
Σχέσθε φίλοι, καὶ μ' οἶον ἐάσατε πένθεϊ λυγρῷ
Τείρεσθαι.——— (*c*) B. 2, 362. β', 321.
——ἐκ χειρὸς χεῖρα σπάσατ' Ἀντινόοιο
ῥεῖα,——— (*d*) B. 2, 259. β', 228. There

There is a part of *Mercury*'s ſpeech in the *Fifth Odyſſey*, and another point in the deſcription of *Lachæa*, an uninhabited Iſland, which (I remember) I mention'd to you formerly, as Examples of this Inconſiſtency. Such indeed they appear'd to me, even after a ſecond and third Reading: but upon conſulting the Original, I at laſt found them to be capable of a conſiſtent Meaning. However it is to be wiſh'd, that the Tranſlator had ſet them in a clearer light: for in one, the reader will be apt to imagine, that the Poet ſpeaks of (*a*) *Inhabitants in a deſart Country*; and in the other, that *Mercury* is ſaid to have been (*b*) *vaſtly delighted* with the ſight of *Calypſo*'s Iſland, and *not to have been delighted at all* with the ſight of it.

In another place (I take it to be in the very firſt Book of the *Odyſſey*) *Telemachus* ſays, that his Father is (*c*) *Dead*, and that he is *wandering* from Country to Country, at the ſame article of time: Thus too we hear the Sea, call'd *the* (*d*) *foaming Flood*, in one Line; and in the very next, 'tis the *Level ſurface of the deep*.

(*a*) Book 9. Compare Verſe 143, with 147.
(*b*) Book 5. Compare Verſe 98, with 124.
(*c*) B. 1, 299, and 309. (*d*) B. 5. 65.

As

As for *meer Miſtakes* (where a Verſe carries ſomething of *Blunder* in the ſound of it) I have taken but little notice of them; and ſhall only mention two or three, juſt to ſhew, that the *greateſt Writers* are capable of falling into ſuch Errors, as will be diſcernible to the *meaneſt Readers*.

(*a*) *I anſwer'd*, Goddeſs! human *is thy breaſt*——

——is a Line of this kind: and the Expreſſions in it will appear to every one that looks upon it, to be improperly put together, on the ſame account, as thoſe in the following Couplet:

(*b*) Some other motive, *Goddeſs*! ſways thy mind,
Some cloſe deſign, or turn of *Woman-kind*.

There is a Verſe juſt come into my head, in which Mr. *Pope* may be thought to talk of (*c*) *ſeeing a Sound*; and in another we are told of *a place ſo* (*d*) *deep, that you cou'd not ſhoot to the bottom of it*.

I know not whether a ſevere Critick would not think that there is a jar between the Expreſſions, where *Ulyſſes* is ſaid, to be

—— ——— Doom'd to mourn,

(*a*) B. 10, 451. (*b*) B. 5, 224. (*c*) B. 6, 40. *See*, from their thrones thy kindred Monarchs *ſigh*.
(*d*) Nor the fleet arrow from the twanging bow, Sent with full force cou'd reach the depth below. B. 12, 102.

(*a*) Bitter

(a) Bitter *Conſtraint*, *erroneous* and forlorn.

And where *Halitherſes* ſpeaks of

(b) *Deeds then undone.*

but theſe, and ſuch like trifles, I ſhall leave to thoſe, who are fond of finding faults; and whom I can own without envy to have a greater Niceneſs, and Curioſity in Verbal Criticiſm, than ever I deſire to have.

Theſe, tho' leſs conſiderable blemiſhes in a *poetical* Character, are much more obvious to every Eye, than the greater defects of a Poem: and will be always obſerv'd upon, with more ſcorn and contempt, than any other: they border on *Ridicule*; and that is a thing, which will ever be agreeable to *little* Minds. That Verſe of Sir *Richard Blackmore*'s, in which he deſcribes (c) the *Veſt* of a *naked Pict*; and that in one of Mr. *Dryden*'s Tragedies, which ſpeaks of (d) *Silence invading the Ear*, has probably been repeated many times more, than the beſt Line he ever wrote. This is low enough

(a) B. 1, 300. (b) B. 2, 201.

(c) A painted Veſt Prince *Voltigern* had on
Which from a Naked Pict his Granſire won.

(d) What horrid ſilence does invade my Ear?

of

o' conſcience, tho' it has been a very faſhionable way of Criticiſing of late Years: it ſhews how ill-natur'd the World is; but people will have their Laugh: and 'tis vaſtly eaſier to *Ridicule*, than to *Admire*.

It is this ſort of Men, *Philypſus*, and a clan of others, equally malicious and more gloomy than the former, who have brought the name of *Critick* into ſuch contempt among us: While thoſe have imagined, that Sneering and Malice are the beſt titles to Wit; and theſe were of opinion, That *to find fault is to Criticiſe*. How different from this was the method of the Antient Criticks of *Greece* and *Rome?* Indeed Criticiſm, as firſt inſtituted by *Ariſtotle*, was deſign'd for a Standard of judging well; to give an inſight into the Excellencies of Authors, and to diſcern their Faults. There was a time, when it was a ſtudy highly rational; far from borrowing its force from Ridicule and Falſe Wit, it ſhou'd proceed upon known Rules and eſtabliſh'd Meaſures. I do not ſay but what the beſt Criticks may have approved of particular Lines, without being capable of aſſigning the Reaſons why they pleas'd them ſo greatly. You often ſee a Face which is very taking, without any regularity

larity of Features: ſuch an one as pleaſes every body, tho' no body can give the Reaſon of his being pleas'd with it. Eloquence has its *Je ne ſcai quoi's*, as well as Beauty. However moſt commonly we can ſpecify the particular *features*, which are ſo agreeable; or know that our pleaſure is founded on the Symmetry of the *whole*.

But it is not enough that Criticiſm is rational; it ſhou'd ever be Human and Good-natur'd. Where the Deſign is great, the Diſpoſition juſt, the Deſcriptions lively, and the Language generally good and poetical, that work is in general to be commended; tho' the Poet, in particular Points, may have fallen into many faults; nay into ſome, which look very groſs, when they are conſider'd ſingly. The greateſt Critick among the *Roman* Poets lays it down for a Rule, That *where there are* more *Beauties than Faults in a Poem, that Piece is to be pronounced good:* And one of the greateſt Criticks among the *Greek*, carries it farther; He ſhews at large, (*a*) *That* there is often a *negligence*, that is *becoming*; ——*That* a greatneſs of Soul will carry a

(*a*) *Longinus* περὶ ὕψους, λγ' &c.

Man above the obſervation of little Circumſtances;——And *That* a Poet of a generous Spirit with faults, is greatly preferable to a low wary Writer without them.

Agreeable to this was the behaviour of theſe great Men in laying down rules, or making obſervations: their intention was to diſtinguiſh the beauties of Language or Sentiments, from the defects and vices of either. You find them to have been in Love with the Charms of Eloquence, and the true Spirit of Poetry, wherever they meet with them. They take not that ſnarling Satisfaction in finding faults, which many of their pretended Succeſſors are ſo full of in their writings. Indeed they very freely pointed out the miſtakes and vices of the greateſt Writers: but their chief deſign in this was, that ſuch of their remarks might ſerve as *Buoys* to ſhew where former ventures had miſcarried, and to prevent others from running upon the ſame Shallows. This was the Spirit of the Antient Criticks. Their Fate was according to their Merit: they ſtill remain among us, and are read with pleaſure and applauſe: whilſt *Zoilus*, the only *Modern Critick of the Antients*, has left nothing behind him, except the odious memory of his Impotence and his Malice.

Our modern *Zoilus's* (interpos'd *Philypsus*) are very easily known. They run down the performances of the best writers with heat and noise: every thing is a fault with them. They will go regularly thorough a Poem, with a constant frown upon them; and think themselves obliged to find mistakes or nonsense in every Line of it: they condemn by Tale, and censure by the Sheet. Nothing is more probable, than that from the *Poem*, they come to quarrel with the *Person* of the Author. Blemishes in his moral Character, and even natural Imperfections, have a share in their observations: and in a word, they labour hard to convince you, that they are bad Christians as well as bad Criticks. The best of it is, their attacks are as weak, as they are violent; they have but little of Courage, tho' they make so great a Noise with it: and are like a sort of Currs that bark most, and run the soonest. The Character that was given of the *French*, as *Warriors*, is true of these People, as *Writers*: They behave themselves fiercer than Men, in the onset; and in the shock, are feebler than Women.

I think you cannot be too ſevere upon them, reſum'd *Antiphaus*: they are a Contradiction to true Criticiſm; as they always ſhew the greateſt malice againſt every thing, that deſerves the moſt to be commended. Mr. *Pope* has had the fate to be attack'd by theſe Animals: and indeed I do not ſee how he could avoid it. He has too many excellencies to let them ſleep in quiet.

'Tis certain that the faults of a Writer (and never was any Writer without faults) ought to be obſerved; and the more excellent an Author is, the more neceſſary is ſuch a Work. But this is the Drudgery of Criticiſm: the Pleaſure and the Profit are on the other ſide.

We ought to ſhew faults, but we ought never to ſhew malice. And beſide the general good Nature which is owing to thoſe Great Men, who have eminently oblig'd the World by their Labours; there are particular allowances to be made in this laſt work of the greateſt Poet of our Age. Nothing in the World is more laborious, than Tranſlation; and eſpecially when the Piece is engag'd for, and muſt go on. 'Tis extremely difficult to keep up the Spirit of Poetry in another's Compoſitions, tho' you catch all the (a) *apteſt Moments*; and never employ the Mind, but when there is an *Impetus* comes upon it toward that particular buſineſs: and this Difficulty is greatly encreas'd, where a Man cannot well ſet down to it, only at ſuch times as his Muſe is in a good Humour; but may be obliged, in a manner, to Write by the Hour, and upon fixt returns. I know not how far this was the Caſe with Mr. *Pope*, in this performance: but wherever it was, the Poet will be little more than a common Man: He is, at ſuch times, much the ſame as a Prophet without his *Afflatus*.

Beſide this, I muſt repeat, what I have ſaid ſo often: The conſtant returns of Rhime unavoidably unnerve a Poem: The Age is in Love with this Weakneſs; and Mr. *Pope*, in indulging their humour has taken much from the ſtrength of his Genius: had he been leſs obliging to the taſte of his Readers, his performance might have been more ſinewy, and more compleat. This ought certainly to be taken into the account: and wherever the Tranſlation falls ſhort of the force and nervouſneſs of *Homer*, we ought con-

(a) Mollia tempora fandi.

ſtantly

ſtantly to ask our ſelves this queſtion; Whether *Homer* himſelf cou'd have carried it farther, had he wrote (as Mr. *Pope* does) in *Engliſh*, and in *Rhime*?

'Tis true, all this may be ſaid of his Tranſlation of the *Iliad*; but if that Piece exceed this of the *Odyſſey*, it is very natural upon other Accounts that it ſhou'd do ſo. *Homer* exceeds himſelf in that Poem.——Great Actions ſtrike the Soul with rapidity; while all the things that relate to lower Life, are leſs vigorous and affecting:——The deſcription of Warriors and moral Precepts have a very different effect, on the writers themſelves; thoſe aſſiſt the Poetical flame, while theſe fling the Mind into a more ſedentary Poſture. 'Tis natural almoſt for People to ſleep at Sermons: But a Battle rouzes and animates the Spectators, as well as thoſe who are engaged in it. Thus there muſt be leſs ſpirit in the Writer, as well as leſs attentiveneſs in the Reader of the *Odyſſey*: and a Tranſlation of it, even from one and the ſame Hand, cou'd not fairly be expected to equal a Tranſlation of the *Iliad*. The Reader and the Poet have both of them the diſadvantage of a cooler and more unactive Subject: A *Poet* (as Age always is) vaſtly talkative; A *Fable* laid infinitely lower; and

and a *Diction*, almost perpetual in moral Sentences and Reflections, give a pattern very different from *Homer*, in all his vigour, describing the Passion of *Achilles*; and sounding out the Wars of the *Greeks*, with an air the most martial and animated, that can be imagined.

Here *Antiphaus* rose up from his seat, and as *Philypsus* perceiv'd that he had finish'd; "I was unwilling to interrupt you (says he) otherwise I shou'd have observ'd on a verse or two, which you repeated, as rough, and of a bad turn. What were those Lines of *the Rocks*, which you mention'd just now?—Of the Rocks? (says *Antiphaus*) let me see---Oh, I remember them;

> No Bird of air, no Dove of swiftest wing
> Shuns the dire rocks: in vain she cuts the skies,
> The dire rocks meet and crush her as she flies.

The same says *Philypsus*: these and that other verse,

> Rich Tapestry, stiff with inwoven gold,

sound indeed rough; but to me their roughness, is their beauty: the turn of them seems design'd; and their manner to be expressive of their sense. If that be the Case, I beg pardon, says *Antiphaus*: Were I the greatest enemy in the World to meer harmony, and the ſtated returns and gingle of ſyllables; I ſhou'd be one of the firſt among the admirers of *Sound*, whenever it is made ſerviceable to nature and true ſenſe. That is the Art (ſays *Philypſus*) and the Maſtery, for which I particularly admire Mr. *Pope*: It is he who took up that great Rule of *the Sounds being a comment on the Senſe*, and enforc'd it beyond any of the Criticks who went before him. To this Writer we chiefly owe the revival of the nobler art of Numbers; and the method of ſignifying motions, and actions, and all that vaſt variety of our own paſſions by *Sounds*. In his incomparable *Eſſay on Criticiſm*, this Writer has given us the beſt Adviſes, and interwove the moſt beautiful Examples into them, in a manner that will always be admired. The firſt *Stanza*, in his *Ode* on St. *Cæcilia*'s Day, is the fulleſt Piece of this kind perhaps extant in any Language: 'tis it ſelf a perfect Conſort. In the Tranſlations of *Homer* we find him very frequent, and very juſt, in the ſame manner of Expreſſing things: I call it ſo; and cou'd almoſt be perſwaded to think it a better way of Expreſſing, than in the common way of *Words*. Theſe have a Senſe affixt to them by Cuſtom; while the other ſpeaks by the Ideas of things;

That

That is a flowing, variable help; this is the Voice of Nature, and a ſort of *Univerſal* Poetical *Language.*

Mr. *Pope* affords us infinite Examples of this Beauty in his Tranſlation of the *Odyſſey*; it wou'd be endleſs to repeat them all, or to admire them as they deſerve. But amidſt all this variety, there is a ſingle Point, which I have obſerv'd more than any of the reſt: Whenever the Poet is ſpeaking of the watry Element, or any thing belonging to it, his management of Sounds is particularly frequent and beautiful.

Tho' it might not be much obſerv'd at the firſt view, I know no place where a greater variety of things are expreſs'd this way, than in the Twelfth *Odyſſey*; 'Tis where *Ulyſſes* is giving an account of his ſetting ſail from the Iſland of *Circe*:

(*a*)——We ruſh'd into the Main;
Then bending to the ſtroke, their oars they drew
To their broad breaſts, and ſwift the galley flew.
Up ſprung a brisker breeze: with freſhning gales
The friendly Goddeſs ſtretch'd the ſwelling ſails;
We drop our oars: at eaſe the pilot guides;
The veſſel light along the level glides.
Then riſing ſad and ſlow, with penſive look,
Thus to the melancholly train I ſpoke.

(*a*) B. 12, 189.

The

The objects ſhift perpetually in theſe Lines; and yet there is not a ſingle period or pauſe in them, the ſound and turn of which does not agree perfectly with the ſentiment: I do not intend to enlarge much upon them; but had it been wrote in the Days of *Dionyſius Halicarnaſſæus*, I doubt not but he wou'd have given us a Diſſertation, on a paſſage which ſo variouſly expreſſes that Art, of which he was particularly fond. That is the Critick, I think, ſays *Antiphaus*, who firſt (*a*) obſerv'd this Beauty in the noted Deſcription of *Siſyphus* his Stone? Yes, anſwer'd *Philypſus*; and every one knows how perfectly well the excellence of that Paſſage is preſerv'd (*b*) in Mr. *Pope's* Tranſlation.

Words give us the bare Ideas of things; but words, thus managed, impreſs them very ſtrongly and ſenſibly upon the mind: Do you not perceive the Storm riſing (*c*) *When the wild Winds whiſtle o'er the main?* and are you not in the midſt of it when (*d*) *Eaſt, Weſt together roar, and South and North roll mountains to the Shore?*

(*a*) Περὶ συνθέσεως ὀνομ. p. 29. Ed. *R. Steph.* (*b*) B. 11, 735. λ', 593. (*c*) B. 12, 379. (*d*) B. 5, 380.

Then

Then are we hurried o'er the Deep, and ſee all the *rocks* and dangers of it:

(*a*) Dire *Scylla* there a ſcene of Horror forms,
And here *Charybdis* fills the ſea with ſtorms;
When the tide ruſhes from her rumbling caves
The rough rock roars; tumultuous boil the waves;
They toſs: they foam.———

The next moment if the Poet pleaſes (like the *Dæmon* he ſpeaks of) He can make all as gentle and ſerene, as it was before rough and boiſtrous.

(*b*) Sunk are at once the winds: the air above
And waves below, at once forget to move:
Some *Dæmon* calm'd the air, and ſmooth'd the deep,
Huſh'd the loud winds, and charm'd the waves to ſleep.

Did you ever ſee a more perfect Calm? Yet ſmooth and huſh'd as theſe Lines are, you may eaſily perceive a difference between the deſcription of a ſtill Sea, and the eaſy beautiful current of a River.

(*c*) Smooth flows the gentle ſtream with wanton pride,
And in ſoft mazes rolls a ſilver tide.

How happy is the hand of the Poet, and what a Command has he of Nature, to make the numbers of his verſe

(*a*) B. 12, 280. (*b*) B. 12, 202. (*c*) B. 11, 286.

ſpeak

ſpeak his Sentiments; Thus to paint even ſounds; and to draw by Meaſures, what does not come under the power of the Pencil? In this Writer, Sir *John Denham*'s Wiſh is effected: His Lines always flow as his Subject;

Tho' deep, yet clear; tho' gentle, yet not dull:
Strong, without rage; without o'erflowing full.

I thank you (ſays *Antiphaus* bowing) I thank you, my dear *Philypſus*, for this unexpected view of one of the greateſt Beauties in Poetry. I cou'd willingly ſtay to hear you farther on this Head, and am perfectly angry with the Night for wearing away ſo faſt. I hope we ſhall ſoon find an opportunity of reſuming the Subject (anſwer'd *Philypſus*) I need not tell you how agreeable it is to me, even to be convinc'd of my Errors by *Antiphaus*; and I'm ſatisfy'd that you take a delight in any occaſion of admiring Mr. *Pope*. I beg you would tell me *Antiphaus*; do you not approve of him in ſome points, more than you have formerly? I do not know how it is, (ſays *Antiphaus*) but I ſeem to be both more pleas'd, and more diſpleas'd with him, than I was before this enquiry: his Excellencies, from the light in which you have ſet them, ſtrike me more agree-

ably

ably than ever; but then this looking ſo cloſely into his Defects has made thoſe too the more groſs and viſible. However (concluded *Philypſus*) you will ſtill acknowledge with me, *That his faults are the faults of a Man, but his beauties are the beauties of an Angel.*—You don't ſeem to like the word: it may ſound perhaps too high; but I mean only of a *Great and Uncommon Genius.*

FINIS.

AN

ESSAY

ON

Pope's *ODYSSEY*:

IN WHICH

Some particular *Beauties* and *Blemishes* of that Work are considered.

PART. II.

———————— Each finding, like a friend,
Something to blame, and something to commend.

Pope's Miscel. Vol. I.

Le choix des grans mots *donne aux choses une espece d'ame & de vie; les* beaux mots *sont la lumiere propre et naturelle de nos pensées: mais un discours* tout simple *exprimera quelquefois mieux la chose, que toute la pompe & tout l'ornement.* Boileau.

Printed for *S. Wilmot*, Bookseller in OXFORD, and Sold by *J.* and *J. Knapton*, *R. Knaplock*, *J. Wyatt*, *D. Midwinter*, *W.* and *J. Innys*, and *T. Astley*, in St. *Paul*'s Church-Yard, *W. Mears*, without *Temple-bar*, *J. Crokat* in *Fleet-Street*, and *J. Roberts*, in *Warwick-Lane*, LONDON. 1727.

Price One Shilling and Six-Pence.

INDEX

OF

Figures, Passions, &c.

* Virgil's

INDEX.

too

INDEX.

The

The Natural Order of the Passages quoted from the ODYSSEY.

523

I N D E X.

INDEX.

INDEX.

N. B. *All the following References belong to the Second Volume of the* ESSAY.

INDEX.

In the time that was taken up by this agreeable Search, he call'd often upon that Friend, with whom he ſhar'd his Studies, as well as his Affections. This was rather a Dividing, than Leaving his Purſuits: for he ſcarce ever ſaw *Antiphaus*, without mentioning ſomething of the *Odyſſey*, and hearing his Sentiments in return. When he had gone entirely thorough the Poem, he went immediately to deſire a Meeting, in ſome place where they might talk more at large upon that Head. By good luck *Antiphaus* was perfectly diſengag'd: "'Tis a fine "Evening, ſays he; and if you pleaſe we "will take a turn together in the Gar-"dens of *Horatio*: ſince we cannot enjoy "his Company, at leaſt let us make uſe "of that Liberty he has left with us. "There we ſhall be retir'd from the "Noiſe, and Buſtle of the Town; and "ſafe from every ſort of Interruption." *Philypſus* was extremely pleas'd to find him ſo ready: they ſtept together into his Coach, which drove immediately to *Horatio*'s, and ſet them down at the Gates which lead into the Great-Walk of the Garden.

After a turn or two there, they ſat down by the ſide of a Fountain, full in ſight of the *Thames*, which paſſes at the

the bottom of the Walk. The Walk itſelf makes a fine Viſto in its Deſcent to the River: at a diſtance, you ſee the Fields and Hills; at firſt in an eaſy Aſcent varied into Paſture and Arable, and then riſing unequally, and cover'd here and there with Woods, till they are inſenſibly loſt in a bluiſh Caſt of the Clouds. The agreeableneſs of the Place made *Philypſus* forget himſelf for a few Moments: he was taken up wholly in wandering with his Eye, ſometimes over thoſe beautiful Gardens, and ſometimes over the irregular Proſpect that lay before them. At laſt recollecting himſelf and turning to *Antiphaus*, "There is a difference (ſays he) "in the agreeable Senſe I feel at preſent "from the delightful Views on all ſides "of us, which may partly confirm what "we were talking of juſt before we ſat "down." Does not this Maſter-piece of Art, with all its Symmetry and Juſtneſs of Proportions, ſtrike the Mind in a feebler manner, than that Landskape of Nature in its infinite Irregularity? Theſe meaſured Riſes and Falls, in Slopes anſwering each other, Thoſe Groves terminating every way in an exactneſs of figure, Theſe Walks intercroſſing without confuſion, and uniting ſo happily, cannot fail of pleaſing the Eye very much: Yet that Wildneſs and Variety abroad, the River, Lawn, Fields and Woods ſo beautifully interſpers'd, compoſe a Scene much finer and more engaging. For my part, I ſhou'd be apt to prefer that ſingle Grot yonder, and the hanging Precipice over it, to a whole Scenary of natural Objects laid out in the moſt regular order imaginable. There is ſomething of this in the Pleaſure which is given us by the greateſt Writers. A Noble natural Genius, however irregular and unconfin'd, delights us in a much higher degree, than the moſt uniform and correct: And the Writer who enjoys this freedom of Soul, amidſt all his Starts and Errors, is greatly to be prefer'd to the Juſtneſs of one, who is too ſevere to commit a Fault, and too cool and phlegmatick to be a Poet.

Such a temper (reply'd *Antiphaus*) can never produce any thing truly Great. The nobleſt Poet in the World has not the feweſt Faults: and the ſame Spirit which qualified *Homer* to be ſo, is what at the ſame time might hurry him away from a nicer Obſervation of ſome little Particulars. The very Negligencies of *Homer* ſhew the Greatneſs of his Spirit: and where there may be any like Neg-

ligencies

ligencies in the Version of *Homer*, methinks, it wou'd be but Justice to attribute them to the same Cause: at least where the Spirit of that Poet is so discernible, as it is in this late Translation.

I cannot but smile sometimes, when I hear a severer Reader very gravely condemning a Poem for a few Faults, which may be evident in it here and there. Nothing can be plainer than that our Judgments ought to be form'd upon the Whole, and not upon Particulars: the Superiority of Beauties or Defects is the only thing that can determine the Character of the Piece. 'Tis possible that Mr. *Hobbes* may have express'd a word or two correctly, where the New Translation has deviated into a Metaphorical or licentious Expression: but what a strange method of Comparison would it be, to settle our opinion of the Writers from hence? By such a way of proceeding we might prefer one, who loses the Life and Vigour of Poetry throughout, to others who preserve it so strongly in the general Turn of their Compositions.

As we go on, *Philypsus*, with our usual freedom of speaking our Sentiments on each particular Passage; I dare say,

that even all thoſe, which may ſeem faulty to us, will make but a ſmall figure, when compar'd to the ſeveral Excellencies of this Piece. As for my part, after a Reſearch of ſome care thro' the whole Tranſlation, I find no reaſon at all to alter my Opinion, "That the Beau-
" ties of it are far more numerous, and
" far more conſiderable, than its Ble-
" miſhes: even taking all thoſe things
" for *real* Blemiſhes, which we may only
" *imagine* to be ſuch.

If the faſhionable Choice of *Verſe* be juſtly blameable; it may as juſtly be ſaid that no one moves with more freedom in his Fetters. In particular Lines, there may be ſome farther diſagreeable *Likeneſſes* of Sound; but the *Variety* of Numbers in general is great and handſome: What Smoothneſs and Harmony do we find thro' the courſe of the Poem; and how ſeldom are they interrupted either by the *Littleneſs*, or the *Vaſtneſs* of the Words? by the *Openneſs* of the Vowels, the *Claſhing* of Conſonants, or any other Roughneſſes whatever: Not to mention againſt theſe, that *Significance* of Sound, which is more frequent, and more happily practis'd by Mr. *Pope*, in particular, than by any other of the Modern Poets.

As to the *Diction*; not only the Poem but our Language itself is enrich'd by it. Where it is once Mean, it is in many instances Great, Noble, and Solemn. Where a Simplicity beyond our Taste is to be preserv'd, we may expect some Flatnesses: And it may be to these perhaps we owe that Justness and Purity, which in so many places makes us imagine, that we are conversing with Persons of those First Ages of the World, in all their Plainness and Honesty of Behaviour. At other times the Narration is rais'd, and the Images strengthen'd by a figurative way of speaking, tho' no doubt, in some cases, to excess: but these Excesses may well be pass'd over, when we consider, that they proceed from Liberties, which are highly useful in rendering the Stile the more various and poetical; so far, as frequently to improve upon *Homer* himself.

Above all, is that *flame* and *spirit* diffus'd thro' the whole Poem; and oftentimes so well kept up, as to make us forget, that we are reading a Translation. When we are engag'd in the Piece, do not the *great* and *generous* Sentiments we meet with perpetually, make a few Thoughts, which have something *cold* or *little* in them, appear inconsiderable

able upon the firſt Compariſon? What *Eclairciſements* have we, and how little *Obſcurity?* What a number of natural Thoughts, Images, and Deſcriptions might be produc'd, to over-ballance ſuch Lines in it, as may ſeem to be Affected, or too Artificial?

Thus which ever way we turn ourſelves, whether we conſider the *Poetical Spirit*, the *Language*, or the *Verſification*; in each of them the Beauties far exceed the Defects. It is with this Notion we ought to proceed in our Enquiries: we muſt carry this Thought all along with us. Let us remember *Philypſus*, "That "all human Excellence ſtands merely on "Compariſon: that no one is without "Faults, and that very few arrive in "any tolerable degree towards Perfecti-"on: That Mr. *Pope* does not only ap-"pear among the Few, but that his Su-"periority is every way viſible: If we "compare his Compoſitions in general "with thoſe of our other Poets, the "Diſproportion is as great, as when we "compare the Blemiſhes of his own "Poetry, with the Beauties which every "where abound in it.

Some of theſe we are now to conſider; and we may enter on this View with the greater Pleaſure, as we have the advantage

tage of Mr. *Pope's* own Obſervations in ſeveral Points, both as to thoſe things, in which he met with the greateſt difficulty; and the Methods he has taken of raiſing his Language, and improving the Verſification.

One of the greateſt Sources of raiſing, as well as enlarging the Poetical Language, is by inventing New Words, or importing old Ones from a foreign Soil. Words, when they are us'd vulgarly, grow mean: Like other Faſhions, when their uſe is once got among the Populace, they ſoon begin to be rejected by the politer Part of the World. This it is (as (a) the *Gentlemen* of *Port Royal* very juſtly obſerve) which neceſſitates the introducing of New Words into every Language; it occaſions a continual Decay, and demands continual Supplies. Thus whoever has a Felicity this way, is a Benefactor to the Publick: he adds ſo much to the Bank; and gives his Aſſiſtance in ſupporting the preſent Credit of Language among us.

It wou'd be equally trifling and laborious, to give all the particular Inſtances of this Verſion's enriching our Language. It is every where viſible; there

(a) *Art de bien Parler.* Part 1. Chap. 4. Sect. 5.

is no reading a Book in the *Odyſſey*, without obſerving it frequently. You will almoſt conſtantly find his new Words to be apt, eaſy, and poetical. Sometimes he introduces the Expreſſions, and even the *Peculiarities* of other Languages into our own: Theſe, when unforc'd, pleaſe us very particularly, by the Variety, and Novelty, they bring along with them. We admire the Stranger in our Habit; and are extremely taken to ſee him look as free and eaſy as if he were a Native, and had been always truly Engliſh.

The Poet has the ſame Art and Delicacy in *Connecting* two Words into one, a thing much more difficult than *Inventing*: The Union is proper and inſenſible; there is no Knot, where they are ingrafted: in ſhort, they (*a*) may be ſaid rather to grow into one another, than to be brought together by Art. I do not ſay, that this hits ſo naturally in all the Inſtances; there may be (*b*) ſome Words leſs tractable, or leſs harmonious than others: But in

(*a*) Thus: *Mellifluous*, *attemper'd*; *ever-ſhady*, *ill-perſwading*, *ſerpent-mazes*, and ſeveral others in this Tranſlation.

(*b*) Thus perhaps: *Sea-girt*, *end-long*, *love-dittied*, *woman-ſtate*, &c. in the ſame.

general

general we may affirm, that as his Tranſlation is wrought off from a Language, which in this Reſpect greatly exceeds all that ever were; So the Imitations of it, this way, are unuſually Beautiful and Harmonious.

To deviate from the ſtrict Rules which Grammarians wou'd impoſe on Words, either ſingle, or as they ſtand in their relations to one another, gives an agreeable uncommon Air to Language; but in the very Notion of it carries ſomething of difficulty, and niceneſs along with it. Mr. *Pope* ſeems to have thought it the ſafeſt way in ſuch Caſes to follow or reſemble thoſe Deviations, which have been already Authoriz'd by ſome Maſterly hand: and where he ſtrikes more boldly into any new Freedom, he is generally careful of giving things ſuch an Openneſs, that they may neither perplex the Senſe, nor embarraſs the Period.

A thing more uſeful and agreeable than either of theſe, is to turn the ſtream of Words out of their common Channel.—There is a good deal of Stiffneſs, which yet attends our Language, from the ſtated order of Words in ſuch a repeated Succeſſion: and tho' we are much freer than our Neighbours the *French* in this particular, I ſhou'd be glad to

ſee

ſee our Poets, at leaſt, go yet farther towards the Liberties of the old *Greeks* and *Romans*. Mr. *Pope* has ſome ſtrokes toward this: he is ſometimes bold in varying the expected range of Words, to give his Sentences a new and agreeable air: he tranſpoſes their order, often by his own Judgment, and often in imitation of ſome of our beſt Poets, who have ſucceeded in it before.

I wou'd not have a certain Grammarian, or two, over-hear me commending theſe Liberties ſo freely: it wou'd certainly coſt one a Diſpute. You know the Men: they are as ſtrict in the Punctilio's of Words, as ſome formal People are in the little Points of Behaviour. I warrant you, your Neighbour, The Doctor, wou'd ſtand as ſtrictly upon the *Nominative Caſe's going before the Verb*, as *Wicquefort* wou'd for the Precedence of an Embaſſador: 'Tis certain he can ſettle all the Rules of Place from undeniable Authorities; diſpoſes of the Upper-hand with perfect Oeconomy; and, upon the whole, would make an Excellent *Maſter of the Ceremonies* among Words and Syllables.

However, with this Gentleman's leave, there are ſeveral juſt *Liberties* which may be allow'd for varying the Poetical

(a) Stile:

(*a*) Stile: and many Aids, proper to enliven and elevate it in the more noble Parts of a Poem.

Among the latter, Mr. *Pope* has made very good uſe of Antiquated Words; and no leſs of Expreſſions borrow'd from our Tranſlation of the Sacred Writings. The Language of Scripture, as it is receiv'd from the firſt with a certain religious Awe, will ſtill retain ſomething venerable, and auguſt: it may therefore be of ſignal Service in giving to the Heroick Muſe that Majeſty, which ſo well becomes the Sublime Air ſhe ought to aſſume. 'Tis much the ſame in the revival of old Words: Antiquity always carries a ſort of Solemnity with it, in its very Roughneſſes and Decays: The *Ruſtick* ſtrikes the Mind, as ſtrongly, as any thing in Architecture; and Ruins themſelves have often ſomething awful and majeſtick in them.

I wou'd not willingly interrupt you (ſays *Philypſus*) but the humour of heaping ſuperannuated Words in ſome late Poems, is too provoking to be paſs'd by. How have our *Miltonick* Writers, in par-

(*a*) Plurimæ ſint locutiones *apud Poetas uſitatiſſimæ*, & in primis *elegantes*, quæ ſcriptis Proſaicis uſurpatæ etiam Grammaticæ leges violant. See *Trapp*'s Præl. Poet. Page 49, *&c.* to Page 53.

 ticular,

ticular, proſtituted them on all occaſions: in what an undiſtinguiſhing manner do they labour to draw into their Works, any word which their great Maſter has adopted into his *Paradiſe Loſt*?--*Erſt*, *Nathleſs*, *Beheſts*, *Welkin*, and a Thouſand other Expreſſions of equal beauty and agreeableneſs of Sound, are repeated ten times in every Sheet of theirs: in ſhort, theſe Gentlemen have made me quite ſick of People's going two Hundred Years backward for their Language; and furniſhing out half their Poems from the Vocabularies annex'd to *Spencer* and *Chaucer*.

As for ſome of thoſe Writers (reply'd *Antiphaus* calmly) You have reaſon to be angry with them; but if we may reject any thing meerly for the *abuſe* of it, there is nothing of the greateſt *uſe*, that we may not fairly reject. *Virgil* made particular uſe of this method in his Poems, and was (*a*) admired by his Countrymen on that account: What is your Opinion of our *Milton*? Are you diſpleas'd with the antiquated Words in his Writings? No, *Philypſus*, I know your Taſte too

(*a*) Cum ſint verba Propria, ficta, tranſlata; Propriis dignitatem dat *Antiquitas*: *eo ornamento* Virgilius *unice eſt uſus*. *Quintil. Inſtit.* Lib 8. Cap. 3. *Again*, Lib. 9. Cap 3.

well

well to imagine any thing of that nature. And even of thoſe, that have follow'd his Example, there is one or two who make good uſe of them. This we ſee in *Philips*'s pieces; not to mention the new (*a*) Poem we were reading the other Day: the Author of which, beſide ſeveral other Beauties, is by no means unhappy in his Management of this ſort of Words. I agree with you, the *Abuſe* of them is frequent, and much to be condemn'd: If perpetual, they run into a meer Barbariſm; and indeed where-ever they are thruſt in, without any other reaſon except their being Ancient, they give a Roughneſs and Diſorder, inſtead of the proper Solemnity: But when they are plac'd here and there with Judgment, they ſupport the greatneſs of our Ideas, and reflect a venerableneſs on the ſubject. Were the Old Oaks, that are left ſtanding in the Gardens of *Blenheim*, more numerous, that Deſign might have too much of the Foreſt in it: but as they are, they ſerve to communicate the nobler air of Antiquity to the things about them; and appear in a Majeſty of Years, equal to the Grandeur of the Place.

I wou'd deſire you to commend the inſertion of Solemn Words, only as they

(*a*) *WINTER*: by Mr. *Thompſon*.

are proper to the Places in which they are us'd. We ſee by Mr. *Pope*'s Obſervations on this Head, that he underſtands the Benefit of them perfectly well; as his Works ſhew that he practiſes up to his own Rules; and ſcarce ever inſerts either the Words of former Centuries, or the Language of Scripture, but where the Subject demands a ſolemn and venerable Turn.

As theſe are the chief Methods of *ennobling* the Poetick Stile; ſo the chief to *enliven* it, is the free and various uſe of *Epithets*. No one thing is of greater ſervice to the Poets for diſtinguiſhing their Language from Proſe. This has occaſion'd that (*a*) large and unreſtrain'd uſe of them, ſo much beyond what we find in Oratory: And tho' *Homer* is more bold and frequent in this, than any of the Poets who have wrote ſince; I know not any of the *Ancient* Criticks who have ever blam'd him on that account. 'Tis partly from his uncommon liberties this way, that Mr. *Pope* looks upon his Epithets, as one of the (*b*) *Diſtin-*

(*a*) Eo (*Epitheto*) poetæ & frequentius & liberius utuntur: Namque illis ſatis eſt convenire verbo, cui apponitur; & ita *Dentes albi*, & *Humida Vina* in his non reprehenduntur. *Quintil. Inſtit.* Lib. 8. Cap. 6. (*b*) Pref. to *Il.* p. 21.

guiſhing

guiſhing Marks of that Poet. In *Homer* they have on ſeveral accounts a peculiar air: and this Tranſlation not only preſerves their proper beauties, but ſhews many Methods of improving upon them. Sometimes the Old are ſet in a ſtronger light, and ſometimes New ones added with a peculiar grace: Sometimes ſeveral are applied to the ſame thing, without (*a*) that ſtrictneſs of connexion, which wou'd (*b*) flatten the energy of them; and where the poverty of our Language will not convey their full Senſe in the Conciſeneſs of the Original, they are enlarged upon in the Tranſlation, and laid more open to our view.

Epithets, *Philypſus*, like Pictures in Miniature, are often entire deſcriptions in one Word. This may be either from their own ſignificance, or by their immediate connexion with ſome known object. We ſee the thing, when the Poet only mentions the *Nodding Creſt* of an Hero; and form a larger Idea of *Jove* from the ſingle Epithet of *Cloud-compelling*, than we might find in a deſcription more diffuſe. It was chiefly from (*c*)

(*a*) Huge, horrid, vaſt! *Od.* 5, 227--175.

(*b*) Τὸ τοιῦτο, Κυρτὰ, φαλκριόωντα, τῇ ἐξαιρέσει τῦ συνδέσμυ μεγαλοπρεπέστερον ἀπέβη. *Dem. Phal.* ξδ'.

(*c*) See Mr. *Pope*'s Note on *Il.* 1, 683.

two Poetical Epithets, that *Phidias* design'd the countenance of his *Olympian Jupiter*; as, in Reverſe, we often ſee the Perſon in his Epithet, from our being acquainted with ſome Statue, or Picture, to which it refers: Thus when *Apollo* is call'd the *Archer-God*, it recalls to our memory the repreſentations we have ſo often ſeen of that Deity: the compleat Figure is rais'd up in the Mind, by touching upon that ſingle circumſtance.

'Tis by the ſame means, that one ſingle Epithet gives us the Idea of any Object, which has been common and familiar to us. Meadows, Fields, Woods, Rivers, and the Sea itſelf, are often imag'd by one well-choſen word. Thus in that (*a*) beautiful Deſcription of *Calypſo's* Bower, you ſee the Groves *of living green*; the Alders *ever quivering*; the *nodding* Cypreſs, and its high Branches, *waving* with the Storm: 'Tis by Epithets that the ancient Poets paint their *Elyſian Groves*; and the Modern, their *Windſor-Foreſts*.

Where our Language will not admit of this conciſeneſs, we find the Image preſerv'd by a Deſcription more full and diffuſive; thus,

(*a*) See *Od.* 5, 85.

——— The Morning Sun encreasing bright
(a) O'er Heavens pure Azure spreads the growing light.

I shou'd think that the Opening of the Sense in a larger Compass may often be approv'd, even where we are not driven to it by the poverty of our Language. *Homer* himself, who has the advantage of single Words so much stronger and more significant, often chuses to draw out his Sentiments, into several Lines: and sometimes (*b*) the very same Sentiment, which upon other Occasions he has express'd in one word only. May not the same Liberty be allow'd to his Translators? Is it not a fine Enlargement for Instance, where *Homer* is speaking of *Penelope's Veil* with the Epithet of *Pellucid* only, to say that "the Transparent Veil

(c) Her beauty seems and only seems to shade."

Tho' these imaging and descriptive Epithets are the more Beautiful, those which add Strength and Emphasis are

---

(*a*) *Od.* 9, 67—56. (*b*) Νήεροψ which is beautifully express'd by *Horace* in three words (*nimium lubricus aspici*) is enlarged by *Homer* himself, on a fit occasion, into three lines: Compare Ιλ. λ, 16, with γ', 340.

(*c*) *Od.* 18, 250—209. λιπαρή.

by

by no means to be contemn'd. This way they are of great Service in all *Satire*; and particularly in that Abusiveneſs, which *Homer* is not over nice in beſtowing upon his Gods: they appear well in the Ridicule of the Suitors; and are ſtrong and vehement in any *Arrogant Character*, particularly in all Contemners of the Gods. I ſhall give you only one inſtance of the latter; from *Polypheme*'s Anſwer to *Ulyſſes*:

Fools that you are! (the monſter made reply,
His inward fury blazing at his eye)
Or ſtrangers diſtant far from our abodes,
To bid me reverence or regard the Gods.
Know, that we Cyclops are a race above
(a)Thoſe *air-bred people*, and their *goat-nurs'd Jove*.

You muſt have obſerv'd (*Philypſus*) ſeveral other Methods of uſing Epithets poetically. I need not mention the peculiar fitneſs and ſtrength, which they may acquire, from the (b)*occaſions* on which they are us'd, or the *Light* they are ſet in: That (c) *Subſtantives* are ſometimes us'd as *Epithets*; and ſometimes (d) *Epithets* as *Subſtantives*: Sometimes the (e) *Metaphor* is convey'd this way with a good Grace;

(a) *Od.* 9, 330--276. (b) *Od.* 23, 217. compared with verſe 227. (c) *Od.* 1, 389--299. (d) *Od.* 19, 110--91. (e) *Od.* 10, 291.

and

and at others, two *Thwarting Ideas* are mixt together in a very agreeable manner. Mr. *Addiſon* is the firſt I know of, that obſerv'd upon theſe, and gave them their Name, and of this kind is the (*a*)*Vegetable Venom* in the fourth *Odyſſey*, which anſwers (*b*) his Inſtance of *Aurum Frondens* from *Virgil*.

I know not whether I perfectly apprehend you, or not (interpos'd *Philypſus*): Do You not mean that particular ſort of Metaphor, when ſome ſtrange *quality* in a thing, is turn'd into an *Epithet*, and directly applied to it? —Either that; or elſe ſome ſtrange Circumſtance applied in the ſame manner: in both 'tis the Novelty and the Surprize, that pleaſe us.-- I take you, ſays *Philypſus*; and believe I now ſee a farther Reaſon, why a very natural Paſſage (in another Poem by Mr. *Pope*) has always been ſo agreeable to me. 'Tis where he ſpeaks of the odd Appearance of things from their inverſion in a River: I think I can repeat it:

Oft in the Stream---The muſing Shepherd ſpies
The head-long Mountains and the downward Skies,
The watry Landskip of the pendant Woods,
And abſent trees that tremble in the floods;
In the clear azure Gleam the Flocks are ſeen,
(*c*)And floating Foreſts paint the Waves with green.

(*a*) Od 4. 320--230. (*b*) *Addiſon's Miſc.* Vol. 1. p. 245. 12°. (*c*) *Windſor-Foreſt*, p. 59. folio.

These are of the kind I mean, ſays *Antiphaus*; they are bold, but they are natural: Indeed with due caution, greater Contrarieties than theſe may be join'd, under ſome particular Circumſtance, to juſtify ſo unexpected an Union. Thus all Epithets, which contradict the general Senſe of the Thing, but agree with the particular Occaſion; Thus is *Grief* call'd *pleaſing*; there are *Kindneſſes* which are *terrible* (*a*): And in many caſes *Death* and even *Diſgrace* may be *deſirable*. Inſtances of this kind, are very frequent, eſpecially among our modern Poets. There are (*b*) many in this Tranſlation: in particular, 'tis this which gives a new Air to that gay (*c*) Speech of *Mercury* in the Eighth Book.

Tho' the *Latins* us'd this agreeable Claſh of Ideas, *the Greek Poets* (as Mr. *Addiſon* (*d*) obſerves on the former Head) *wanted Art for it*; They, at leaſt the more Ancient of them, never join things that ſeem to diſagree, in ſo cloſe an Union. Unleſs where Nature her ſelf

(*a*) As when the *Cyclops*, in the height of his good nature, promiſes *Ulyſſes*, that he ſhall be the laſt he will devour. *Od.* 9. (*b*) *Od.* 1, 449---353. 15, 435---399. *otherwiſe* 12, 52. 18, 284 &c. (*c*) Verſe 380---342. (*d*) *Miſc.* Vol. 1. p. 245. 12°.

has

has led the way in an (*a*) actual mixture of Contrarieties: in any point, except that single one, these must be entirely Improvements on the Original.

The Misfortune is, that in all Human Excellencies there will be an Alloy: Faults spring out of our Improvements themselves; and the very methods of Beautifying lead often into Blemishes. The way to any Perfection is full of Difficulties and Windings on each side; and every step out of the right Path (tho' they cross each other every Moment) is a wandering from our Design. In a word, *Philypsus*, 'tis much the same with Errors and Improvements, as it is with Pleasure and Pain in the Philosopher's Fable: they are blended together in such a manner, that it is impossible to come at the one, without touching upon the other.

All the Methods which are us'd in Mr. *Pope*'s Translation, and which are so often of great Efficacy towards beautifying and improving the Diction, may sometimes fall under a different Character.

(*a*) Thus in the *Twilight*, when we have really a sort of *visible Darkness*, *Homer* uses an Epithet of the same contrariety: Ἀμφιλύκη νύξ, i.e. Darkness ting'd every way with Light. Ιλ. ή, 433.

Among

Among the Words which are introduc'd from other Languages into our own, there may be (*a*) ſome, which ſtill retain too much of the air of Foreigners: As antiquated Words may (*b*) look too Groteſque, or have a rough diſagreeable ſound. The very Solemnity of Scriptural Expreſſions may ſometimes require that they ſhould not be (*c*) alienated: at leaſt it may make them look (*d*) too high for the Paſſages in which they are inſerted.

Next to the importing of Words New to the Poetical Stile, is the varying the uſe of the Old. To deviate from the ſtrictneſs of Grammar, is what gave a riſe to Rhetorick; and ſurely there are few who wou'd not prefer all the beautiful Forms and Figures of the latter (at leaſt for Poetry and Oratory) to that bare correctneſs, which alone is the Province of the former: Yet there may be Innovations on this too harſh or daring; and Figures, that may look more like Patchwork, than true Ornaments in the Dreſs of Poetry.

(*a*) Dexter, circumfuſile, variegated *Od.* 15, 145.
(*b*) Seneſchal, viands, bev'rage, irefull 3, 179.
(*c*) *Jupiter* is ſtil'd, *God* (ſimply; *Od.* 3. 190---158, Θεὸς) *Neptune*, A God above the Gods. *Od.* 13, 167.
(*d*) To thee a Son is giv'n—*Od.* 18, 207. And-- Food in the deſart land, behold, is giv'n. *Od.* 10, 204--175.

The

The greater danger is, when the Poet aſſumes (*a*) any common Word in a new unuſual Senſe. The worſt Fault of any Language is, Ambiguity; that great cauſe of Darkneſs in Verſe, and the continuer of every Diſpute that has been kept up for any time in Proſe. The various Appearances of words, *Philypſus*, ſhould not be multiplied unneceſſarily; the Reader is apt to be diſtracted between ſo many Lights: and in ſuch a Variety may follow the falſe, as well as the true.

I have obſerv'd this particularly in Words deriv'd from other Languages: Theſe, you know, often prevail among us very differently from their native ſignification. The *Latin ſenſe* perhaps is one thing, and the *Engliſh uſe* another: When this has obtain'd univerſally, we ought not to run back to the Latin (*b*) ſenſe of the word, in our uſe of it. If you ſhould, the Learn'd themſelves may not readily fall into your meaning, and the Unlearn'd will inevitably miſtake it.

It may be enquir'd too, how far this Tranſlation, may make a wrong uſe of Terms borrow'd from any of the Arts and Sciences: As where we read of *Ar-*

(*a*) *Flown* (with Inſolence) *Od.* 1, 292. *Filial* (for a Daughter) 6, 67. (*b*) *Partial Od.* 8, 185. *Succinct* 17, 200. *Objected* 7, 54. *Implicite* 9, 514.

 chitraves,

chitraves, *Colonnades*, and the like. I would not produce theſe as undoubted faults in the Poetical Stile: tho' the baniſhing *all Technical Words*, be laid down by ſome Criticks as a Rule never to be tranſgreſs'd; I ſhould imagine they might be admitted in ſome Caſes; even where there is not that abſolute neceſſity, either of uſing them, or loſing the Senſe of the Original.

Will not the very thing, on which the Rule is founded, allow the departing from it ſometimes? "*That the Poet writes to all Mankind in general*; And "*That he ſhould avoid all appearance of Labour, as well as Affectation*, is very true; and very good reaſons they are for his not uſing Technical Words, while they carry difficulty and an Air of Affectation about them: But if ſuch words ever happen to be perfectly Familiarized by the Writings of former Poets, or become of common Uſe in the World, I ſhould think they have the ſame Right to be admitted into Poetry (and if not mean, the ſame propriety) as any other Words, the moſt obvious and intelligible. Any one may diſtinguiſh their greater, or leſs fitneſs, on this Account, in the deſcription of *Alcinous*'s Palace: in which there are ſeveral Inſtances, both of Terms familiariz'd, and

and of ſuch as are leſs allowable, under one and the ſame view :

The *Front* appear'd with radiant ſplendors gay,
Bright as the lamp of Night, or orb of Day.
The walls were maſſy braſs: the *Cornice* high
Blue metals crown'd, in colours of the sky :
Rich plates of gold the *folding-doors incaſe* ;
The pillars ſilver, on a brazen *baſe* ;
Silver the *Lintels deep-projecting* o'er,
(a) And gold the *ringlets* that command the door.

Some of theſe Terms are certainly allowable ; And you will think perhaps I carry the matter too far in another Point, which may ſeem as allowable to the full. You muſt know, I am apt to imagine, that not only the more difficult Terms of Art, but even ſuch Words as are (*b*) *uſurp'd* more particularly in any ſingle

(a) Od. 7, 117---90. *(b)* Thus there is ſomething which does not ſound entirely right in theſe lines ;

Full ſhines *the Father* in the *Filial Frame*, *Od.* 4, 199.
He ceas'd : the *Filial Virtue* made reply. 22, 167.
Mean time *Arete* for the hour of reſt
Ordains the fleecy couch——7, 428.
The Peers reproach the ſure *Divine* of fate. 20, 432.

Within the *Stricture* of the palace wall 22, 186.
Impoſthumate with pride.——20, 358.
With *Venial* freedom let me now demand
Thy name.——1, 219.
There cling *implicite*, and confide in *Jove*. 9, 514

The *Seneſhal* rebuk'd in haſte withdrew, 4, 47.
A *Cenotaph* I raiſe of deathleſs fame. 4, 794.

 Province,

Province, may become leſs fit to be uſed in Common. If ſo, it may require caution in inſerting ſome, that are *appropriated* to particular Perſons or Things; Many that are us'd much in the *Profeſſions*, eſpecially in the *Scholaſtick* way of Diſtinctions: and all in general that are perplex'd, or not to be underſtood without Difficulty.

I'm afraid I have tired you, *Philypſus*, with ſuch a ſtring of dry Obſervations; they muſt have their Turn in a view of this Nature; and to omit what is Neceſſary, for fear of an imputation of Pedantry, is perhaps the worſt Pedantry one can be guilty of.

Give me leave to enlarge more upon the Abuſe of Epithets, as I did before upon the Uſe of them. 'Tis the ſame with theſe, *Philypſus*, as with all other Ornaments of Speech; their being ſo very ſerviceable, may lead to a larger Uſe of them than is proper: but there is this Advantage too; the very thing which makes them ſo ſtrong and beautifull, will help to diſcover any Error in their Application. They are each connected ſo immediately to their Subject, that their Impropriety, as well as Agreement, is very eaſily diſcern'd.

On

On (*a*) this Account, we ſhould be the more cautious how we mix the Epithets of the *Proper*, with any *Metaphorical* Expreſſions: Theſe, for the Time change their Nature, and may ſignifie things very different from what they ſtood for before. That Metaphor, which puts the Name of a *Place* or *Country* for its *Inhabitants*, is reckon'd a great and agreeable one; but wherever it is uſed, we muſt remember it ſtands now for *Men*, and is not to be conſider'd in its proper ſtate, as a *Part of the Earth*. If its old Epithets are ſtill applied to it, the Senſe muſt be diſagreeing and confus'd.

I fear we meet with ſomething of this where *Penelope* complains of the Numbers and Importunity of her Suitors: after this manner:

Zacynthus green with ever-ſhady groves,
And *Ithaca*, preſumptuous boaſt their loves;
Obtruding on my choice a ſecond Lord
(*b*) They preſs the *Hymenæan* rite.———

(*a*) Δεῖ καὶ τὰ ἐπίθετα καὶ τὰς μεταφορὰς ἁρμοττούσας λέγειν· τοῦτο δ' ἔσται ἐκ τοῦ ἀναλόγου· εἰ δὲ μή, ἀπρεπὲς φανεῖται, διὰ τὸ παράλληλα τὰ ἐναντία μάλιστα φαίνεσθαι. *Ariſtot. Rhetor.* Lib. 3. Cap. 2.

(*b*) *Od.* 19, 155—131.

Longinus, (*a*) ſomewhere in his Treatiſe on the *ſublime*, gives us an inſtance of this ſort of Metaphor, from *Herodotus*, where that Hiſtorian is ſpeaking of a very moving Tragedy, *at the Acting of which, the Theatre burſt into tears:* This the Critick judges to be ſo taking, from the ſurprize that Turn of Expreſſion carries with it. The Metaphor itſelf has certainly ſomething great in it: But had *Herodotus* join'd ſome of its proper Epithets or Deſcription with this Mataphor, and ſaid, that "*The Theatre, raiſed all on* "*Columns of the Corinthian Order, burſt into* "*Tears at the deepneſs of the Tragedy*" *Longinus* might have thought the paſſage more *Surprizing*, but I dare ſay he would not have thought it ſo worthy of his Commendation.

To mix theſe things in a Deſcription is really as Abſurd, as to paint a *River-God*, not with his *Urn*, to ſignifie what he is; but guſhing all over into Streams, like ſome of the odd Figures in *Ovid's Metamorphoſis:* and by the way, it may be a very good (*b*) Rule that is given, to try mixt Metaphors at any time; by forming in one's Mind a Picture, from what is ſaid; and conſidering how the

(*a*) Cap. 24. Ed. Oxon. 1718. (*b*) *Spectator*, N. 595.

Parts

Parts of it would agree, were they delineated upon Canvass.

There is another disagreement in Epithets, when two Expressions, proper in themselves, are yet join'd together improperly. After a great Slaughter we may very well have a Notion of *Heaps, or* (as it is in the Poetical language) *Mountains of the Slain*; 'tis natural on the same Occasion to imagine to ourselves their Wounds, and the *blood ebbing* out of them: these are very proper separately; but to join them under the Notion of a (*a*) *Bleeding Mountain* does not look so reconcileable to the Mind.

An Error yet more frequent is, when we give a word that Epithet, which is proper to it on some Occasions, indifferently at all times, and without any Occasion.

This, in some Measure, has been always allowable in Verse: however such a Liberty is not without its bounds, nor should it be used intemperately. *Purple* (for instance) is an Epithet very frequent in the Ancient Poets for the Habit of Princes: yet it is not to be given to that of all Great Men; nor of Princes equally,

(*a*) *Od.* 22, 135---118.

whether (*a*) young or old; nor of the very ſame Prince, under ſeveral Circumſtances: tho' a Remark of this kind may ſeem inſignificant, an Impropriety in this Caſe might be very groſs and ſhocking.

Again: What is proper in one Language, may not be ſo in another. Was any one to Tranſlate the *purpureis Oloribus* of *Horace*, *Purple Swans*, would not he be ſo *Literal*, as to miſs the *Senſe* of his Author entirely?

There may be another Impropriety from the difference of time and circumſtances: It may do very well to give the Epithet of *browzing*, to a Goat; or *grazing*, to the Ox: it helps to deſcribe them in the Fields, or to diſtinguiſh them from ſome other Creatures; and if neither of theſe, at leaſt it gives the Language a Poetical Air: Yet theſe Epithets have ſome reſtraints, they belong to Life and Action; they do not ſuit with thoſe very Creatures, when Dead; and leſs ſo, when they are cut out in the Shambles, or ſerv'd up at a Feaſt: this is the Caſe in a Paſſage relating to *Penelope*'s Suitors; they,

(*a*) Δεῖ σκοπεῖν, ὡς νέῳ φοινικὶς, αὕτω γέροντι· οὐ γὰρ ἡ αὐτὴ πρέπει ἐσθής. *Ariſt. Rhet.* l. 3. c. 2.

A

——— A Luxurious race, indulge their cheer;
Devour the *grazing Ox* and *browzing Goat*,
(a) And turn the generous Vintage down their throat.

As Epithets ſhould be proper to the *Things*, or *Perſon*, they are ſpoken of; ſo muſt we take Care that they are ſtill proper to the *Metaphors* we add; and in Allegory, not to confound the Epithets of the *Real*, with thoſe of the *Fictitious Perſon*.

In the Preface to the *Iliad* (b) we have an Excellent Diſtinction to this Purpoſe, on a known (c) Epithet of *Apollo*; "Which "(as we are there told) is capable of two "Explications; One Literal, in reſpect "of the Darts and Bow, the Enſigns of "that God; the other Allegorical, with "regard to the Rays of the Sun: there"fore in ſuch Places, where *Apollo* is re"preſented as a God in Perſon, I would "uſe the former Interpretation; and "where the Effects of the Sun are de"ſcrib'd, I wou'd make Choice of the "latter." You ſee the juſtneſs of the Obſervation: it may ſerve to explain my Meaning better than I could expreſs it my ſelf.

(a) *Od.* 17, 621---535. (b) Page 22. 12*mo*.
(c) Ἑκηβόλος.

'Tis

'Tis Evident, by the Way, that Mr. *Pope* form'd this Obſervation upon his Experience in the Progreſs of that Tranſlation: This appears from the firſt Part of that Work, in which we ſometimes find the Properties and Effects of the Sun, blended with the perſonal Acts of *Apollo*: thus it is in the firſt Appearance of that Deity in the Poem. I ſhall read the Paſſage to You, tho' ſomething long: it begins with that beautiful line,

Silent * he wander'd by the ſounding Shore:
Till ſafe at diſtance to his God he prays,
That God, who *darts around the World his rays*.
O *Smintheus* ſprung from fair *Latona's* line,
Thou guardian power of *Cilla* the Divine,
Thou *ſource of Light*, whom *Tenedos* adores,
And whoſe *bright* preſence *gilds* thy *Chryſa's* ſhores;
God of the Silver bow! thy Shafts employ,
(*a*) Avenge thy ſervant, and the *Greeks* deſtroy.

The Original here does not once Attribute any thing to the Deity but what is perſonal: 'tis certain the Sun and its Effects are hid under this Allegory; but then they muſt be hid; for ſo far as it appears, it will ceaſe to be Allegory. *Homer* never mixes ſhadows and reality; and as Mr. *Pope* perceiv'd this in his going on with the Poem, I preſume he built upon it that excellent Obſervation.

* *Chryſes*. (*a*) *Il*. 1, 60--42.

Any

Any mixture of this Nature is more evident in Epithets, for that obvious Reason I mention'd before. And thus, you see, there are Inconveniences attend each Method of improving the Poetical Diction; and that the danger bears some Proportion to the Excellence. Where the finest Colourings are most visible, the faulty strokes of the Pencil are the sooner perceiv'd: and when we meet with the greatest Improvements in a Piece, we must not imagine it to be wholly without defect. Of all Doctrines, I shall never hold that, which supposes any Man to be Infallible: and of all Men, the Poet of a true, free, glowing Spirit, must naturally be incapable of that Character. No, *Philypsus*, the most *correct* Writer is he, that has the *fewest* Faults: and he is the *noblest* Poet, that has most distinct Excellencies.

You need not repeat, says *Philypsus*, what you have throughly convinc'd me of long since. Yes, 'tis the (*a*) Condition of every human Performance not to be absolutely perfect. I can allow of seeing Faults in any the most favourite Piece: and find a fresh and greater Pleasure e-

(*a*) Whoever thinks a faultless Piece to see,
Thinks what ne'er was, nor is, nor e'er shall be.
Pope's Essay on Criticism.

very

every Day in reading an Author without that Biaſs, which uſed to make me admire every thing I read. Yet I muſt own my Infirmity to you; I ſtill find it very Difficult to arrive to that Indifference, you would perſwade, in any Tolerable degree.

A perfect Indifference (anſwer'd *Antiphaus*) is no more attainable, than a perfect Excellence, by a Creature made up of ſo many Paſſions, as is Man. We muſt poiſe ourſelves with all the Steadineſs we are Maſters of; and when thoſe Diſturbers will be interfering, the beſt way is to turn their own Artillery upon them: and to play one Paſſion againſt another. If the ſuperiour Merit of a Writer, or his engaging Way, is apt to captivate us ſo far as to raiſe any partial regards in us; we muſt ſtop, and Conſider what we owe to Truth, the moſt beautifull and commanding thing in the World: On the contrary, where-ever we begin to feel a malicious Pleaſure in finding out the Faults of great Men, we muſt break off that humour as ſoon as perceiv'd, by turning immediately to ſome of the fineſt Paſſages in their Works, and indulging that Delight and Admiration they raiſe in us.

I do thus (reply'd *Philypſus*) and yet it is but too frequently that I find my ſelf more

more engag'd than I ought to be, after all my Endeavours: How happy should I be, cou'd I have that command of my Temper, which *Antiphaus* shews upon all Occasions.

If you have observ'd any thing in me of that Nature (says *Antiphaus*, interrupting him) it is chiefly owing to the Observance of this Rule, "When we "are thinking of any particular Passage, "to forget the Character of the Author: "and when we are speaking of the Cha-"racter of the Author, to forget the "Turn of any particular Passage." Our Notion of a Poem is not to be influenc'd by a few Lines, taken here and there from it: the only thing by which it can be justly determin'd is the Ballance of the Account, after reckoning up all its Beauties and all its Defects against one another. I mean, not only as to their *Number*, but according to the real *Value*, or *Alloy* that is in them. But what am I doing, *Philypsus*? to talk at this rate, while I might be enjoying your Observations?——The things I have heard you speak of at Different Times, make me long to see them in one collected View. We are here safe from the Impertinence of Business, or Visits: and may enjoy our selves at Large, without being interrupted by either.

I am ſenſible (anſwer'd *Philypſus*, after a ſhort pauſe) that what you particularly mean, is the Improvements in Mr. *Pope*'s Tranſlation, from the many Figures and Variations added in that Work: but as I am not prepared for a regular Account of them, You will give me leave to mention them juſt as they come into my Thoughts. My happineſs is, that I ſpeak to ſo generous a Friend: I know *Antiphaus* too well to make Apologies for the Weakneſs of my Obſervations, or the looſe manner in which I may lay my Thoughts before him.

(*a*) "To be *Clear* and *not* to be *Mean*, "is the great Excellence of Language. "A Stile that is made up wholly of *pro*-"*per* Words, will be the cleareſt of any, "but at the ſame Time it will neceſſarily "be mean: On the Contrary, the im-"prov'd *figurative* Stile is great, but if "it be Crowded every where with Fi-"gures and new Terms, it muſt grow "dark and barbarous.

If this Rule be juſt, as it has ever been allow'd to be (quite down from the Great Father of Criticiſm at *Athens*, to thoſe who Flouriſh now in the Academy of *Paris*) all Additional Figures in this

(*a*) From *Ariſtotle's* Lib. de *Poet.* Cap. 22.

Tran-

Tranſlation, which neither darken nor perplex the Senſe, are ſo many new Beauties and Improvements upon the Original.

For my part I ſhould not ſtick at carrying this Point farther. I ſhould imagine, That Figures are the Language of the Paſſions. The Body it ſelf is agitated, and our Features diſcompos'd, when the Mind is ſtruck violently with any Object: and if we ſpeak upon ſuch Occaſions, 'tis with rapidity and diſorder. We burſt out into Exclamations: our Sentiments are quick and violent; and our Language interrupted frequently with ſuddain Starts, and as ſuddain Pauſes. Things appear then more ſtrong and largely to the Mind; and we paint them in more expreſſive Colours, with a greater Energy of Words. 'Tis this way of ſpeaking, that gave riſe to what the Criticks afterwards call'd Figures. Theſe are the beautiful Diſorders of Language; they are in our Words what ſuddain Agitations are in our Minds; and tho' we may think them chiefly the effect of Art, they are really the moſt natural things in Poetry.

When we are ſtruck ſuddainly with Joy or Sorrow, Hopes or Fears, we break out in a ſhort quick manner of

Expreſſion.——*Ulyſſes*, in the Habit of a ſtranger, finds the good old *Laertes* ever ſorrowing for his Abſence, and buſying himſelf in his Garden, to divert the melancholly of his Thoughts. The Hero does not diſcover himſelf immediately; only juſt mentions to him, that he had ſeen *Ulyſſes* in his Travels. That is the point *Laertes* fixes upon: *This Iſland you are landed upon* (ſays he) *is Ithaca*;

But tell me Stranger, be the Truth confeſs'd,
What years have circled ſince thou ſaw'ſt that gueſt?
That hapleſs gueſt, alas! for ever gone!
Wretch that he was! and that I am! my Son!
If ever Man to miſery was born,
(*a*) 'Twas his to ſuffer, and 'tis mine to mourn!

Ulyſſes in his Anſwer informs him where he had met with his Son; and that when they parted, he flatter'd himſelf with hopes of ſeeing him again; but now, he found, he muſt deſpair of that happineſs. This was too much for *Laertes* to bear: we ſee him overcome with Sorrow. 'Tis now *Ulyſſes*'s turn to be agitated, and to ſpeak his Paſſions in the ſame impetuous manner:

He ran, he ſeiz'd him with a ſtrict embrace,
With thouſand kiſſes wander'd o'er his face,
"I, I am he; Oh Father riſe! Behold,
"(*b*) Thy ſon! ———

(*a*) *Od.* 24. 339--289. (*b*) *Od.* 24. 376-- 320

I can ſcarce leave the pleaſure I take in repeating theſe Paſſages only to tell you, that they are extremely improv'd by Mr. *Pope.* No one will imagine how much, that has not compar'd them with the Original.

You ſee theſe Paſſions break out in ſhort violent Flaſhes: ſometimes they are ſo ſtrong as to permit no more than one word or two. When *Euryclea* by accident diſcovers *Ulyſſes*, ſhe can only cry out (a) *My Son!--My King!*---And where any go farther, they rather *hint* at things, than *mention* them: Their Thoughts are full of ſtarts, and hurry; they ſpeak with vehemence; and often end abruptly. Thus *Ulyſſes*, when he diſcovers himſelf to *Telemachus*:

I am thy Father. O my Son! my Son!
That Father, for whoſe ſake thy days have run
(b) One ſcene of woe. &c.——

And in another place, from a different Paſſion:

O curſt event! and Oh unlook'd for aid!
Melanthius, or the women have betray'd ——
(c) Oh my Dear Son! ——

(a) *Od.* 19, 554---475. (b) *Od.* 16, 208---189.
(c) *Od.* 22, 166---152.

These passionate *Breaks* are one of the finest things in Poetry. They are as natural in Anger, as they are in Sorrow or Suprizes; and indeed in the former are proper sooner, and upon less motives far, than in these. I know not how it is, they have a particular aptness in all Threats; and either intimate very strongly, or are very well fill'd up with some menacing Action:

This choice is left you to resist or die;
(a) And die I trust, Ye shall.———

Or, as in the *Nineteenth* Book,

Vagrant be gone! before this blazing brand
(b) Shall urge---and wav'd it hissing in her hand.

You have puzzled me, says *Antiphaus*: Now for my Life can't I tell which to approve of most, the expressing, or the intimating the Action in such Cases: this requires the greatest strength in the Poet, and the other has greater force in his Performance. Oh, give me leave to mention one thing---Have you not observ'd a Larger sort of Break, which is used artificially in a Poem, to incite the Attention of the Reader? I mean, when

(a) Od. 22, 81---67. (b) Od. 19, 85---69.

the

the Narration is dropt in the most engaging parts of it, or just before some very material Incident: This adds a double desire of hearing: the Audience generally make it their Request, that the Speaker would go on, and inform them of the Sequel. Thus it is in the Eleventh *Odyssey*. *Ulysses* in the midst of his Account of the Infernal Regions (*a*) makes a feint of concluding: we are immediately told, that the *Phæacians* were eager to hear him on; and 'tis observable, that the very (*b*) same Break, and the very same Sentiment after it, is imitated by *Virgil*. 'Tis indeed improv'd in the latter: he has all the Use of *Homer's* suspence, without the Tediousness of it.

I have often taken notice of this Artifice, says *Philypsus*. 'Tis very usual in the Close of the particular Books, not only of this Poem, but equally of the *Iliad* and *Æneid*.---Were it not a thing pretty obvious in itself, I should be apt to imagine, that it was from this practice of *Homer* and *Virgil*, that those prudent

(*a*) *Od*. 11, 408---328.——Κηληθμῷ--ἔσχοντο, Verse 333. And V.369. *Alcinous* desires him to proceed.

——(*b*) Donec Calchante ministro——
Tum vero ardemus scitari.——*Æn*. 2, 100 and 105.

Authors,

Authors, who write for Sale, had learnt what is ſo common among them: Thus in our Books of Adventures and Romance, we ſeldom meet with a Firſt Part, which does not break off in ſuch a point of the Story, as may be moſt apt to engage the Expectation of the Reader; and to draw him in for that moſt tedious thing in the World, vulgarly call'd, *A Second Part*.

There is yet another ſort of Breaks, *Antiphaus*, which proceed not from the Artifice of the Writer, but the Paſſion he feels upon ſome great or unexpected Calamity. There might be Inſtances of this given from the Poem before us: but we muſt go to another Piece of Mr. *Pope's* for the fineſt that ever I met with in my Life. 'Tis in his Charming *Ode* on *Muſick*, where he is ſpeaking of that great Maſter of it, *Orpheus*:

(*a*) See wild as the winds o'er the mountains he flies,
Hark *Hæmus* reſounds with the *Bacchinals* cries!
——— Ah, ſee! he dies.

Thoſe Paſſions, which break off our Language in this manner, and confine it to ſhort catches and ſtarts; when they are wrought up to the higheſt pitch, or croud in many of them together upon

(*a*) *Stanza* the 6th.

the

the Mind, are best exprest by *Silence.* Such Silences as these (pardon me a Paradox as old as (*a*) *Pythagoras* his times) are the voice of Nature. 'Tis true in the common Method of speaking, there are only a few particular Organs concern'd: but in stronger Emotions, in the violence of any Passion, the whole Body may be *talkative.* Every Look, and Turn, and Motion is significant; and each Nerve can have its share in making up (what our *Shakespear* calls) *A kind of Excellent Dumb Discourse.*

To be more plain: Our Passions are often too strong to be express'd immediately by words; they often choak up the passage for them: and yet at the same time they are most apparent. The more any one is a stranger to art and disguises, the more is he moved on these Occasions: these Silences are the pure effects of Nature; and the Descriptions of them are some of the most natural, as well as most beautiful Passages in the whole Poem.

(*a*) Ἡ σιωπὴ ὑπὲρ τοῦ θείου σφισὶν (the Disciples of *Pythagoras*) ἐπέσχητο· πολλὰ γὰρ θεῖά τε καὶ ἀπόρρητα ἤκουον· ὧν κρατεῖν χαλεπὸν ἦν, μὴ πρῶτον μαθοῦσιν, ὅτι καὶ ΤΟ ΣΙΩΠΑΝ ΛΟΓΟΣ. *Philostratus* de Vita *Apol*: Lib. 1, Cap. 1.

The

The Recovery of *Ulysses* is the Incident of the greatest concern to all his Friends, and must be attended with the strongest flow of Passion in them: accordingly they are each too much mov'd with the discovery, to utter their Sentiments on that Occasion. *Telemachus* is the first to whom *Ulysses* makes himself known: He falls on his Father's Neck, and they continue embracing each other, without speaking (*a*) for a considerable time.--We have a like Scene, (*b*) when he discovers himself to two or three select Friends: Good old *Laertes*, on the same Occasion is not only silent, but scarce (*c*) able to support himself, under such an excess of Passion, And the fond, tender *Penelope*, is quite overcome with it:

(*d*) She sickens, trembles, falls, and faints away.

A Great Surprize, or Extraordinary Fright, has the same Effect: as in *Homer's* (*e*) *Eurylochus*, and the Sir *Trevisan* of *Spencer*, which the (*e*) Notes mention as a Parallel to *Eurylochus*. Never was any Image set in a fuller Light than this of *Spencer's*: 'tis presented to our View

(*a*) *Od.* 16, 243---220. (*b*) *Od.* 21, 240---226. (*c*) *Od.* 24, 404---346. (*d*) *Od.* 23, 212---205. (*e*) *Od.* 10, 288---246.

with

with all the ſtrength that Poetry is capable of. I muſt beg leave to read it to you.

> He anſwer'd nought at all, but adding new
> Fear to his firſt amazement, ſtaring wide
> With ſtony eyes, and heartleſs hollow hue,
> Aſtoniſh'd ſtood, as one that had eſpy'd
> Infernal furies with their chains unty'd:
> Him yet again, and yet again beſpake
> The gentle Knight; who nought to him reply'd
> But trembling every joint, did only quake.

Admirable Imagery! and admirable Silence! cry'd *Antiphaus*. But I hope you will not be ſo poſſeſs'd with the excellence of our Poet, as to forget (*a*) the *Ajax* of *Homer*; whom *Ulyſſes beſpeaks again, and yet again*, without any Anſwer at all? Or perhaps this has been obſerv'd upon ſo often, that you think it needleſs to repeat its Beauties: I don't queſtion but you admire it very much. I do ſo (anſwer'd *Philypſus*) and agree entirely with the Obſervation. (*b*) "That "*Ajax* has more the air of Grandeur "when he ſays nothing, than when the "Poet makes him ſpeak.

Mr. *Pope* does not only follow *Homer* very finely, wherever he has led the Way in theſe beautiful Figures; he ſometimes

(*a*) *Od.* 11. 665---537. (*b*) Note *ibid.* and *Longinus*, 9.

heightens,

heightens, and ſometimes adds them with a great deal of Propriety. Every one ſees how unwilling *Calypſo* is to part with *Ulyſſes*: But the Command of *Jove* muſt be obey'd: and the ſame fondneſs which makes her look on the departure of that Hero with extreme regret, engages her, at the ſame time, to aſſiſt him in the conveniences for it. She is always directing him, when employ'd; and when not, ſecretly diſſwading him from his Voyage. We ſee her buſy, even to Officiouſneſs, in bringing him the Inſtruments for his Work: guiding him to the Foreſt, and ſhewing what Trees are fitteſt for his Purpoſe:

(a) On the lone Iſlands utmoſt verge there ſtood
Of poplars, pines, and firs, a lofty wood,
Whoſe leafleſs ſummits to the skies aſpire,
Scorch'd by the ſun, or ſear'd by heavenly fire.
Already dry'd. —— Theſe pointing out to view,
The nymph juſt ſhew'd him, and with tears with-[drew.

This is much better expreſs'd than in the Original: indeed there we ſcarce diſcern that it is a paſſionate Silence. Improvements of this kind, *Antiphaus*, are the more to be valu'd, becauſe there is not any one thing in Poetry of greater Beauty and Energy. The Criticks look

(a) *Od.* 5, 305--238.

upon

upon it as the most (*a*) sublime, unusual part of Eloquence: and 'tis none of its least Advantages, that it hits that excellent Rule they give us, *Of* (*b*) *Leaving some things for the Audience to perceive of themselves:* Tho' it be not told him, every Man very easily finds out the heightning of such a Circumstance; and is sure to value it the more, because he finds it out himself. In short, these are Masterly strokes, and few hands arrive to them in their true Excellence. Tho' it requires the greatest Art and Judgment to introduce it, the Writer when he has chose the proper Point, seems to be put to no pains to rule our Affections: he governs all our Passions without the *Labour* of Words; and looks as *Archimedes* would to one's fancy, moving the whole World, while he *sits still* himself.

Suspence and Doubt have something of this Figure intermixt with them. A Speaker hesitating and unresolv'd, is in a State of *Half-silence:* As we see the former poetical Silence is observ'd in *Homer* every time *Ulysses* discovers himself

(*a*) φωνῆς δίχα θαυμάζεται ποτὲ ψιλὴ καθ' ἑαυτὴν ἔννοια δι' αὐτὸ τὸ μεγαλόφρον. *Longinus*, θ'. And *Cicero*: Rarum est eloquenter loqui; rarius, eloquenter tacere. Ep. ad *Atticum*. L. 13.
(*b*) See *Dem. Phal.* Σκδ'.

to any of his nearer Friends; so is there a mixture of this Doubtfulness also in each of those Interviews: Thus *Telemachus*, on that Occasion;

Thou art not---no, thou can'st not be my *Sire*;
Heaven such illusion only can impose
(*a*) By the false joy to aggravate my woes.

The *Unravelling* of the Doubt is what strikes us most, both in *Laertes* and *Penelope*: in the latter Case, this is deferr'd for too long a time: However as they are, they afford us some of the most pathetick Passages in the whole Poem. In what an affecting Manner does *Laertes* appear to us just at the point of his being convinc'd, that the Stranger he is conversing with, is his Son?

Smit with the signs which all his doubts explain,
His heart within him melts; his knees sustain
Their feeble weight no more; his arms alone
Support him, round the lov'd *Ulysses* thrown:
He faints, he sinks with mighty joys opprest:
Ulysses clasps him to his eager breast.
Soon as returning Life regains its seat,
And his breath lengthens, and his pulses beat;
Yes, I believe, he cries: Almighty *Jove*! ——
Heaven rules us yet, and Gods there are above.
(*b*) 'Tis so. ——————

(*a*) *Od.* 16, 217---195. (*b*) *Od.* 24, 411---351.

As

As to *Penelope*: Where a modern would have been overjoy'd, and caught immediately at an Occasion for so many raptures, the *Greek* Poet chuses rather to shew her Prudence, than her Passion. I believe every body will agree, that this *still Interval* is not ill-chosen: the fault of it is, its being carried through too many Lines. The Queen, no doubt, struggled hard all the while; She had difficulty enough in restraining herself; And the moment she is convinc'd, she is all Tenderness and Passion.

While yet he speaks, her powers of life decay,
She sickens, trembles, falls and faints away:
At length recovering to his arms she flew,
And strain'd him close, as to his breast she grew;
The tears pour'd down amain: And oh, she cries,
Let not against thy Spouse thine anger rise!
O vers'd in every turn of human art,
Forgive the weakness of a woman's heart——
O let me, let me not thine anger move,
That I forbore---thus---thus---to speak my love;
Thus in fond kisses, while the transport warms,
Pour out my Soul, and die within thy arms!—
(a) I yield, I yield! my own *Ulysses* lives.

This unravelling of a *Doubt* is generally follow'd by what is the most contrary to it of any thing in the World, *Precipitation*. To doubt of any happy

(a) *Od.* 23, 240---230.

Circumstance, is to fear that it should not prove true. When we are agitated by the Expectation of some Bliss, we long to indulge that Flow of Spirits which it Occasions; only some particular Caution forces us to restrain them in the midst of their Career: The moment our Doubt is clear'd, and the Obstacle remov'd, they rush on with the greater Violence and Impetuosity. Then are our Words quick and vehement; We speak short, and fast; A Thousand things We want to say, and are so eager we don't know which of them to say first. I know nothing in Musick that strikes me equally to those *suddain Pauses*, when the Consort stops at once; and after the still Interval, breaks out unexpectedly into a full Tumult of Harmony. This Pause, and the Impetuousness that succeeds upon it, is the case (to carry on a Scene, which we have touch'd upon twice or thrice already) when *Telemachus* recognizes his Father: *Telemachus* wants to know every thing at once; and *Ulysses* wants to tell him every thing as fast:

> All, All, *Ulysses* instant made reply,
> (*a*) I tell thee All, my Son! ———

(*a*) *Od.* 16, 249---226.

Such

Such an Hurry of Spirits, the more violent it is, makes us ſpeak in the more broken and interrupted manner. You always ſee that a Croud is the longeſt in getting out of a place, where they are in the greateſt Haſte, and preſs moſt. When the Paſſions are leſs diſturb'd, they go in Train, and follow one another eaſily; but if they move all of them for a Paſſage at the ſame time, they hinder one another: This ſort of Precipitation, is very well expreſs'd in *Penelope*, upon receiving *Telemachus* after his Voyage:

Few words ſhe ſpoke, tho' much ſhe had to ſay,
And ſcarce thoſe few for tears cou'd force their way.
Light of my Eyes! He comes!--Unhop'd-for Joy!
Has Heaven from *Pylos* brought my lovely Boy?
So ſnatch'd from all our cares! Tell, haſt thou known
(*a*) Thy Fathers Fate, and tell me all thy Own.

You cannot imagine, *Antiphaus*, the full heightning of this Paſſage, without comparing it with the Original: 'Tis the ſame caſe in moſt that I have mention'd; They are ſome of the juſteſt Improvements in the Poem; as well as Inſtances of the beſt ſort of Figures, ſuch as ſhew the Paſſions of the Mind in a ſtrong and lively manner. There are o-

(*a*) *Od.* 17, 55--44.

ther, which the Poet makes ufe of, fometimes to raife and diverfify his Language; fometimes to give ftronger Colours to the things he defcribes; And fometimes to engage or poffefs his Readers. I need not enter into a long Enquiry concerning the more known Figures of either kind; but fhall touch upon one or two, which as yet have not been introduc'd by the Criticks into their *Syftems*.

Poetical Prophecy, is when we acquaint the Reader before-hand of fome Events, which will happen in the Progrefs of the Poem: *Prevention* is when we fpeak of fuch things, yet to come, as if they were already prefent. *Prevention* gives an uncommon Greatnefs and Energy to the Language: It places diftant Actions full before our Eyes; and carries a certain Boldnefs and Affurance with it, that is very becoming: The *other* is of great Strength in poffeffing and captivating the Reader; We love to look on into Futurity: Thus it flatters the Powers and Capacity of our own Minds, at the fame time that it gives an Air of Superior Knowledge and Authority to the Poet.

From the Invocation of the Mufe in the entrance to his Poem, the Poet has a Right of Prophecying; and it might be *partly* from this, that the Name of

Prophet

Prophet and *Poet* has in ſome Languages been us'd in common. But tho' he may, and does, prophecy in Perſon, things of this Nature are uſually introduc'd from others: as from Superior Beings; from Prieſts and Augurs; from (*a*) Perſons in the other State, or juſt at the (*b*) Point of Departing from this. This latter Method perhaps may carry the greater *Sanction* with it; but the other is the more *Poetical*.

Some of the ſtrongeſt Speeches in *Homer* and *Virgil* are deliver'd after this manner, by Men of the Prophetick Character; It is to this Figure (if you will give me leave to call it ſo) that the *Sixth Book* of the *Æneid*, and the *Fourth* of the *Odyſſey* owe the greateſt ſhare of their Beauty. Even the frightful Raptures of *Theoclymenus*, and the *Harpye* of *Virgil*, engage the Reader with a ſort of pleaſing Terrour. There is ſomething horribly delightful in theſe Lines.

Floating in gore, portentous to ſurvey!
In each diſcolour'd vaſe the Viands lay:
Then down each cheek the Tears ſpontaneous flow
And ſuddain Sighs precede approaching woe.

(*a*) As *Tireſias* in the 11th *Odyſſey*; or *Anchiſes* in the 6th *Æneid*. (*b*) See *Il*. π', Ver. 844 and 852. *Æn*. 10, 739.

In

In vision rapt, the * *Hyperesian* Seer
Up-rose, and thus divin'd the Vengeance near.
O Race to Death devote! with *Stygian* shade
Each destin'd Peer impending Fates invade:
With tears your wan distorted cheeks are drown'd,
With sanguine drops the walls are rubied round:
Thick swarms the spacious hall with howling [Ghosts,
To people *Orcus*, and the burning Coasts!
Nor gives the Sun his golden Orb to roll,
(*a*) But universal Night usurps the Pole!

I beg pardon (says *Antiphaus*) but the Speech of *Theoclymenus* is a particular Favourite of mine: and now you repeat it in *English*, I seem to want something of that strong Pleasure it used to afford me, Where the *Greek* speaks (*b*) *Of the Sun being perisht out of Heaven, and of Darkness rushing over the Earth*; I cannot express the Fulness of the Words---But you know the Original; and I fear will never see a Translation equal it. This whole Prophetical Vision of the Fall of the Suitors is the *True Sublime*: and, in particular, gives us an higher *Orientalism*, than we meet with in any other part of *Homer*'s Writings. You will pardon me a new Word, where we have no old one to my Purpose: You know what

---

* *Theoclymenus.*

(*a*) *Od.* 20, 430---357.

(*b*) ————————Ἠέλιος δὲ
Οὐρανοῦ ἐξαπόλωλε, κακὴ δ' ἐπιδέδρομεν ἀχλύς.

I

I mean; That *Eaſtern way of expreſſing Revolutions in Government, by a Confuſion or Extinction of Light in the Heavens.* It is this manner of Thinking which works up that Speech the neareſt of any to thoſe noble Paſſages in holy Scripture; (*a*) "*I* "*will ſhew Wonders in the Heavens and in* "*the Earth, Blood and Fire, and Pillars of* "*Smoak; the Sun ſhall be turn'd into Dark-* "*neſs, and the Moon into Blood.*—(*b*) *I* "*will cauſe the Sun to go down at Noon,* "*and I will darken the Earth in the clear* "*Day.*—(*c*) *All the bright Lights of Heaven* "*will I make Dark over thee, and ſet Dark-* "*neſs upon thy Land.*

I have often wondered, *Philypſus*, at ſome particular Perſons, who are ever raviſh'd with any thing of the Sublime in common Authors, and yet ſeem to have no taſte for the fineſt touches of this kind, thoſe which are ſo frequent in our ſacred Writings. With what Greatneſs, and Sublimity, do they abound? Such, as might perſwade, that weare not only bleſt with *Inſtructions*, but favour'd too with a *Language* from Heaven. Thoſe ſacred Pages want only to be read with a common regard, that all Men might acknowledge them to contain the great-

(*a*) *Joel* 2. 31. (*b*) *Amos* 8. 9. (*c*) *Ezek.* 32. 8.

est

eſt Maſter-pieces of Eloquence. Yes, *Philypſus*, it is there, that Eloquence ſits beſide the Throne of Truth, in all her nobleſt Attire, and with a Look, that ſtrikes us at once with Reverence and Delight. I long to expatiate on ſo glorious a Subject: but perhaps we may find a time of joining together in ſome View of this Nature: There has been a very good (*a*) Example ſet the World this laſt Summer; and if ever we ſhould follow it, and enter thoroughly into this ſort of Criticiſm, I dare ſay it will make any other kind look poor and inſipid, when compared with it.---But at preſent we are in another Sphere; and I have already interrupted you too much.-----

Philypſus, deſirous as he was to launch immediately into thoſe noble Depths of Eloquence, comply'd for the preſent, and return'd to the point in hand. " My laſt " Inſtance from the *Odyſſey* prevents what " I had deſign'd for the next; You ſee, " it ſpeaks all along of future things, as " if they were actually preſent. *Theoclymenus* has the whole fact paſſing ſucceſſively before his Eyes: The Deſtruction of the Suitors is pictur'd in his Mind; he ſees their *blood* ſprinkled upon the Walls;

(*a*) *Blackwall*'s Sacred Claſſicks.

their

their *bodies* floating in Gore, and their *souls* sinking to the Regions of the Dead.

Now I am upon this head of *Prophecy* and *Prevention*, I should be very defective, were I to omit the other Branch of it; which takes in all cases where the Poet forewarns us of Events in his own proper Person. This is to be found in the very same point, the Fate of the Suitors; but it is not deliver'd with the same Air of Enthusiasm: The *Poet* is inform'd by the Muse of things to come, while the *Prophet* is possess'd by Vision: The knowledge of one, is from Instruction; of the other, from a sort of Frantick Possession of Mind. The Poet therefore anticipates Events with less emotions of Language; and seldom rises into any fervor, above what we meet with in these Passages:

——— Incens'd they spoke
While each to chance ascrib'd the wondrous stroke;
Blind as they were—For death even now invades
(*a*)His destin'd prey, and wraps them all in shades.

And before:

——————In his Soul fond joys arise,
And his proud hopes already win the prize.
To speed the flying shaft thro' every ring,
Wretch! is not thine: the arrows of the King
(*b*)Shall end those hopes, and fate is on the wing.

(*a*) *Od.* 22, 38—33. (*b*) *Od.* 21, 104—98.

You

You obſerve, *Antiphaus*, that this Event which is ſo often anticipated by the Poet, is the great Point on which the Completion of his Fable turns: and I believe you may have obſerv'd, that *Virgil* puts on the Prophetick air, (*a*) exactly in the ſame Caſe. *Virgil* oftentimes improves upon his Maſter: the Circumſtance that introduces that Paſſage in the *Æneid*, and the greater diſtance of time, give it a much finer and a nobler Air, than we find in *Homer* himſelf.

Theſe Figures (for ſo I beg leave to call all unuſual manners of Speech) are of more difficult Obſervation, as they lye out of the common road: I am afraid of wandering too far; and ſhall therefore return very readily to the more beaten Path.

All Paſſions warm the Imagination, and make its Images more ſtrong and ſenſible. It is this, in my Opinion, that might render *Metaphors* very proper in the Pathetique: Tho' you and I, perhaps, ſhould not agree entirely on that Head.

At leaſt this is certain, that they ſtrengthen and enliven the narrative Part of Poetry, beyond any other Method

(*a*) See *Æn.* 10, 501.

what-

whatever; when the Poet treats of the most common things, he does not treat of them in the common manner:

Fame ſpeaks the *Trojans* bold, they boaſt the skill,
To give the feather'd arrow wings to kill;
To dart the ſpear, and guide the ruſhing car,
With dreadful inroad thro' the walks of war.

(*a*) Strip theſe Lines of the Metaphor, and they loſe their greateſt Force and Beauty. To ſay barely (as it is in the Greek) *That the Trojans are good Warriors, that they lauch the Spear, and handle the Arrow well; that they manage their Horſes dextrouſly, and in general, that they are very Strong and Succeſsful in Battle:* This declares the whole of the thing; but, with Submiſſion, 'tis more like a Proſe, than a poetical Narration; at leaſt, when compar'd with the ſame Sentiments in thoſe Lines I have juſt repeated.

There are many Innovations of this kind, which make the Engliſh *Homer* appear with Advantage: A naked relation of Fact is enough for Hiſtory; but Poetry requires ſomething more than bare Truth: It has a thouſand ways of raiſing and beautifying its Subject: *Phœbus*, like the Luminary over which he preſides,

(*a*) Od. 18, 308---263.

does not only ſhew, but ſets a Luſtre too, on every thing he touches: The Poet is not ſo much to declare Events, as to give its Colours and Life to every Action: in doing this, nothing is ſo requiſite as ſtrong animated Figures; as of all Figures the Metaphor affords the moſt ſenſible Strokes, and comes neareſt to the Pencil.

Even in common Caſes they are not without their Beauty: thus in that Enterview between *Ulyſſes* and *Laertes*:

Beneath a neighb'ring tree, the chief divine
Gaz'd o'er his Sire, retracing every line,
The ruins of himſelf! now worn away
(a) With age, yet ſtill majeſtick in decay.

Thus *Agamemnon* (after all his dangers, murther'd by the hands of Villains in his own Kingdom) is not ſaid barely *to die*, but *to end*,

(b) *The ſad Evening of a ſtormy life.*

When this Figure expreſſes ſome ſtrange Particularity, or includes any magnifying Compariſon, one ſingle Word is very powerful in raiſing the Narration, and enlarging our Ideas up to the Occaſion:

(a) Od. 24, 272---232. (b) Od. 4, 116---91.

With

With dreadful shouts *Ulysses pour'd* along,
(a) Swift as an Eagle, as an Eagle strong.——
Now by the *Sword*, and now the Jav'lin fall
(b) The rebel Race, and Death had *swallow'd* all &c.

I know no Case, in which Metaphors of a bold Sound are more proper, than in arrogant Speeches; When Men defy the Gods, or quarrel with the Dispensations of Providence. *Philætius* in the *Odyssey* is no arrogant Character: Yet in one place (upon considering the Afflictions of his Prince, whose Piety and Virtue he was so well assur'd of) he falls into a Rant against Providence; in which the Language is as lively and vigorous, as the Sentiment is ill-grounded and absurd:

O *Jove*! for ever deaf to human cries;
The tyrant, not the father of the skies!
Unpiteous of the race thy will began:
The fool of Fate, thy manufacture, Man,
With penury, contempt, repulse, and care:
(c) The gauling load of Life is doom'd to bear.

These Metaphors (which are of that kind we may call *The audacious*) come very near the Spirit of *Oldham* and *Dryden*; who undoubtedly, in their Satirical Works, flash out into the greatest Boldnesses this way of any of our Writers: indeed, in both, there are some which

(a) *Od.* 24, 622---537. (b) *Od.* 24, 612---527.
(c) *Od.* 20, 256---204.

may come too near to Prophaneness: but we must always take care not to attribute to the Poet, what he speaks under some other Person. A Devil is no longer a Devil, unless he be haughty, impenitent and blaspheming: and *Dryden* is no more to be condemn'd than *Milton*, for making such impious Spirits speak according to their true Character.

What you assert, I take to be perfectly true, says *Antiphaus*: but were I blest with any Genius for Poetry, I own that a shocking Impiety should be one of the last things I would *chuse* to describe. And where it is chosen, there is room to be moderate, without injuring the Character with too great a shew of Goodness: We see that *Milton* is not so gross, as *Dryden*: Nor (*a*) *Virgil* so blunt, as *Homer*.

(*a*) *Virgil* seldom descends to particulars: he chuses rather to say in general, *Atque Deos, atque astra vocat crudelia mater.* Even his *Mezentius* is more reserv'd than *Homer's* Deists: He rather ridicules than affronts; *Ast de me Divum pater atque Hominum Rex Viderit.*—— Afterwards he grows a little Warmer, and more Metaphorical;

Dextra mihi Deus, & telum quod missile libro,
Nunc adsint ——

Where he speaks plainest of all, *Virgil* touches upon his miserable fate in the very next line:

Nec mortem horremus, nec Divum parcimus ulli:
Desine. Jam venio moriturus. —— *Æn.* 10.

Well,

Well, ſays *Philypſus*, there are other Points which you might chuſe, and which ſerve as well for this ſort of Metaphor: Thus all pious Frauds, infamous Prieſts, or any prevailing Superſtition. Here the Figure retains much of the audacious Air, without any thing of Impiety in it. *Agamemnon* indeed goes too far in the *Iliad*, where he ſeems to neglect *Apollo*, as well as his Prieſt:

Hence, with thy lawrel crown, and golden rod,
Nor truſt too far thoſe enſigns of thy God:
(*a*) Mine is thy daughter, Prieſt ——

Here is ſomething of Irreverence to the God, and an evident Injuſtice to Man: and the Poet very prudently condemns the Speech, before he delivers it in his Poem. But there is no ſuch Mark ſet on one of *Hector's*; nor does it at all infringe that Hero's Character, which is remarkably Pious all through the Poem: He is ſpeaking againſt a very popular Superſtition, the Trade of Augury:

Ye Vagrants of the Sky! your wings extend
Or where the Suns ariſe, or where deſcend;
To right, to left, unheeded take your way,
While I the dictates of high Heaven obey.
Without a ſign his Sword the brave man draws,
(*b*) And asks no Omen but his Country's cauſe.

(*a*) *Il.* 1, 39--29 (*b*) *Il.* 12, 284--243.

This has the *audacious* Air, becauſe it ſpeaks contemptuouſly of a Practice, which was vulgarly look'd upon as religious and ſacred: and is *juſt*, becauſe it ſhews at the ſame time the greateſt Reverence to the Gods: He obeys the Dictates of *Heaven*, but he contemns the Artifices of *the Prieſt*.

Whatever reſtraints this kind of Metaphor may deſerve, there is another ſort which has always been receiv'd with the greateſt Liberty. The *animating* Metaphor, tho' the (*a*) moſt Sublime, and the moſt Daring of any, except what was laſt mention'd, is very common; and that even in the chaſteſt Poets, and in the ſofteſt Pieces. It is this by which we give Action and Spirit to things that are Still and Inſenſible. This will raiſe the meaneſt Points in the World: it may treat meer *Names*, as if they were *Things*; and Things ſtill and inanimate, as if they had Thought and Action. What might ſeem the moſt ſurpriſing is, that this method of raiſing things above their

(*a*) Præcipuè ex his oritur mira ſublimitas, quæ *audacia proxima* periculo tranſlationis attollitur: Tolluntur quum rebus ſenſu carentibus actum quendam & animos damus. *Quintil.* Lib 8. Cap. 6. *Ariſtotle* and *Phalareus* ſay exactly the ſame; ſee the latter Περὶ Ἑρμ. Πιθ.

Nature,

Nature, has nothing of ridiculous in it. We easily perceive this to be true: but I own, for my part, I should have been at a loss for the reason of it, had not I met with a (*a*) fine Observation in Mr. *Pope's Appendix* to this Work. I wonder now why I cou'd not before perceive, That *Ridicule is confin'd to moral Agents, and obtains only where Choice and Freedom is directly concern'd.* That this is the Case is the more plain; because, even among moral Agents, the very same thing, which if brought on by our own Folly, is a certain subject for Ridicule; when it proceeds from some inevitable Misfortune (or Necessity) is the farthest from being Ridiculous.

I am pleased to see that this Figure stands on such good reason; for it is the very Life and Soul of Description. And might it not be of a larger Use, *Antiphaus*, than has commonly been observ'd? It is chiefly mention'd indeed of enlivening things inanimate; Whereas possibly it may hold thro' the whole Chain of Beings in the World, as they rise gradually above one another. Thus when we attribute any thing of absolute Perfection to the highest Orders of created Beings,

(*a*) *Od.* Vol. 5. Pag. 238.

any

any thing which we think Angelical to Man, or any thing like Humanity or Virtue to Beasts; it might as well be included in this Branch of Metaphor, as when we give the Powers of Motion to things, Still; or Passions, to things Inanimate.

Nay, it may even return from the Lower to the Higher; when the Species of a lower Rank, upon the whole, has any (*a*) particular Excellence which the higher wants: Or partakes of any (*b*) Excellence, which is common to them both, in a greater and more excellent Degree.

But it must be observ'd, that where this Figure, in its higher Notion, is applied to Intelligents, it must not be done with the same Indifference; or rather it requires the strictest Caution.

The Poet is at liberty to attribute Action and Passions to any part whatever of the mute Creation: he may make the Woods, or any such Insensible, Sympathize with his Grief, with the same freedom as any inferiour Animals; we find it thus used particularly in all the *Pasto-*

(*a*) As when we amplify the Swiftness of an Hero, by comparing it to the Flight of an Eagle; or (*b*) the Swiftness of an Eagle, by comparing it to the Swiftness of the Winds.

ral Writers, whether Ancient or Modern. Every Beaſt may have the Compaſſion of Man; but few Men can ſuſtain the Properties of an Angel: Nothing would make a common Mortal ſo mean and ridiculous, as ſuch an Elevation: the ſame holds in the higher Intelligents; The Firſt of the Angelick Order looks monſtrouſly ridiculous (as well as monſtrouſly impious,) when he would imagine an Equality, where there was an immutable Diſproportion.

However, in ſome Caſes, the Property of an Angel may be given to a Man. The Heathen Poets compare their greater Hero's to their Gods; And when the Chriſtian Poet extols any ſuperiour Genius, any Character that has ſomething in it above the common race of Mortals, he may well draw ſome Expreſſions from the Order of Beings next above the Human. Had not Mr. *Addiſon* thought this Juſtiſiable, we ſhould have loſt one of the fineſt Amplifications imaginable.

(*a*) So when an Angel by Divine command
With riſing tempeſts ſhakes a guilty land,
Such as of late o'er pale Britannia paſt,
Calm and ſerene he drives the furious blaſt;
And pleas'd th' Almighty's orders to perform,
Rides in the whirl-wind, and directs the ſtorm.

(*a*) See *Addiſon's* Works, Vol. 1. Pag. 78. 12°.

But

But whither am I wandring, my *Antiphaus?* You will think ſuch Flights as theſe too Airy; ſurely, I am got into the Wilds of Criticiſm!---I don't know what the World might think of You at preſent, ſays *Antiphaus*: but if ever Mr. *Dryden's* Scheme ſhould take place, and the Poetical Characters of Angels be generally eſtabliſh'd; what you may think the wildeſt of your Flights now, might then be of good Service this way in Poetry.---Be that as it will, ſays *Philypſus*, I believe I had better draw in my thoughts a little for the preſent; and keep to things, that are more obvious and ſecure. All agree, that the giving *Thought* to things *inſenſible*, and *human* Paſſions to the *brute* part of the Creation, is equally juſt and beautiful: and at the ſame time nothing is of greater Efficacy in rendring our Sentiments Rais'd and Poetical. That *The Sufferings of our Fellow-creatures affect our Souls by a natural Sympathy*, is a very good moral Sentence: but the Poet is to Elevate this effect of Miſery; he inveſts her with a ſort of new *Being*; and then gives her *Addreſs* and *Action*. In Poetry our Tears (*a*) *ſpeak*; our Misfortunes are

(*a*) *Od.* 10, 291---248.

(a) *Eloquent*; and *Misery appears* (b) *in Person to plead for the distress'd.*

When more uncommon things are transfer'd this way, the Metaphor may be safer, if it has some grounds in the Fact; tho' it will bear very often without it. 'Tis allowable to represent the Sea, as flying back, and astonish'd, at the *terrible* (c) *Voice of the Cyclops*: but 'tis more close to attribute this Fear and Flight to it, when its Waves are (d) *drove asunder by the same Cyclops flinging a Rock into the midst of it.*

Another thing, which made this Figure the stronger among the Ancients, was their Notion of *Genii*, or *presiding Deities*. In particular, there was scarce a River or Brook amongst them, but what had its *Genius*; and in speaking of these the Poets carry this Metaphor farther than in any other case whatever. What an Appearance does *Xanthus* and *Simois* make in the *Battle of Rivers*, which takes up the 21*st Iliad*? What a bold Draught is that of the *Nile*, in the Sea-fight at *Actium*, by (e) *Virgil*? And how much more Sublime than either, is our Translation of the Sacred Writings,

(a) *Od.* 6, 374--311. (b) *Od.* 6, 204--169.
(c) As *Æn.* 3. 672. (d) *Od.* 9, 581--495.
(e) *Æn.* 8, 712.

where

where it makes *the Deep* (a) *utter his voice, and lift up his hands on high?*

You may perceive I am run into another Figure: but it is of a kind, ſo nearly allied to the *animating Metaphor*, that one often finds ſome difficulty in diſtinguiſhing the one from the other. Indeed when any of theſe *Perſonages* are introduced diſtinctly in full State, then it is ſomething beyond Metaphor; but in ſhort Sketches, it may paſs very well under that Figure. There is nothing but a ſtronger Name adapted to the thing, than its ſtrictly proper Acceptation affords. I think, for inſtance, that we need not ſeek for a new Figure in this Paſſage:

Aw'd by the Prince ſo haughty, brave and young,
(b) *Rage gnaw'd* the Lip, *Amazement chain'd* the [Tongue:

Or for this:

In every ſorrowing ſoul I pour'd delight,
(c) And *Poverty ſtood ſmiling* in my ſight.

In the cloſe of this Poem, the Narration is elevated, by a ſucceſſive Chain of theſe *Metaphors*, or *Fictions*, call them which you will. When the *Ithacenſians*

(a) *Habakkuk* 3, 10. (b) *Od.* 20, 335---268. (c) *Od.* 17, 506---421.

are

are rang'd in Arms against their Prince, 'tis not said, that they *shall Die*, but that (a) *Death attends them in the Field*:---To express *Ulysses*'s aptness to forgive them: (b) *Oblivion is ready to stretch her Wings over their Offences*: As when they are shockt with their Crime, and fling down their Arms, there is this Voice from Heaven to effect it:

" Forbear ye Nations! your mad hands forbear
(c) From mutual slaughter. *Peace descends to spare.*"

These, *Antiphaus*, are the most remarkable things, I have taken notice of, as to the Figures. I could have produc'd a greater number of excellent Lines from this Translation, had not I endeavour'd chiefly to give such Instances as contain'd, at the same time, some peculiar Improvements in them: You would be surprized to see how many Beauties they have, that are wanting in the Original.

Surely they who are the most rigid for Close-translating, will allow such beautiful Variations as these; which, without losing the Sentiments of the Original, only set a finer Turn upon them.

(a) Od. 24. 540---470. (b) Od. 24. 558---484.
(c) Od. 24. 618---534.

Let them call them, if they pleaſe, glorious Offences, or beautiful Wandrings from the Letter: theſe are ſuch Offences as one would wiſh to ſee more frequent than they are; and of which the beſt Tranſlators are the moſt guilty.

For my part I am particularly pleaſed, when I ſee a Tranſlator reflect new Light upon his Original: where-ever this is done juſtly, it does not alter the Objects; it only makes them more bright and viſible.

I believe, *Antiphaus*, you will not diſapprove of ſome other Methods, us'd in the Engliſh *Odyſſey* for this Purpoſe, which I am juſt going to lay before you. Sometimes the Language is rais'd and ſtrengthen'd; ſometimes the Order tranſpos'd to Advantage; in ſeveral Caſes we have *Homer*'s Thoughts inſpirited by collateral Thoughts from other Authors: ſome little things are omitted, and ſome ſhort ſtrokes added, to correct the Sentiment, or to heighten the Colours in the Original.

Before you enter upon thoſe Points, ſays *Antiphaus*, give me leave to mention ſome few things, which look like Blemiſhes, under the Subject you have juſt concluded.

It is allow'd, that Metaphors are the most useful of Figures to raise the Poetical Stile, to give their Colour to our Descriptions, and a just Swelling and Relief to our Images; 'Tis allow'd, that a Translator may add these Colours, where the Original is less Lively and Expressive, than the Subject may very well bear. The Faults then must lie, either in the Excess, or Impropriety of such Additions. Some things will not bear a strong Light; and others require to be flung into Shades.

Where there is no Occasion for Figures, they are at best only so many unnecessary *Ornaments:* I cannot see why a Quiver full of Arrows should be call'd (a) *A Store of flying Fates*; why a Fire should be term'd (b) *A burning Bed:* or a Libation, (c) *The Sable Wave of offer'd Wine.*

'Tis not the Disproportion of the Metaphor to the Thing, which might render these Expressions blameable; If any thing, 'tis the want of Occasion. When the Poet is to aggrandize small Subjects, we can bear with much bolder Metaphors than these: tho' it may not be proper to

(a) Od. 22, 136--119. (b) Od. 9, 449--378. (c) Od. 14, 499--447.

call a ſtream of Wine, by the Title of a *Sable Wave*, on common Occaſions; Yet when the Work requires heightening, we may go ſo much farther, as to call a (*a*) *ſmall River by the Name of the Ocean.*

If we judge by the *Occaſion*, there can be but few liberties for Metaphor in common Converſation; I mean, the common Converſation of Poetry. Not that they are to be baniſh'd thence entirely; rather it will require them frequently: but it requires only ſuch as are ſingle, and not far remov'd from the Subject. When a Perſon is ſpeaking to *Penelope*, in Commendation of *Ithaca*, he might be allow'd to ſay, that *Its Soil is* rich; *that it abounds in Corn; and that its Trees are* laden *with Fruit: Homer*'s Expreſſions ſcarce carry this ſo far; and yet I ſhould think them preferable to theſe in the Tranſlation:

(*b*) In wavy Gold thy ſummer vales are dreſs'd;
Thy autumns bend with copious fruits oppreſs'd.

Where the Original ſays, that *Eurynomus was among the Suitors of Penelope*, does not it ſeem better, as well as plainer, than this Tranſlation?

(*a*) As does *Virgil*, Georg 4. 29. (*b*) *Od.* 19, 131---112. See V. 565 ib. 482.

—— To

——— To climb with haughty fires
(a) The royal bed, *Eurynomus* aſpires.

A Metaphor may be continu'd too far, as well as carried too high: a long Chain of them leads us away from the proper Senſe; and flings that into *Allegory*, which we intend for *Reality ſtrongly expreſs'd.* This is very common, eſpecially in our *Pindarick* Writers: indeed few of our Poets, but what have (b) faln into it ſome time or other; but in thoſe, you find the moſt groſs and inſufferable Inſtances of it, that can be imagin'd.

In theſe *ſtrings* of Metaphor, nothing in my Opinion is ſo faulty, as that Point which has been ſo often touch'd upon: the ſhifting of Circumſtances in the ſame Deſcription; and repreſenting a Thing confuſedly, ſometimes in its *figurative*, and ſometimes in its *proper* Appearance. While an Actor is upon the Stage, his own private Character muſt be wholly laid aſide: he muſt be entirely *Booth*, or entirely *Cato.* Nay, even in the Scenary itſelf, things muſt be of a piece; and Mr. *Addiſon* has the juſteſt Occaſion for his frequent Severities upon this (c) con-

(a) *Od.* 2, 28---21. (b) See *Od.* 19, 286---251. And 20. Verſe 19, to Verſe 30---13, to 23.
(c) See *Spectator*, Numb. 5.

tradictory Mixture's prevailing so monstrously in our Theatre: How would the Wits of King *Charles's* time have laugh'd to see *Nicolini* sailing in an open Boat, upon a Sea of Past board? What a field of Raillery would they have been let into had they been entertain'd with painted Dragons spitting Wildfire, enchanted Chariots drawn by Flanders-Mares, and *real Cascades* in *artificial Landskips?* the making things after this manner, partly real, and partly imaginary, is to join Inconsistencies. Shadows ought never to be mixt with Realities in the same Piece, whether in poetick Scenary, or that of the Stage.

A Poet is never more apt to fall into this Confusion, than when he is speaking of Allegorical Persons; as, particularly, the Deities of the Heathens. When we speak of them personally, we are apt to mix something of their mystick Character: this is certainly vicious in Writing; and 'tis more so, to confuse the Properties of those things, over which any of those Deities were suppos'd to preside, with the Personal Acts of any particular Deity.

The Poets are allow'd the priviledge of elevating every Subject they take into their management: if they please they

may

may repreſent the Sun, as guided by an Intelligence: and 'tis but one ſtep farther with them, to give that guiding Intelligence, a Name; they call him *Phœbus*; and obviouſly enough, feign to themſelves, that he drives round the World in a Chariot of Fire. By degrees the Allegory is form'd regularly, and enlarg'd with more Particulars: he has ſo many Horſes aſſign'd to his Chariot: His own Appearance is well known: Beardleſs and Young, A Glory round his Head, and a Quiver full of Arrows o'er his Shoulder: *Thetis* is ready to receive him at the End of his Journey; and when he is to ſet out again, *Aurora* riſes from the Ocean to open the *Gates of Heaven*, that are kept for him by the *Hours*.

How very regular can Fiction be upon Occaſion? The eſtabliſhment of this Allegory under theſeParticulars, has prevented a world of Confuſion: this we may ſee by any Allegory, which is not yet ſettled on ſome Uniform Plan. To ſhew how far, I ſhall beg leave to enlarge a little on one of the ſame Nature, That of *Aurora*, the Goddeſs of the Morning.

Phœbus is never repreſented on this Occaſion, but in his Chariot I was ſpeak-

ing

ing of ; As for *Aurora*, I know not whether ſhe rides, ſits, or walks : Sometimes ſhe is in Heaven , and ſometimes upon Earth : In ſhort, the Poets ſeem to leave it undetermin'd how, when, or for what time ſhe makes her Appearance. I have laid together ſeveral Paſſages relating to this, but they leave the Point as confus'd as it was before :

Now did the roſy-finger'd Morn ariſe,
(a) And ſhed her ſacred light along the skies :

There, ſhe is plainly in Heaven.

———— When o'er the Eaſtern lawn
In ſaffron robes the daughter of the dawn
(b) Advanc'd her roſy ſteps ————

And here, as plainly upon Earth.

———— With her orient wheels
(c) *Aurora* flam'd above the Eaſtern hills.

Here I cannot abſolutely determine, whether ſhe be in Heaven , or upon Earth ; but 'tis plain, ſhe is got into her Chariot now, as ſhe was pleas'd to Walk the time before.

But when it is evident, that ſhe is not upon Earth ; 'tis ſtill difficult to know

(a) *Od.* 13, 22--18. (b) *Od.* 4, 587--431.
(c) *Od.* 16, 380--368.

whe-

whether ſhe is near it, or in the higher Heavens: whether ſhe

——— ——— Aſcends the Court of *Jove*,
(*a*) Lifts up her light, and opens day above:

Or, only

(*b*) ——Heaves her orient head above the waves.

There is the ſame difference in the degrees of that Brightneſs, which is attributed to her appearance: ſometimes ſhe only (*c*) *bluſhes with new-born Day*, and ſometimes ſhe is encompaſs'd with (*d*) *the full ſplendor of it:* When I read one Deſcription, I take it for granted, that the Glory round her Head ſhould be of *a* (*e*) *glimmering Light*; but when we come to another, 'tis of *a ſtrong* (*f*) *Flame:* You are at the ſame loſs to know, whether her *Robes* are (*g*) *Roſe-colour'd*, (*g*) *Saffron*, or (*h*) *Purple:* In fine, It would puzzle the Criticks to anſwer directly, whether ſhe has a *Quiver* on her Shoulders; and whether ſhe is to appear in a (*i*) martial, or in a gentle, peaceable Poſture.

This unſettledneſs in the preſent Caſe, runs through almoſt all the Poets ſince

---

(*a*) *Il.* 2, 60---49. (*b*) *Il.* 19, 1. (*c*) *Il.* 11, 1. (*d*) *Il.* 8, 83---66. (*e*) *Od* 9, 515---437. (*f*) *Od.* 16, 381---368. (*g*) *Od.* 4. 587---431. (*h*) *Od.* 19. 500---428. (*i*) Compare *Od.* 19, 500, with 6, 58.

Homer.

Homer. The moſt correct that ever wrote are not entirely free from it. *Virgil* himſelf often-times (*a*) continues her Courſe ſo far, that his (*b*) Commentators, to ſalve the matter, ſay, we muſt underſtand *Phœbus* by *Aurora*. In him the very *Horſes* that draw her Chariot are (*c*) *Roſe-colour'd*; as in *Theocritus* they are (*d*) *White*: ſometimes ſhe has the (*e*) Horſes of *Phœbus*; ſometimes (*f*) Four of her own; ſometimes (*g*) Two; and ſometimes ſhe is forc'd to ride only, and that upon (*h*) the Wings of *Pegaſus*.

It may be left to the Poets themſelves to determine, whether this Management be juſt towards Perſons of their own making: I ſhall only ſay, that the greateſt Criticks have ever thought, that *conſiſtency* is requir'd in the moſt *unbounded Fictions*: And, if I miſtake not greatly, *Homer* is more regular in this very Fiction before us. A Perſon better vers'd in his Writings, than I have the Happineſs to be, might, I believe, form from them as ſettled a Scheme in relation to this Goddeſs,

(*a*) *Æn*. 6, 536 &c. (*b*) Thus *Donatus*, *Ruæus*, &c. (*c*) *Æn*. 7, 26, and 6, 536. (*d*) —— Λεύκιππος ἀνατρέχοι ἐς Διὸς ἀώς. *Idyl*. 13. (*e*) *Æn*. 5, 105. (*f*) *Æn*. 6, 536. (*g*) *Æn*. 7, 26.

(*h*) Κραιπνοῖς ὑπὲρ νώτοισι Πηγάσου πτεροῖς. *Lycophron*.

deſs, as has been drawn up for any other of his Deities. This is certain, that he has preciſely fixt the *time* of her appearance; 'tis that (*a*) Interval, which commences after the firſt Dawn of Light, and ends juſt before the actual Riſing of the Sun. She always aſcends (*b*) from the Sea, to the Eaſtern *extremity*, or (as it is in the Language of Poetry) the (*c*) *Gates of Heaven*: there ſhe ſits in her (*d*) Golden Chariot, which has two Horſes aſſign'd to it, diſtinct (*e*) from thoſe of *Phœbus*, and there ſhe waits to (*f*) prepare the way for the Chariot of that Deity.

The Dreſs, and the Epithets, which *Homer* gives to this Imaginary Being are, as they ought to be in all ſuch Allegories, *at the ſame time evidently* (*g*) *drawn from the Nature of the Thing, and fairly applicable to the Fictitious Perſon.*

So much for Allegory: 'Tis a dangerous Topick, and we are apt to be loſt

---

(*a*) The Twilight is reckon'd into the Night. *Iliad* η', 433. And the firſt *direct* appearance of Rays attributed to the Sun; *ibid.* 422. (*b*) *Il.* τ', 2. (*c*) See Mr. *Pope's* Note on *Il.* 5, 928. (*d*) *Od.* ψ' 244. (*e*) See Note on *Od.* 23, 260. (*f*) φόως ἐρέουσα. *Il.* β', 49, &c. (*g*) This *Euſtathius* ſhews at large in his firſt Note on the ſecond Book of the *Odyſſey*: particularly, as to the Epithet ῥοδοδάκτυλος.

in

in the Clouds of it: Either the natural Defcription, or the Allegory, by it felf, may have a thoufand Beauties; but when they are dafh'd together, every thing is dark and confus'd. They put me in mind, *Philypfus*, of the two Liquors Sir *Ifaac Newton* fpeaks of, which from a fine Azure, and a beautiful Red, if you mix them, produce no Colour at all; The tranfparence and glow, which each had feparately, is immediately loft; and their Beauties vanifh away into one thick impenetrable Shade.

Before thefe confus'd Allegories and mixt Metaphors, I fhould have mention'd fome other Inftances, in which fingle Metaphors are faulty, either as they are Improper or Affected.

Is it proper to fpeak of *Penelope's Wit and Beauty* (or her Beauty alone) under the Notion of (*a*) *Drooping Verdure*? is it proper to talk of (*b*) *Raining Kiffes*? or of (*c*) *Storing a Veffel with* profperous Gales?

Is not the Metaphor and the Turn of Expreffion fomewhat affected, or overwrought, in this Paffage of the Nineteenth *Odyffey*:

(*a*) *Od.* 19, 149---128. (*b*) *Od.* 17, 49---39.
(*c*) *Od.* 5, 213, and 216---167.

These

These ſwarthy arms among the covert ſtores
Are ſeemlier hid; my thoughtleſs youth they blame
(a) *Imbrown'd with vapour of the ſmouldring flame.*

And a little farther, in the ſame:

My woes awak'd will violate your Ear;
And to this gay cenſorious train, appear
(b) *A winy-vapour melting in a Tear.*

Again; upon *Telemachus*'s return:

All crowded round the family appears,
With wild entrancement, and exſtatick tears.
Swift from above deſcends the Royal Fair;
Her beauteous cheeks the bluſh of *Venus* wear,
(c) Chaſten'd with coy *Diana*'s penſive air.

In the following Lines ſhe hangs o'er him,

——In his embraces dies;
(c) Rains kiſſes on his neck, his face, his eyes.

You have here (ſays *Antiphaus*) what has appear'd to me as Blemiſhes in this Poem, under theſe ſeveral Heads. I have endeavour'd, *Philypſus*, to read it with ſeverity: and when my Regards for the Author, or the Influence which ſuch Writers will always have over ones Soul,

---

(a) *Od.* 19, 22---18. (b) *Od.* 19, 143---122.
(c) *Od.* 17, 49---38.

began at any time to ſway my Mind; I have call'd up all the Ill-nature I am Maſter of to my Aſſiſtance; I'm fully ſenſible how difficult it is to keep the ballance ſteady: ſometimes our Admiration may warm us too much; and ſometimes a little Malice will prevail. If any thing I have been ſaying ſeems diſcolour'd with this Temper of Mind, point out my Faults to me, dear *Philypſus*; Correct me like a Friend; and ſhew that openneſs I have deſerv'd at your hands.

When I have time to conſider the Notes, I ſee you have taken down (anſwer'd *Philypſus*) and to compare ſome Paſſages with the Original, You ſhall know more of my Mind: as yet I ſee no reaſon for your Requeſt; but think you have dealt with that Fairneſs which I ſo much admire in my *Antiphaus*.

In the mean time I have a word or two to add on thoſe other Excellencies of this Tranſlation, which I mention'd to you before.

That Method of Improving the Original, by *Transferring Beauties* from one fine Writer to another, is carried on thro' this remaining part of the Poem, in the ſame frequency, as it was us'd in the former Volumes.

These

These *Foreign Infusions* of Thought and Language (to use the Name which Mr. *Addison* has given them) are very discernible to any one of a tolerable Taste: 'tis true, they must have something of a new Air; but they still retain a distinct Resemblance of the Old, something like that of the Sister *Nereids* in *Ovid*;

——— Facies non omnibus una,
Nec diversa tamen; qualem decet esse sororum.

In pointing out these Resemblances to some People, I shou'd be apprehensive, that they might think me taken up in an Imaginary Chase: but any one of much less Discernment, than *Antiphaus*, will perceive immediately, that this Likeness is real, and design'd by the Poet himself. There is an (*a*) eminent Critick, who has wrote a whole Treatise on this single Point, in Praise of a (*b*) particular Favourite of his: In the present Case, Mr. *Pope* tells (*c*) us, "That he read the Ancients with this Design; that he serves himself of them as much as he can; and that they have been his chief Inspirers in Poetry." I believe the Gen-

(*a*) *Casaubon.* (*b*) *Persius.*
(*c*) Preface to his Works, Fol. and Pref. to the Pastorals. p. 10.

tlemen, who are concern'd with him in this Tranſlation, would give me leave to ſay the ſame of them: 'Tis too evident to be denied: it appears both in their (*a*) Obſervations, and in their excellent Works.

In theſe laſt Volumes, how finely are (*b*) ſome Thoughts wove into this Tranſlation from the ſacred Pages? from the *Iliad*, and *Æneid*; from *Dryden*, and *Milton* among ourſelves; and from ſeveral others, both Ancient and Modern?

The Tranſlator is ſometimes as Artful in adding, of himſelf, ſome ſhort Strokes to what *Homer* has ſaid. We meet with ſeveral of theſe little Inſertions, which are very juſt and improving. I ſhall mention but one. As Mr. *Addiſon* (*c*) propoſes a Correction of *Paradiſe Loſt*, by cutting off the two laſt Lines; Mr. *Pope* improves this Poem, by adding a Line in the Concluſion of it: This Inſertion poſſibly is better choſe, than that

(*a*) See Note on *Odyſſey* 11, 152—18, 207.
(*b*) From Ss. Book 16, 237. *ibid.* 420. B. 18, 158. B. 19, 99 &c.
Virgil. B. 15, 250. B. 16, 189. B. 17, 227.——
Ibid. 523. B. 18, 121. B. 24, 131. &c.——
Homer. B. 17, 613. B. 24, 513.——
Milton. B. 19, 694. B 20, 370. B. 24, 498. &c.——
Dryden. B. 23, 322. B. 24, 309. *ibid.* 632.——
(*c*) *Spectator*, Numb. 369.

Altera-

Alteration so modestly propos'd by Mr. *Addison.* The Reader, indeed, would willingly go off with some Hopes and Satisfaction, after the Melancholly Scene in *Milton's* last Book: but it may be said that, considering the Moral and chief Design of that Poem, Terror is the last Passion to be left upon the Mind of the Reader. On the contrary, the *Odyssey* ought on all Accounts to terminate *happily:* and Mr. *Pope's* Addition, in the close of it, is therefore an Improvement, because it forwards the Moral; it gives us a (*a*) fuller View and Confirmation of the *Happiness of Ulysses*, and leaves it upon a firmer Foundation.

In the beginning of the Evening, *Antiphaus*, You were speaking of the Poets *transposing Words* to Advantage. I believe

---

(*a*) So *Pallas* spoke: the mandate from above
The King obey'd. The Virgin-seed of *Jove*
In *Mentor's* form confirm'd the full accord,
And willing Nations knew their lawful Lord.

Homer himself does not end in so full and compleat a manner: His last Line does not rest well; and *Chapman* seems resolv'd to shew the infirmness of it, as much as he could possibly in his Translation, which breaks off in these Lines.

——— Twixt both parts the seed of *Jove*,
Athenian *Pallas*, of all future love
A League compos'd; and for her form, took choice
Of *Mentor's* likeness; both in limb, and voice.

 this

this may ſometimes be of greater Uſe in altering the Order of *Sentences*, or the Succeſſion of ſome *Incidents* in the Poem; tho' I own, this muſt be attempted but rarely, and with the greateſt Caution: Difficult as it is, You will find a good Inſtance of the Former in one of the Suitors ridiculing Speeches; and of the Latter in *Euryclea*'s Tranſports.

Euryclea, You know, diſcovers *Ulyſſes* by a Scar upon his Leg, while ſhe is Bathing him. The Moment ſhe makes this diſcovery, ſhe drops the Jarr of Water, and is ready to faint away with Surprize and Joy. Tho' theſe, in the Nature of the Caſe, muſt follow immediately upon one another, *Homer* has inſerted a long Story (how the Scar was occaſion'd) *juſt after* the Diſcovery, and *before* thoſe Paſſions, which are the immediate Effect of it. Thus is a ſuddain Event *declar'd* fourſcore Lines before it is *deſcrib'd*——A Succeſſion of *time* taken up in the Narration, contrary to the time of the Fact——An *Impetuous* Paſſion kept in ſuſpence; in a word, Two things inſeparable in their Nature, are diſjointed in the Deſcription. I know not whether I ſee this in a wrong Light; but at preſent it puts me in Mind of *Mahomet*'s flinging his Baſon down, travelling

to

to Heaven, feeing the Lord knows what there, and returning again before the Water is run out.

If I miftake not, this Impropriety is avoided very Artfully. *Euryclea* is not made to difcover this Scar before that long Digreffion. (*a*) It is rather faid (in the Prophetick manner of the Poets) that fhe would foon Difcover it, than that fhe has actually Difcover'd it. 'Tis after the Digreffion, that it is mention'd directly as Fact: fo that in the Tranfla-tion, This Fact is not dif-jointed from thofe Emotions which it immediately raifes in *Euryclea*; We are not told four-fcore Lines after the Jarr is flung down, that the Water is *running* out of it.

If this be really the Cafe, fays *Anti-phaus*, I think the Alteration is much to be commended. But why may not *Homer* himfelf be underftood to fpeak in the Pro-phetick manner too? for I fuppofe that fingle Point would falve all: You do not blame the Digreffion itfelf?

No, fays *Philypfus*, 'tis not the Di-greffion which I blame, but the Point in which it is introduc'd; juft between a Fact, and what in Nature muft be im-mediately confequent upon that Fact.

(*a*) *Od.* 19, 461. And 547---392, and 467.

If, as you ask, *Homer* ſpeaks at firſt, only in the Prophetick manner, then it is all clear'd up: But I fear his Expreſſions confine it directly to a thing *then done*, and cannot be taken in the Prophetical way.

Philypſus was ſo engag'd to this Moment, that he had not once obſerv'd how the Day wore away: He was ſurpriz'd to find the Night was juſt coming on. "Why did you ſuffer me (ſays he "to *Antiphaus*) to keep you here ſo long: "I did not imagine the Night had been "ſo near us: You know I am an Eternal Talker——However I ſee the "Coach is at the Door; and we may "reach our Lodgings, I believe, before "it is quite dark.

An

An ESSAY &c.

EVENING the FIFTH.

BEFORE they parted the last Evening the two Friends agreed, that their next meeting shou'd be in the same place; and as this was to be the last which they intended to set apart for this Enquiry, they set out for *Horatio*'s earlier than usual. When they alighted, *Philypsus* order'd his Servant before them to the *Dome* of *Apollo*, with a Book or two he had brought in the Coach; whilst He and *Antiphaus* walk'd on gently to enjoy the Freshness of the Air, and the Beauties of the Place. The Sun (which now began to be in its decline) as it shot thro' the Trees, made a thousand wavering Mixtures

Mixtures of Light and Shade: The Birds, on all ſides were anſwering one another in their little natural Airs: every thing look'd Freſh about 'em; and every thing was Agreeable.

Delighted with ſo many calm undiſturb'd Pleaſures, they wander'd on from one Walk to another; and chatted, as they went, of a Thouſand indifferent Things. Among the reſt *Philypſus* fell into an Account of the Company he had to Dine with him. You know *Morforio*, ſays he?——— *Perfectly well, anſwer'd Antiphaus.*———He was there too; and made it his Buſineſs, as uſual, to contradict every thing that was offer'd againſt any of our celebrated Poets.——— *I am very glad, ſays* Antiphaus, *that I was not of the Company; his way of arguing is too General to be Anſwer'd, and too Poſitive to be Born with.*———Yes, ſays *Philypſus*, it was his old way. If one Perſon blamed ſome particular *Littleneſs* in *Milton*, he wou'd immediately ask him how he cou'd blaſpheme ſuch a *Sublime* Poet? and when another mention'd a groſs Line from *Addiſon*'s Works; How abſurd is that, ſays he, to charge ſuch a thing on the chaſteſt and moſt *correct* Compoſitions in the World?——— *Right! and I ſuppoſe the very next thing he muſt ask was, How You*

cou'd

cou'd dislike such Glorious Men, as Addison *and* Milton——You have him exactly. It was in vain to tell him that you disliked only *this Line*, or *that Thought:* He would have his way: and, I doubt not, but in his Opinion we are all a Set of Hereticks, or at least Free-thinkers in Poetry. What an egregious Fault is it, *Antiphaus*, with some Men, only to have ones Eyes open?——*But there are times* (says *Antiphaus*, assuming as he spoke, the imperious air and manner of *Morforio*) *there are times sure, when they had better be shut*——And therefore I should wink always——*Not so neither: Your Betters may direct you what to look upon, and what not*——That's a good Thought, truly: 'tis great Pity the Legislator has not consider'd of it. I should be in Love with an Act of Parliament about the *Use of Eyes.*——*Why where would be the great harm of the Matter, if you were order'd to wink hard, or to turn away from every disagreeable Object, that offer'd it self?*——How may I behave, if the Object be agreeable? ——*Look as long as you please*——And How, if there be a Mixture of disagreeable in it?——*You suppose then, that there may be something disagreeable, in that which is beautiful?*——Really, Sir, that is my Notion. Nay, I am apt to think farther

farther, that there is nothing so Beautiful, as to be without Defect; without some Mixture of the Disagreeable. By your Rule then, we must lose the sight of a Thousand fine Objects. How can I look on that Lady, you were admiring so much the other Day in the Ring, without seeing that her Hair is of a disagreeable Colour? Or must I swear that her *Eyebrows* are *Black*, because she has a *fine Shape?*——*That's over-straining the matter: but I think you might pass by such a Trifle, if it were only in Complaisance. Where there are such exact Features, so charming a Complexion, and a Make so delicate, 'tis barbarous not to let such a small Affair, as the Colour of an Eyebrow, escape your Observation.*——Depend upon it, I would not be so blind as to think the Lady was Disagreeable on that Account——*But I cannot allow any thing disagreeable about her*——Where are your Eyes then?——*I would not believe them*——That's one way——*Or what would you say to the new Invention*——What Invention I beseech you——*Only of a sett of Glasses, which shall make each favourite Object appear exactly the same to every Eye*——And exactly beautiful?——*That too*——An hopeful project, truly! Let but *Morforio* be the Designer, and some things

things would appear all Glaring and Beautiful; while all the reſt, I ſuppoſe, only upon turning the Tube, might be nothing but Deformity.

In the midſt of this roving ſort of Talk, they were got to the *Dome*, before they thought of it: " Well, ſays *Philypſus* " (as he enter'd) till I meet with the " Perſpectives you were talking of, I " ſhall not be aſham'd to confeſs, that I " find my Eyes at preſent to be of a diffe- " rent Turn. I cannot help perceiving " ſome little Blemiſhes in our moſt de- " lightful Poets; and yet I am far from " an Inſenſible to their Beauty: I view " them with delight; I admire them paſ- " ſionately: Nay, I believe, I have all " of *Morforio*'s Love, except the Blindneſs " of it. 'Tis there that you have open'd " my Eyes, *Antiphaus*: You have taught " me to Love not only with Paſſion, but " with Reaſon——Rather ſay (reply'd *Antiphaus*) that your own Mind aſſerted its true Prerogative; and roſe up to guide your Paſſions to none, but proper Objects.——However that be, ſays *Philypſus*, I am ſenſible of an Alteration for the better; and can now indulge a Paſſion for any Writer with the greater Appetite, as I am perſwaded it gives the Mind a ſufficient Pleaſure, without making ſo great a Fool of it. Do I not love this Writer, added he, (taking up one of the Pieces that lay before him) I read him with the ſame Eagerneſs, and find new Charms in him continually. Nay, I think my Love of him more ſecure, than ever: Since I can ſuffer my ſelf to ſee his Faults; and by that means, am ſatisfied that they can never be ſufficient in the leaſt to cloud his Perfections.

I am entirely of your Opinion, (ſays *Antiphaus*) and doubt not, but in our finiſhing this Enquiry, we ſhall have the greater Security in admiring Him. I only ſpeak of our ſelves. There may be many other Beauties, and other Faults, viſible to Men of better Eyes: but we may ſafely fix our own Sentiments on what we have been able to diſcover our ſelves. I hope, we have endeavour'd ſincerely to hold the Ballance ſteddy; and when we have done what we can, we have done what we ought.

I wiſh you would have left that *Sentence* for me, ſays *Philypſus*; It would have ſerv'd admirably to introduce what I am to enter upon this Evening.——It is at your ſervice (ſays *Antiphaus*) and therefore I beg you would proceed.

Tho' I might begin very well with the *ſententious manner* in Writing; my Subject,

ject, says *Philypsus*, is so various, that I do not well know what I ought to chuse first: The Prospect widens rather too much upon me; and indeed takes in most of the Faults and Vertues of any Poem. I own that, in general, the Great and First Excellence of a *Poet*, is to be *natural*: but it will be allow'd me, that the chief, and distinguishing Beauty of an *Epick* Poem, as such, is a true Air of *Greatness*, and a Stile that carries *weight* and *emphasis* with it: as the Vice most opposite to it, is *trifling*, *vulgarity*, and *meanness*. I wish I may manage these Points as fully, as I doubt not *Antiphaus* will display the *natural* strokes that are so frequent in the *Odyssey*.

Sentences carry much efficacy with them in a Poem; they are usually of the perceptive kind; tho' they seem rather to insinuate, than to command: As they are general Truths and Maxims of Life, well adapted to some particular occasion in the Poem, they appear with Authority; and contain the most useful Instructions, without the Stiffness and Odium of personal Advice.

'Tis a Mistake (to use a Maxim of Lord *Shaftsbury's*) *to think that no body knows how to take Advice; the Fault is, that few know how to give it.* To do this

agreeably, and at the ſame time with Weight, is the great Art of Sentences in Poetry.

Poetry in its Birth was calculated for the Service of Religion. The deſign of the *Epick* Muſe was to paint the Succeſſes of Vertue, or the Puniſhment of Vice. Hence the *Tragick*, that follow'd the very ſame Purpoſes; and afterward the old *Comedy*, whoſe buſineſs lay in encouraging leſſer Domeſtick Vertues, and ridiculing the Foibles of Mankind. *Satire*, the Off-ſpring of both theſe, partakes of either kind; ſhe Smiles in *Horace*, looks Severe in *Perſius*, and Commanding in *Juvenal*: The Satiriſt may uſe different Methods, but whether he Laſhes or Ridicules, 'tis ſtill the *vicious*, who are to ſuffer.

All the other Species of Poetry either fall in with theſe, or follow the ſame Ends: ſuch, as forget this, deſerve not the Name of Poets: they proſtitute the Muſe; and whatever they produce muſt be of a Baſtard-Kind.

Among many other Excellencies, this ought particularly to be obſerv'd in Honour of the true genuine Poets of Antiquity, that they ſeem to treat of Morality, even better than thoſe who profeſs'd that Study. Were it not for the Works

of

of their Poets, we might very well imagine *Benevolence*, for Inſtance, That which gives its Life and Spirit to the whole Family of Vertues, was ſuppreſs'd to the laſt Degree among the Heathens. In reading their Philoſophers, one is almoſt perſwaded, that they teach Revenge; and make it their buſineſs to limit and reſtrain that Love, which Men have naturally to one another. In ſhort, He that wants to find the true Philoſophy muſt go to their Poets. They break out into warmer Notions, and more exalted Leſſons of Humanity. Among them the Face of Charity is leſs veil'd, and clouded; and Goodneſs appears with a Countenance more generous and erect.

The *Odyſſey*, as a *Moral Poem*, exceeds all the Writings of the Ancients: it is perpetual in forming the Manners, and inſtructing the Mind: it ſets off the Duties of Life more fully, as well as more agreeably, than the *Academy* or *Lyceum*. *Horace*, who was ſo well acquainted with the Tenets of both, has given (*a*) *Homer's* Poems the Preference to either.

(*a*) Quid ſit pulchrum, quid turpe, quid utile, quid non, Plenius ac melius Chryſippo & Crantore dicit. Lib. 1. Ep. 2.

Surely, *Antiphaus*, Men were more Virtuous in the days of *Homer*, than they were in the time of *Plato* or *Cicero*; at leaſt, they were more charitable, and tender to Strangers. How elſe could the Poet ſpeak in ſuch a Spirit of Goodneſs, whenever he touches upon this Duty? Nothing is inculcated by him, more frequently; and nothing, with greater Strength and Emphaſis.

Homer (in relation to *Strangers*) does not ſtint the Charity of his Countrymen to the common *Uſe of Fire and Water*: he ſeems rather to proportion the *bounty* to the *want*;

'Tis ours the Sons of ſorrow to relieve,
(*a*) Chear the ſad heart, nor let affliction grieve.

He ſcarce looks upon this as *bounty*, he rather thinks it a *debt* owing to every one of the ſame nature with us:

'Tis what the happy to the unhappy owe;
(*b*) 'Tis what the Gods require.

What is given to them (ſays he) is paid to, and will infallibly be rewarded by, the Divine Power.

By *Jove* the Stranger and the Poor are ſent;
(*c*) And what to *thoſe* we give, to *Jove* is lent.

(*a*) *Od.* 6. 245---207. (*b*) *Od.* 9, 321---269.
(*c*) *Od.* 6, 247---208.

As

As the neglect of this will be aveng'd by the same,

> To *Jove* their cause, and their revenge belongs.
> (*a*) He wanders with them, and he feels their wrongs.

I doubt not, but this Notion of the Gods wandering on Earth in a disguis'd manner, was a very common motive to Charity in those times: it is mention'd very strongly in the Original, in this place; and (*b*) afterwards, when *Ulysses* appears as a Suppliant among the *Phæacians*.

Such high exalted Thoughts of this Duty have carried the Poet so far as (*c*) to teach, "That we shou'd not value any "labour of our own in assisting others:" but as that is not deliver'd in the *Sententious manner*, I shou'd go out of my way to repeat it at present.

To us, who have always enjoy'd so clear and steady a Light, in regard to every branch of this Duty, these *sentences* may appear common and obvious: but I imagine any one, who shou'd compare these Passages, by the rules of Benevolence in the Philosophical writings of the Ancients; would upon such a view al-

(*a*) *Od.* 9, 329---271. (*b*) *Od.* 7, 265---199.
(*c*) See *Od.* 7, 256---194.

low

low them to contain thoughts highly noble and extensive.

I shall mention but one more, which tho' it run thro' several lines, is but one entire *sentence*: and which, by the way, if I forget not, contains a motive to Charity, not to be found even in (a) *Cicero*'s Catalogue.

Who calls, from distant nations to his own,
The poor, distinguish'd by their wants alone?
Round the whole world are sought those men divine,
Who publick Structures raise, or who design;
Those to whose Eyes the Gods their ways reveal,
Or bless with salutary arts to heal:
These states invite, and mighty Kings admire,
Wide as the Sun displays his vital fire.
It is not so with Want! How few that feed
(b) A Wretch unhappy, merely for his need?

I ought not to dissemble one thing; That the Translation is not to be trusted entirely in this Argument: we find these Passages improv'd in the Handling; and those Lines, in which they resemble our sacred Writings, may be drawn more strongly. However, the Original it self may give us a great deal of reason to suppose, either that *Homer* had borrow'd some lights from thence; or that he cou'd discern the Light of Nature more

(a) *De Officiis*, p. 20. In beneficentiâ delectus esset dignitatis &c. (b) *Od.* 17, 471---387.

clearly,

clearly, than any other of the Heathen Writers.

Before I compar'd Paſſages, I muſt own to you, that I was in particular expectation of Improvements from Mr. *Pope* under this Article. A virtuous generous Soul is certainly as neceſſary to conſtitute a Great Poet, as a Great Orator: and in Sentiments like theſe, we may diſcover that temper of Mind, which I dare ſay has contributed much towards making that Gentleman ſo good a Poet, as well as ſo good a Friend.

There is one particular more extremely frequent in *Homer*: it runs thorough all his Works; and is ſcarce once omitted, where there is any occaſion for it. I believe your Thoughts outrun me, and might prevent my ſaying, that I mean His Reflections on the Miſeries of this Life. They are moſtly very emphatical; and lead to a very eaſy and uſeful inference.

——To his native land our charge reſign'd, [hind.
Heaven is his life to come, and all the woes be-
Then muſt he ſuffer what the Fates ordain;
For Fate has wove the thread of life with pain,
(*a*) And Twins ev'n from the birth are Miſery
[and Man!

In another place we have the ſame Thought as ſtrongly expreſs'd, tho'

(*a*) *Od.* 7, 264---198.

branch'd

branch'd out into ſeveral other Particulars: Let us ſuppoſe *Ulyſſes* before us: A Prince, Great for the Ages in which he liv'd, and greatly diſtreſs'd: How much does he ſpeak like one, born to Wiſdom, and long inſtructed by Adverſity?

Of all that breaths, or grov'ling treads on earth,
Moſt vain is Man! Calamitous by birth.
To day with power elate in ſtrength he blooms;
The haughty creature on that power preſumes:
Anon, from Heav'n, a ſad reverſe he feels;
Untaught to bear, 'gainſt Hea'vn the wretch rebels.
For Man is changeful, as his bliſs or woe;
Too high, when proſp'rous; when diſtreſs'd, too [low.
There was a Day, when (with the ſcornful Great)
I ſwell'd in pomp and arrogance of ſtate;
Proud of the pow'r, that to high birth belongs;
And us'd that pow'r to juſtify my wrongs.
Then let not Man be proud; but, firm of mind,
Bear the beſt humbly, and the worſt reſign'd:
(*a*) Be Dumb, when Heaven afflicts!——

Of all *Sentences*, there are none which ſtrike the Mind more forcibly, than thoſe which carry a bold air, a certain nobleneſs of Thought with them. There is a *Moral Heroiſm*, greatly to be preferr'd to that which generally uſurps its Name; a Generoſity of Soul, that looks beyond the Vulgar, and ſpeaks up to the Truth of things: It is this Generoſity, which animates thoſe Lines in *Virgil*:

(*a*) *Od.* 18, 171---141.

Eſt

Est hic, est animus, lucis contemptor; & istum
(a) *Qui vitâ bene credat emi, quo tendis, honorem.*

The same Spirit is infus'd into this Line:

(b) Death, ill-exchang'd for bondage and for pain!

The noblest Sentiments, are not such as make an *Eclat*, but those which are *solidly generous and good.* We have frequent instances of both from two Persons in the *Iliad*: *Hector* speaks things, that are *great*; *Ajax* often, what is *marvellous* and *surprizing*: Both speak loftily: but one is more solid, and the other nearer to a Rant; both shew Courage and Generosity in what they say; but they seem to *talk*, as they *act*; *Ajax* fights merely for fighting sake; while *Hector* engages always for the good of his Country.

I shall beg leave to close this Head with two Sentiments, as much celebrated as any in the *Iliad*, and spoke by the two Heroes we have been talking of. The one, in the mere Spirit of an Hero;

If *Greece* must perish, we thy will obey,
(c) But let us perish in the face of day.

(a) *Æn.* 9, 206. (b) *Od.* 17, 523---441.
(c) See Note on *Il.* 17, 731---647.

The

The other, in that of a Patriot too;

Without a ſign his ſword the brave man draws;
(a) And asks no omen, but his country's cauſe.

I am ſorry, ſays *Antiphaus*, you have quitted this Point ſo ſoon, methinks you might afford a little more room for a thing of ſuch conſiderable Uſe. *Sentences* are fitted by their Nature to carry on that Chief deſign of Poetry, to mix the *Uſeful* with the *Agreeable*. ——Together with a certain air of Authority, they ſerve to eſtabliſh the Poets Moral Character; which, according to a (b) late Hypotheſis, may render him at the ſame time more *delightful*, as well as more *inſtructive*.—Beſides this, they often flatter the Vanity of the Reader; And (as the (c) Firſt of Criticks tells us) "take the "more readily with this or that Perſon, "as they confirm in general, what he "has before concluded from his own Ob-"ſervation on particular Occurrences in "Life."

I wonder at one thing, ſays *Philypſus*; That ſo many of the Criticks ſhou'd blame Sentences, and look upon 'em as particularly unfit for Poems of the *Epick*

(a) *Il.* 12, 284---243. (b) *Origin* of our Ideas of *Beauty* and *Virtue*. (c) See *Ariſt. Rhet.* Lib. 2. Cap. 21.

Kind:

Kind: (*a*) *Rapin*, I think, condemns them, as they ſeem to jut out of the Structure of the Poem, and are apt to interrupt the Narration too much: *Boſſu*, who is rather on their ſide, yet obſerves there is a kind of *Calm Wiſdom* in them, that is contrary to the *Paſſions*. Even the Perſon, whom you juſt now call'd the *Firſt of Criticks*, puts us in mind of your Ruſticks, that are always (*b*) ſtringing of Proverbs together: and a very good Critick of our own ſays, in ſo many words, that (*c*) *they are generally ſome of the heavieſt pieces in a whole Poem.*

Let them add, if they pleaſe, ſays *Antiphaus*, that they ſound aukwardly from the mouth of a *Young Perſon*, and prepoſterouſly from an *Atheiſt*. I own the charge: the beſt Writers themſelves ſeem to be ſenſible of it; and where they do any thing of this kind, are the firſt to correct themſelves. *Addiſon* (*d*) puts a Sentence into the Mouth of *Portius*; but he corrects him for it, in the next Line, tho' the Son of a *Cato*; and when *Virgil*

(*a*) See Note on *Od.* 7, 379. (*b*) *Ariſt. Rhet.* Lib. 2. Cap 21. (*c*) *Addiſon*'s *Miſc*. vol. 1. p. 237. 12°. (*d*) *Port.* 'Tis not in mortals to command ſucceſs; But we'll do more, *Sempronius*; We'll deſerve it. *Semp.* Curſe on the ſtripling how he apes his Sire! Ambitiouſly ſententious. —— *Cato.* Act 1. Sc 2.

K (*a*) makes

(*a*) makes his Atheiſt ſententious, there is ſtill a mixture of the Atheiſt to be diſcover'd in what he ſays.

But grant that Sentences are not proper from Perſons that are Young, or Vicious; Grant, that they are not proper in a *Mezentius*, or a *Portius*: What then? may they not be proper in *Cato* himſelf, or in *Æneas*?

'Tis the ſame Caſe in every particular you have produc'd from the Criticks: they ſpeak rather againſt the Abuſe of this Ornament, than againſt the Ornament itſelf. There can be no doubt of it; *Sentences* are certainly faulty, when they appear too groſsly, and ſtand off from the reſt of the Work: But what is this to Sentences, which are fitly applied, and wove in Artfully with the other Parts? *Homer* and *Virgil* are very happy in this particular: they give them a ſufficient Fulneſs; but they never glare ſo, as to attract the Eye ſingly to themſelves: You admire them as much from their Relation to the things about them, as for their own particular Beauty: in ſhort, they might be Beautiful by themſelves, but they are much more ſo in the *Tout-enſemble* of the Piece.

(*a*) *Æn.* 10, 860.

We

We may add to this, that their Sentences are ſo far from hindering the Narration, that they are almoſt conſtantly a part of it, and help to carry it forward: But tho' they are uſually wrought into the Speeches of the Poem, we do not receive them from Perſons improper; or hurried by any violent Paſſion: and where the Subject is ſtill and gentle, that *calm Wiſdom*, that has been objected to them, cannot be very prejudicial. Indeed in any place, or on any Occaſion, a long thread of them is inſupportable; theſe are worſe than the *Sanchoiſms* of *Cervantes*, becauſe they are not ſo ridiculous: We can laugh at *Sancho* all the time he is multiplying his Proverbs upon us; but in Poetry, ſuch dry Preachments are, of all other, the greateſt Opiates, and have the quickeſt effect on the Audience. *Lucan's* Poem and *Seneca's* Tragedies, notwithſtanding all their Beauties, are Inſtances of this to a great degree.

There is another way of murthering Sentences, for which we are wholly oblig'd to thoſe ingenious Gentlemen, the *Editors*. It is that Art of cutting off Sentences from the Body of a Work, and forcing them *to jut out* from it, whether they will or no, by Printing all ſuch, where-ever they can catch them, in *Ita-*

ick Characters. Mr. *Addison*, if I remember, is condemning this Practice in that very place where he says, that *Sentences are some of the heaviest Pieces* in a Poem: and I imagine nothing could make him speak so severely of them in general, but this Practice that is so destructive of their Beauty.

In short, Sentences that are cold, affected, or ill-placed, such as are either too distinct, or too much throng'd, may be blam'd with a great deal of Justice: but such as are handsomely wove into the Narration, at proper Intervals, and from none but proper Speakers, will not only be safe from the Censure of the Criticks; but are allowed by them in general, to be highly serviceable towards giving its proper Weight and Emphasis to an *Epick* Poem.

I think you have defended this Beauty sufficiently, says *Philypsus*; and shall go on to the next under this Head, *Conciseness*: There is no greater Symptom of weakness in a Writer, than his being apt to say *a little in a great deal*; as nothing is more strong and emphatical, than to say *a great deal in a little*.

Hence the Force and Emphasis of this Line of Mr. *Pope*.

(*a*) Oh

(a) Oh every ſacred Name in one, my Friend!

And of this,

[King.
(b) The Great, the Good; your Father and your

The want of a ſcrupulous Connexion, draws things into a leſſer Compaſs; and adds the greater Spirit and Emotion:

(c) He ſhrieks, he reels, he falls.——

The more Rays are thus collected into a Point, the more vigorous the Flame: Hence there is yet greater *Emphaſis*, when the Rout of an Army is ſhewn in the ſame contracted manner; As that in the 24th of the (d) *Odyſſey*: which has ſome reſemblance to *Salluſt*'s Deſcription of the ſame thing (agreeable to his uſual Conciſeneſs) in theſe four Words only: (e) *Sequi, fugere, occidi, capi.*

There may be a contraction of many Circumſtances to a Point, which turns more on the *Sentiment*, than the *Diction*: as when we place the Succeſs of a Thouſand important Events on one Effort, or one Moment of Time: Thus *Antinous*,

(a) *Od.* 22, 226---208. (b) *Od.* 2, 54---47. (c) *Od.* 18, 443---397. (d) V, 610. (e) *Bel. Jug.* p. 106. Ed. *Mattaire.*

the Chief of the Suitors, to his Companions,

(a) Arise, (or you for ever fall) arise.

Which has such an Air of *Milton's Lucifer* :

Awake, Arise, or be for ever faln!

Those Lines, says *Antiphaus*, serve the purpose for which you repeat them very well ; but is there not something too much like a *Turn* upon the words in them? I was sensible of that (answer'd *Philypsus*) but I follow your Example, *Antiphaus*, in viewing a thing only in one Light at a time, to prevent the infinite Confusion that would happen in turning each Line every way. This is brought as Emphatical : You allow it to be so; if it answer the end for which it is produced, that is all that I intend : and I beg once for all to be understood under this view in every Instance that I have, or may use, on particular Occasions.

This masculine nervous Conciseness, I am speaking of, is very usual from Generals to their Soldiers : but among a multitude of Instances, I am particularly pleas'd with that Speech of *Henry*

(a) Od. 24, 499--436.

the

the *Great*, before the Battle in the Plains of *Ivry*, "*I am your King, You are French-*" *men, and there are the Enemy.*

Sometimes we find an Emphasis and Vigour impress'd on every particular word of a Sentence:

(a) *Now, Grief, thou all art mine!*

And in these Lines, which we have often admired for their peculiar Strength and Efficacy; They speak of *Ulysses*'s extream Love of his native Country:

To see the *smoak* from his lov'd palace rise,
While the dear Isle in *distant* prospect lies,
(b) With what *contentment* would he *close his eyes?*

This is not only of use in the Grand or Pathetick: there are excellent Instances of it from *Terence* (c), in the Tender and Familiar, as there are others from *Virgil* in the Natural, and even in the Satirical; and that so strongly in the latter, that (d) some have been apt to

(a) Od. 18, 299—255. (b) Od. 1. 77—59.
(c) Hæc verba mehercule *una falsa lachrumula*, Quam, *oculos terendo misere, vix vi expresserit*, *Restinguet.* ——— *Eun.* Act. 1. Sc. 1.
(d) Thus *Dryden*: from his
——— Non tu in *triviis, indocte, solebas*
Stridenti miserum stipula disperdere carmen. Ecl. 3. 27.
As others from this Line:
Qui Bavium *non odit, amet tua carmina*, Mævi. ib 90.

imagine

imagine from them, that *Virgil* might, if he pleas'd, have made the greatest *Satirist* that ever wrote.

Sometimes this very Emphasis is encreas'd by a certain *Opposition* of the words us'd in it: there is a Passage in the *Iliad*, which I have particularly admir'd on this Account: Give me leave to repeat it from the Original; because the *Greek* Tongue is particularly Emphatical, and has more Nerves than perhaps our Language is capable of:

Οὐ γὰρ πω ἰδόμην, οὐδ' ἔκλυον αὐδήσαντος,
Ἄνδρ' ἕνα τοσσάδε μέρμερ' ἐν ἤματι μητίσασθαι,
(a) Ὅσσ' Ἕκτωρ ἔρρεξε.——————

The Emphatical manner in writing flies all Dress and Ornament, all superfluous and descriptive Epithets, all turns and elegancies of Thought. Hence that Conciseness, which generally attends it. The most obvious fault in Conciseness is Obscurity; what is obscure, can never be sufficiently emphatical: This makes the concise way the most difficult of any. 'Tis easy to follow the Stream of one's Imagination, and write on with an unthinking Rapidity; but to express every

(a) Ιλ. κ, 48. The *Opposition* is carried on farther in the next Lines, between ἐν ἤματι, & δηθά τε καὶ δολιχόν.

thing

thing fully, and to ſay nothing that is needleſs, requires a great Judgment, and much force in our Expreſſions. The great *Monſieur Paſcal* had a particular happineſs of comprizing *much* in a *few* Words: he had a very Mathematical Turn of Thought; and of all things hated an idle Prolixity. You will be pleas'd with an Excuſe of his in a certain Caſe, where he had been guilty of it: 'Tis in the cloſe of one of his Letters, where he begs his Friend to pardon the unuſual length of it, by ſaying, *that he really had not time to make it ſhorter.*

Some emphatical Paſſages are not only ſo conciſe, as to contain juſt as *many Ideas* as *Words*; they have often force enough even to *intimate* ſeveral Ideas more than they *expreſs*.

Thus it is in all Intimations of Power. One of *Homer*'s greateſt Excellencies lies in this. In ſetting off the Hero of his *Iliad*, he does not ſay in Words, that he was vaſtly Terrible to the Enemy; he mentions the effects, and leaves the Reader to collect what Terror muſt attend him. After the Death of *Patroclus*, the whole Army of the *Trojans* is put into Confuſion, only (*a*) *at hearing his Voice*:

(*a*) Ιλ. σ', 224.

They

They are all trembling, and diſpirited: (*a*) *they had ſeen Achilles.* 'Tis not a ſudden Panick; it continues upon them: When they pour'd down in ſuch Numbers from the City, it was becauſe (*b*) *they did not behold the Creſt of that Hero*; and now they are all conſulting, whether they ſhould not quit the Field, becauſe (*c*) *he had ſhewn himſelf at a diſtance, and might poſſibly enter into the next Engagement.*

Homer has the ſame addreſs in intimating the Power of his Deities; when he introduces them as effecting their deſigns with a (*d*) *Touch*, with a (*e*) *Voice*, with a (*f*) *ſingle Thought.*

It is the ſame Sentiment that gives their Air of Grandeur to theſe Lines:

(*g*) Declare thy purpoſe; for thy Will is Fate.
Let all be Peace.——He ſaid; and gave the nod
(*h*) That binds the Fates, the Sanction of the God.

And this, of the ſame import, from our *Shakeſpear*;

——What he bids be done,
Is *finiſh'd* with his bidding.——

(*a*) Ιλ. σ', 248. (*b*) *ib.* π', 70. (*c*)--σ', 262. (*d*) Ιλ. ν', 60, 75. (*e*) *ib.* ξ, 150. (*f*) *ib.* ο', 242. (*g*) *Od.* 24, 547---475. (*h*) *Od.* 24, 561---485.

On

On this turns the Greatneſs of that Thought in the Sacred Hiſtory of the Creation: *God ſaid, Let there be Light, and there was Light:* Tho' I ſhould imagine this to exceed every Inſtance above; becauſe it *intimates,* all that they *expreſs,* and intimates it as *fully* and *ſtrongly,* as they *expreſs* it.

Let the Greatneſs of this Sentence ſtand or fall by the Rules of Sublimity. We need not mention, that (*a*) *Longinus* choſe it for an Inſtance of the *Sublime:* whether that great Critick ever ſaw it or not, is not material: but I wonder, that ſome later Writers, of very great Name, cannot be perſwaded to ſee any Force or Energy in it. I own, I have never read what *Monſieur Le Clerc* offers againſt the Sublimity of this Paſſage: Surely it would not be very difficult to anſwer it, if it be of a Strain with what (*b*) *Monſieur Huetius* offer'd before him; Where he ſeems to argue, that (*c*) *This Paſſage cannot be* Sublime, *becauſe the Language is* Simple.

It is this Art of leaving more for the Reader to collect, than you expreſs in Words, which runs through ſeveral of

(*a*) Cap 9. Ed. *Oxon.* 1718. (*b*) See Preface to *Boileau*'s Works. (*c*) See *Huetij Dem. Ev.* Prop. 4. Sect. 53.

Ulyſſes's

Ulyſſes's Speeches; both at the Court of *Alcinous*, and before the *Suitors*. Whether the Hero tells his own Story, or feigns ſome other, he is equally carefull in laying before them ſomething of the High Station he once enjoy'd: and hence his Speeches have generally a great Air of that celebrated Anſwer of *Marius* to a Meſſage ſent from the Roman General: (*a*) *Go, and tell*, Sextilius, *that you ſaw* Marius, *ſitting among the Ruins of* Carthage.

Intimation is ſo ſtrong and nervous, that the (*b*) Ancient Criticks confin'd the Name of *Emphaſis* to this one Point; tho' (as we uſe the word) the very contrary of this, may be of great Service in making a Diſcourſe *emphatical*. The Soul is ſometimes poſſeſs'd by the *Number* of great Circumſtances. Thus in that Paſſage of *Homer*, which Mr. *Pope* tranſlates after the following manner;

> *Men*, *Steeds*, and *Chariots* ſhake the trembling [ground;
> The *Tumult* thickens, and the *Skies* reſound:
> *Victors* and *Vanquiſh'd* join promiſcuous cries,
> (*c*) Triumphant *ſhouts*, and dying *groans* ariſe.

(*a*) *Plutarch*'s Life of *Marius*. (*b*) See *Quintil. Inſtit.* Lib. 8. Cap. 3. and Lib. 9. Cap 2. (*c*) *Il.* 8. 80---65.

We

We meet with the ſame *tumultuary Figure* in the Deſcription of the Field after the Battle :

[of *Slain.*
(*a*) Thro' *Duſt*, thro' *Blood*, o'er *Arms*, and hills

This Paſſage (we are told) is imitated by *Xenophon* ; and I am ſure the Hiſtorian has not weaken'd it, by drawing it into a greater length, and expreſſing the Circumſtances more fully ; Allow me the Satisfaction of reading it to you. (*b*) *When the Battle was over, one might behold thro' the whole extent of the Field, the Ground dy'd Red with Blood, the Bodies of Friends and Enemies ſtretch'd over each other, the Shields pierc'd, the Spears broken, and the drawn Swords, ſome ſcatter'd on the Earth, ſome plung'd in the Bodies of the Slain, and ſome yet graſp'd in the Hands of the Soldiers.*

Now we have faln upon an Hiſtorian, give me leave to obſerve one thing ; That, both with Poets and in Hiſtory, (*c*) *There may be ſome Fraud in ſaying only the bare Truth.* In either, 'tis not ſufficient to tell us, that *ſuch a City*, for Inſtance, *was taken and ravag'd with a great deal of Inhumanity :* There is a *Poetical*

(*a*) *Il.* 10, 356---298. (*b*) Note on *Il.* 10, 356.
(*c*) Minus eſt totum dicere, quam omnia.

Falsity, if a strong Idea of each particular be not imprinted on the Mind; and an *Historical*, if some things are passed over only with a general mark of Infamy or Dislike. It was in (a) *Quintilian* I first met with this Observation; and I wish our Historians, of all Parties, did not give us so many Examples of it, as we find every where in their Works.

'Tis the same in Poetry: when all the *Circumstances* are laid out in their proper Colours, and make a compleat Piece; its Images strike us with greater Energy, than when the *Whole* of the thing is only mention'd in general. Thus the *diffused Style* has its Propriety under this Head; and makes a larger and more continu'd Impression: as the force of its contrary Excellence, a just and emphatical *Conciseness*, may be more collected, and pierce the deeper. I do not mean when we *mention* a thing, but when we *shew* it in a few words. There are just Miniatures of Great Objects in Poetry, as well as in Statuary or Painting. A *Hercules*, in little, may have all the Nerves of a *Colossus*: and even that prodigious Design of (b) *Dinarchus* might not

(a) *Instit.* Lib. 8. Cap. 3. (b) To form Mount *Athos* into a Statue of *Alexander* the *Great*; so design'd, as to hold a City in one hand, and to have a River run thorough the other.

have

have been more *Gigantick*, than *Timanthes* (a) his *Polyphemus*. Noble Images, whether in a large or ſmaller Compaſs, ſtrike the Mind very ſtrongly. Either muſt be according to the Occaſion. Things ſometimes demand to be drawn at full Length, and the Soul requires to expatiate over them: Sometimes they chuſe a more contracted Space; But tho' they loſe from their Size, they loſe nothing of their Spirit. It fills us with a noble and enlarg'd Pleaſure, to conſider the Heavenly Bodies, their Courſes, and their immenſe Diſtances: at the ſame time, we are ſtruck with a very particular Admiration, when we view their Situation and Meaſures in the *Orrery*.

Any uncommon extenſive Image cauſes an Enlargement of our Ideas, and poſſeſſes the Mind more compleatly: In ſuch Caſes 'tis obſervable, that even the Turn of the Verſe may aſſiſt theſe Images. I may ſeem too particular if I ſay, that *large* Words and Lines which conſiſt chiefly of *long* Syllables, may be of uſe to extend our Thoughts in conceiving any Gigantick form: and yet perhaps both will be found not unſerviceable in Mr. *Pope*'s Deſcription of his *Cyclops*.

(a) His Picture of that Giant in Miniature.

A Giant-ſhepherd here his flock maintains;
Far from the reſt he ſolitary reigns,
In ſhelter thick of horrid ſhade reclin'd;
And gloomy miſchiefs labour in his mind.
(a) A Form enormous! ———

Or, where we ſee him

(b) Stretch'd forth in length, o'er half the cavern'd [Rock.

Or, when

He ſends a dreadful groan; the rocks around,
(c) Thro' all their inmoſt, winding caves reſound.

Whether you think this length and heavineſs of the Syllables neceſſary in the preſent caſe, or not; I am ſure, you will allow it to be ſo in Melancholy Images.

Where heavenly-penſive Contemplation dwells,
And ever-muſing Melancholy reigns ———

And a Thouſand more.

Homer too in deſcribing a large Object, makes uſe of a word, which of it ſelf is (*d*) above half a Verſe: and *Ovid*, on a like Occaſion, joins ſeveral together of an unuſual length. We behold his *Ægeon* beſtriding his Whale, even in

(a) *Od.* 9, 217. (b) *Ibid.* 354. (c) *Ibid.* 469.
(*d*) *Il.* 6, 676.

the

the Turn (*a*) of the Words which are to describe him.

Delay and *Repetition* are sometimes proper for the same Reasons; There is a Delay almost in every Syllable, where Mr. *Pope* intimates the vast *size* of a Stone, as well as the *difficulty* in heaving it up;

Then heav'd the Goddess in her mighty hand
A stone, the limit of the neighbouring land,
(*b*) There fixt from eldest times; black, craggy, vast.

Virgil adds a Repetition in his Imitation of this very Passage in *Homer*: *Saxum circumspicit ingens, saxum antiquum, ingens*——And Mr. *Pope* commends the Beauty of this Repetition, as (*c*) *it makes us dwell upon the Image, and gives us leisure to consider the Vastness of it.*

It may seem strange, that the Vastness, the *mere Bulk* of an Object, shou'd possess the Mind in the manner I have been speaking of: but tho' there is no real Excellence in Largeness, 'tis certain that we are apt to apprehend it as excellent. This puts me in Mind of a Point, that always strikes me very much in Poetry;

(*a*)——— Balænarumque prementem
Ægeona suis immania terga lacertis. *Met.* 2, 10.
(*b*) *Il.* 21, 470—404. (*c*) See Note *ibid.*

A ſort of *Comprehenſion*, as I ſhould chuſe to call it, for want of ſome better Name. 'Tis when any Great View is compleatly contracted into a few Lines; but to come up perfectly to my Notion, it ſhould be ſuch a View as is ſufficient to fill the whole Mind: We are, in a manner, ſurrounded with it on all ſides; and which ever way we turn our Eyes, we cannot look out of it. This is the Caſe, where *Ulyſſes* is repreſented in his Shipwrack on the Coaſt of *Phæacia*;

Above, ſharp Rocks forbid acceſs; *around*,
(*a*) Roar the wild Waves; *beneath*, is Sea profound!

If you can fancy yourſelf in the Place of *Ulyſſes*, at that Juncture; you will apprehend what I mean the more fully. You can then ſee nothing, but what is painted out in this Couplet.

I apprehend you, (ſays *Antiphaus*) and indeed have obſerv'd this Beauty often in Reading. There is a Thought, (if I miſtake not) repeated twice in the Eleventh *Odyſſey*, of this kind:

(*b*) Above, Below, on Earth, and in the Sky.

I know not whether the Image be Total, but it cannot want much of it, in

---

(*a*) *Od.* 5, 529---413. (*b*) *Od.* 11, 139 and 373.

that

that Deſcription of a ſhipwreckt Perſon, juſt before the Lines you repeated:

> Amidſt the rocks he hears a hollow roar
> Of murm'ring ſurges breaking on the ſhore;
> Nor peaceful port was there, nor winding bay,
> To ſhield the veſſel from the rolling ſea;
> But cliffs, and ſhaggy ſhores, a dreadful ſight,
> (a) All rough with rocks, with foamy billows white.

If this be not Total, at leaſt it will engroſs Two of your Senſes, whilſt you keep in the ſame Poſture; but thoſe, as you ſay, ſeem the moſt compleat, which take up the Eye what ever way you turn. ——As this (reſum'd *Philypſus*) to keep to the ſame Element:

> (b) And all above was sky, and ocean all around.

Theſe Total Views are much more vigorous and affecting, when the Objects are not inanimate: or at leaſt, when, ſome more moving Conſiderations are annext to them. Thus in the Picture of a rough Sea, terminating in craggy Shores, and Rocks, and a tempeſtuous Sky, every Object has an additional Terror from our ſeeing *Ulyſſes* painted in the midſt of theſe Dangers, and ſtruggling to make ſo difficult a Shore.——I

(a) *Od.* 5, 521. (b) *Od.* 12, 474.

re-

remember a Paſſage of this kind in a Writer of a very ſtrong Imagination, which is heighten'd by the ſame Method. We have it in a Deſcription of Mount *Atlas*, tho' I believe the Author took his Ideas from the *Alps*: 'tis deliver'd in this bold Poetical kind of Proſe: (*a*) "*See, with what trembling ſteps poor Man-*" *kind tread the narrow Brink of the deep*" *Precipices! from whence with giddy Hor-*" *ror they look down, miſtruſting even the*" *Ground which bears them; whilſt they hear*" *the hollow ſound of Torrents underneath,*" *and ſee the Ruin of the impending Rock,*" *with falling Trees, which hang with*" *their Roots upwards, and ſeem to draw*" *more Ruin after them.*——

In theſe Caſes, our Paſſions, as well as our Senſes, are engag'd: and I take ſuch Views to be then entirely compleat, when all our Paſſions, as well as all our Senſes, may be engroſs'd by them. Were I to give an Inſtance of ſuch a View, I ſhould prefer that Paſſage in *Virgil*, where he places you in the midſt of a City, cover'd with the diſmal ſhades of Night, taken and fir'd in a Thouſand places by the Enemy, and every where fill'd with Ruin, Terror, and Confuſion:

(*a*) *Characteriſticks.* Vol. 2. Pag. 389.

---*Cru-*

(*a*) ——— *Crudelis ubique*
Luctus, ubique Pavor, & plurima mortis image.

I have dwelt the longer on these *Comprehensive Views*, as they fill and delight the Mind very strongly. There is another Case, much of this Nature, and of particular Energy: I do not mean, when we *surround*, but when we carry the Mind out to a vast *extent*: As in this Sentiment;

(*b*) By Heaven above, by Hell beneath.

There is a Thought of this Nature, very justly reckon'd among the Sublime, which appears with a perfect Uniformity in (*c*) *Virgil*, in *Homer*, and in the *Book of Wisdom*, formerly ascrib'd to *Solomon*: For my part, I do not at all wonder at this exact Resemblance in them. It is such a Thought, that when it is once set before one, it possesses the Mind so strongly, that it will leave its Image behind it: And indeed 'tis observable, that a great Critick, where he

---

(*a*) *Æn.* 2, 369. (*b*) *Od.* 23, 369.
(*c*) *Ingrediturq; solo & caput inter nubila condit Æ.* 4, 177.
Οὐρανῷ ἐστήριξε κάρη καὶ ἐπὶ χθονὶ βαίνει. Ιλ. δ',
Καὶ οὐρανοῦ μὲν ἥπτετο,
Βεβήκει δὲ ἐπὶ γῆς. Lxx per *Grabe*. Σοφ. Σολ. ιη', 16.

wou'd

wou'd applaud it in *Homer*, (*a*) repeats it himſelf in the very turn of his own Criticiſm. *Longinus* is the Perſon I mean: who in a thouſand Inſtances, as well as this,

(*b*) —— *Is himſelf the great Sublime he draws.*

One of the moſt common Topicks for this among the Poets, is in ſpeaking of the diſtance of *Tartarus*. *Homer* makes it as far from Hell to Earth downwards, as it is upwards from Earth to Heaven: It has been (*c*) obſerv'd, that Two of the beſt Poets ſince have enlarg'd it gradually, *Virgil* to Twice, and *Milton* to Thrice that Depth: but, if I miſtake not, *Heſiod* of old has carried the Mind further than either of them: It wou'd pleaſe you to ſee, how exact he is in his Meaſures: (*d*) "An Anvil (ſays he) will be Nine "days compleat in falling from Heaven "to our Earth; and as many in falling "from our Earth to *Tartarus*."---This is the Diſtance from us to the Gates of *Tartarus* only: he afterwards carries the Mind much farther, in this Deſcription:

There lye the Treaſures of the ſtormy Deep,
Of Earth, and Water, and extended Darkneſs.

(*a*) Τὸ ἐπ' οὐρανὸν ἀπὸ γῆς διάστημα. De *Subl.* θ'. Edit. *Oxon.*

(*b*) Eſſay on *Criticiſm*. (*c*) Note on *Il.* 8, 16.

(*d*) Θεογ. V, 722.

A dreadful Chasm! squalid, and uninform'd,
And hateful even to Gods. Whoe're, within
The dreadful Opening of its Gates, shou'd plunge
Prone thro' the great abyss; twelve times the course
Of the Pale Moon, should feel its Storm and Tempest
In dire Descent; still hurried on precipitate,
Amidst the various Tumult and Confusion
Of disagreeing Natures. Oft the Pow'rs
Immortal cast their Eyes upon these regions,
(*a*) And shudder at the Sight.———

This Imagination seems to be imitated in *Milton*, where *Satan* meets with that violent shock, in Travelling thro' *Chaos*; but the Fall here strikes us more, because it has no Bounds: It is still continuing lower and lower; and the Mind, in endeavouring to conceive it, is lost in its *desired Infinitude*.

When our Bodies are all so straiten'd and confin'd, what must the Soul be made of, *Antiphaus?* and what might be its Powers, if unrestrain'd? Since even in such dull Company as the Body, with all these Weights and Incumberments about it, it betrays on every the smallest Occasion such an Appetite to Infinity?

Mr. *Addison*, in one of his finest Works, the Essay on the Pleasures of the Ima-

(*a*) *Hesiod's* Θεογ. 744.

gination, reckons *Greatness* as first among those things, which give that (a) Pleasure: "Nothing (says he) (b) gratifies *the Mind* "so much, as those large growing Ideas, "which lead her on almost to an Infini-"tude. (c) Our Imagination loves to be "fill'd with an Object, or to grasp at "any thing that is too big for its Capa-"city: We are flung into a pleasing "Astonishment at such unbounded Views, "and feel a delightful Stillness and A-"mazement in the Soul, at the Appre-"hensions of them."

Every one may know this Pleasure by Experience: 'Tis not a dry Maxim laid down by the Philosophers: Whoever will consult his own Mind, when he looks only on a Prospect, may say as much as Mr. *Addison*, or Mr. *Locke* have on this Occasion. When I had the Pleasure of Conversing with the Gentleman, who design'd these Gardens, (as indeed the Finest in the Nation owe their Beauty to his Directions) I was very much pleas'd with a Maxim which he then mention'd; "That as the greatest *fault* in a Prospect "was Confinement; So the *meanest* thing "too in a Design, was to have the

(a) Spectator, Numb. 412. (b) Numb. 420. (c) Numb. 412.

"Bounds

"Bounds and Reſtraint of it immediate-"ly viſible."

There may be ſeveral other Points to be conſider'd under the Character of Emphatical, whether from the *Strength* of the Language, the *Nobleneſs* of the Sentiment, or the *Greatneſs* and *Extent* of the Object itſelf: but I am only giving a few Sketches of the Kind: You will give me leave, in the ſame manner, to take a ſhort View of its Contrary, the *Low* or *Mean Stile.*

It has been ſaid, That (*a*) *Lowneſs has juſt as many Cauſes, as Elevation; ſince whatever raiſes the Sentiment or Diction has its Oppoſite, which is Mean.* This has the Appearance of Truth; but if one general Meaſure muſt be giv'n, I ſhould think that it is an Exceſs either way, which cauſes Meanneſs. Things over-wrought, as well as things under-wrought, will be Mean.

When the leaſt Object is expreſs'd in juſt and proper Terms, it will not of itſelf come under the Character of Meanneſs: Nay, ſmall things may be manag'd ſo, as to change their Nature, and to com-

(*a*) Eadem fere eſt ratio minuendi: Nam totidem ſunt deſcendentibus, quot aſcendentibus gradus. *Quintil. Inſtit.* Lib. 8. Cap. 4.

compose the *Grand Air*. We meet with Dissertations on the late Discoveries in the lesser World of Animals, which have something Great and Sublime in them. Littleness itself may be assistant too in Amplifying a Subject: *Homer* uses it thus in his Character of *Tydeus*; and 'tis visible to any one, That bold Martial Atcheivments look greater in a *Nassau*, than they wou'd in a *Maximin*.

Such Considerations as these have induc'd me to imagine, That all Meanness arises from some *Disproportion*, or other. When a Person is represented in a View beneath himself, or any Action of Force is express'd weakly, the Expressions fall short of the Nature of the Thing: Again, that Meanness, which arises from the Language, may have the same Measure. The Close of a Sentence may fall beneath the Expectance rais'd in the Beginning of it, and then will necessarily have a mean Air. Some sorts of Poetry are of a nobler kind; and Descriptions of things, that would not be Mean in a *Sonnet* or *Satire*, may become so in *Epick*. In general, all vulgar Terms, and all very disagreeable Descriptions, are beneath the Heroick Stile: as all Triflings, or any Affectation of Ornament, argue something beneath the Care of a Poet,

who

who has taken upon him to rule the nobler Passions, and to sing of Heroes and of Gods.

When any thing has an Epithet higher, than its own Nature and the Occasion requires; or lower, than the proper Idea of the thing might very well demand; 'tis much the same; in both there will be a Disproportion, and a Meanness. Thus,

Be mindful of yourselves draw forth your Swords,
(*a*) And to your Shafts obtend these *ample boards*.

And this Line,

(*b*) His Shoulder blade receiv'd th' *ungentle shock*.

The same Critick, who observes on a certain Writer, for saying, That some Persons who were Shipwreckt met with *an Unpleasant Death*; is equally severe on those, who carry things too far; he ranks any vain (*c*) *Elevations*, and the *Puerile Stile*, under one and the same Head.

Indeed Both are frigid, and Both are mean. A little or pretty Thought dress'd up in grand Words, is like the *Cupid*, in

(*a*) *Od.* 22, 88---75. (*b*) *Od.* 17, 549--461.
(*c*) *Longinus*, Cap. 3.

one of *Coypel*'s Pieces, who is crept into *Mars*'s Armour, and looks as if he was endeavouring to ſtrut about in it: Whilſt a great Thought in little Words, puts one in Mind of that tall Gentleman we ſaw one Night at the Maſquerade, dreſſed like an Infant; and dangling its Hands, as if it were perfectly helpleſs.

A Mixture of *Mean* Language with the *Grand*, makes the Meanneſs more viſible; as poſſibly in this Line,

(a) Stript of his rags —— *He blaz'd out like a God.*

Thus where a Libation to the Gods, is call'd (b) *An Holy Beverage* in the *Odyſſey*; and *Mars* (c) the *Heavenly Homicide* in the *Iliad*.

There ſeems to me to be ſomething too mean for the Idea we form of a Giant, in this Expreſſion;

(d) Her * Husband *ſcowr'd* away ——

And juſt after;

The Men like fiſh, they ſtuck upon the flood,
(e) And cram'd their filthy throats with human [food.

(a) Od. 22, 2. (b) Od. 3, 435---339. (c) Il. 21, 471. * *Antiphates*. (d) Od. 10, 131---115. (e) Od. 10, 144---124.

In

In the ſame manner we hear of *Ulyſſes*'s Companions, being (*a*) *daſh'd like Dogs* by the *Cyclops*.

I doubt not this was expreſs'd thus, to give us the larger Idea of that *Monſter*: but might not it have been expreſs'd ſo, as to ſerve that purpoſe, without giving us at the ſame time too low an Idea of the *Men*?

The Dignity of the Perſon will make any mean Language appear yet meaner. Whether we conſider *Ulyſſes* as (*b*) *ſo great an Hero*, or as *the* (*c*) *Godlike Gueſt* of *Alcinous*, this Couplet ſounds beneath his Character!

(*d*) —— Shrunk with pining faſt,
My craving bowels ſtill require repaſt.

Nothing can be more juſt than *Horace*'s Obſervation, (*e*) *That a King in Exile, or Diſtreſs, muſt lay aſide that Air of Grandeur, and thoſe ſwelling Words, which might become him in his Power*: Yet muſt he remember, that he has been a King: there's a Greatneſs even in Diſtreſs; and a due Medium between Words *of a Foot-and-a-half Long*, and *Monoſyllables*. Be that as it will, there is certainly much

(*a*) Od. 23, 337--313. (*b*) Od. 7, 228. (*c*) Od. 7, 191. (*d*) Od. 7, 296--215. (*e*) De *Arte Poet.* V. 96.

Reason, that he should reassume his Style with his Dignity: and (whatever may be said for that Speech of *Ulysses* in his Wanderings) after he is reinstated, he ought certainly to speak like a Monarch. I am afraid he fails in this respect, in the following Lines:

Be it my care, by loans, or martial toils,
To throng my empty'd folds, with gifts or spoils:
But now I haste to bless *Laertes*'s eyes,
(a) With sight of his *Ulysses* e're he dies;

When the God of the Ocean sees *Ulysses* escap'd from his Dominion, he is so much provok'd, that he flies immediately to the Throne of *Jupiter*, to lay his Complaints before the *Father* of the *Gods*; Let us hear part of his Speech on this grand Occasion;

Against *yon destin'd head* in vain I *swore*,
And menac'd vengeance e're he reach'd the shore;
(b) Behold him landed—*careless and asleep.*

When an Expectation is rais'd by the preceding Verses, and little or nothing follows upon this Expectation;——We need not quote (c) *Horace* to prove that it will be *Mean*; every one will see it;

(a) *Od.* 23, 387—360. (b) *Od.* 13, 156—135. (c) De *Arte Poet.* V. 139.

and

and every one may see, that it arises from the Disproportion.

I have often observ'd, how fatal this Particular is to that sort of People, who are known by the Character of *Story-tellers*. The greatest baulks these Gentlemen meet with, are occasion'd by their bespeaking Attention too much; and after all, ending in some inconsiderable Circumstance: There is a certain Passage in the *Odyssey*, which puts me in Mind of this Disaster so common to them:

Prepare then said *Telemachus*, to know
(a) *A Tale*, from falshood free, not free from woe.

What follows upon this? *No earthly thing, I'gad*, as Mr. *Bays* has it; only that he is *the Son of Ulysses*, and that he is searching *after the King his Father*.

There is another (b) Instance of this Nature, in that important Dialogue, between *Neptune* and *Jupiter*, just mention'd.

Of this kind also is a certain Figure, which Mr. *Addison* (c) calls an *Anti-climax*: A Downfall in the Close, where a Passage has been very promising in the

---

(a) *Od.* 15, 295---270. (b) See *Od.* 13, 164 to 172---140 to 147. (c) *Misc.* Vol. 1, p. 300, 12°.

Begin-

Beginning. I remember he quotes a (*a*) *French* Couplet upon that Occasion, which I suppose was design'd for Ridicule; but there are many Instances of it, from more serious Writers. Such is what a Grave Doctor has said in his Character of your *Miltonick* Friend, Mr. *Philips:* 'tis deliver'd in this grand air of Prophecy. Mr. *Philips*'s *Poems* (says he) *will last, as long as Blenheim is remembred, Or* (*b*) Cyder drunk in *England*.

I beg leave to mention one thing, says *Antiphaus*,——What You have been saying, may afford the reason, why that Species of Criticism, which goes upon Ridicule (in the *manner* of the *Hind* and *Panther*) is not to be depended upon: The best Lines that ever were wrote, may be render'd Ridiculous, only by raising too great an Expectation in the Reader, just before they are introduc'd in the Criticism.

There is another kind of Littleness (proceeded *Philypsus*) when the Language does not become the Poetick Stile; all *Prosaick Poetry*, or (as Dr. *Garth* us'd to call it) *a Diction loytering into Prose*, carries something of meanness with it; some-

(*a*) Allez vous, luy dit-il, sans bruit chez vos parens, Ou vous avez laisse votre honneur & *vos gans* ib.
(*b*) *Dis*. on the *Classicks*. p. 217.

thing

thing below the Harmony, the Emotion, the Majesty, that is requir'd from the *Epick* Muse.——Here are two or three Couplets which I think descend too near to Prose;

And now *Telemachus*, the first of all,
(a) Observ'd *Eumæus* entring in the Hall.

—— Let *Eurymachus* receive my guest.
(b) Of nature courteous, and by far the best.

His food an herald bore; and now they fed,
(c) And now the rage of craving Hunger fled.

It might be thought too trifling to observe, that this Meanness is often owing to an ill-judg'd use of Monosyllables. (d) A Long Run of these little *Pigmy* Words, beside an unavoidable Air of Meanness, often makes a Line rough, and hobling; and almost ever keeps it from being firm, and compact.

'Tis very rare, that you meet with a *Latin* Verse terminating in a single Monosyllable; and sometimes, where we do meet with it, 'tis evidently (e) design'd to assist in expressing the Littleness or Ridiculousness of the Subject.

(a) *Od*, 17, 400—328. (b) *Od.* 15, 560—517. (c) *Od.* 8, 68—69. (d) From *Vossius* de Carm. Cantu. p. 45. (e) As in *Horace*'s Art of Poetry. V. 139 and *Virgil*'s 1 *Georg*. V. 181.

Unless

Unless it be thus design'd, or be significant, a Verse (even an *Hemistick*) may be render'd Mean, merely by consisting of these little Words. I know there are entire Lines of them that are tolerable, nay, that run with some degree of Vigour; as this in the *Odyssey*,

(*a*) 'Ere yet he loos'd the Rage of War on *Troy*.

And that *Close* in *Shakespear*,

Cry'd Havock; and *let slip the Dogs of War*.

The Sentiments here are so great, that they take us off from observing the Littleness, which the Diction might otherwise Occasion: Yet, to speak my Mind, I believe that these very Thoughts wou'd appear more Majestically in large adequate Expressions.

Beside this Littleness from the Nature of words, there is oftentimes a Meanness annex'd in our Thoughts to such particular Words and Phrases. All mere *Vulgar* ways of speaking are mean in Poetry.——The Muse shou'd reject any low *Proverbs*, and the Language of the Croud——Even the *Ideas* of things, in which they particularly are employ'd,

[*a*] *Od.* 8, 78.

are

are sullied and debas'd——I believe I may add, that whatever has an Air of *Burlesque*, or has been markt for ridiculous on any other Occasion, will be apt to retain something of the *Mean*, where-ever it is us'd.

His Shoulder blade receiv'd th' ungentle shock;
He stood and mov'd not, like a marble rock,
[a] But shook his thoughtful Head.——

I doubt not, I have formerly met with something in *Burlesque*, to which this Passage has a distant Resemblance: tho' the thing itself be gone out of my head, the distast to such a particular Expression still remains with me. 'Tis true, this wou'd not justify a Criticism; and yet it leads one unavoidably to dislike the Passage.——This sort of *Acquir'd Meanness* may be sometimes more general: as where *Menelaus* calls *Telemachus*, [b] *The Mirror of constant Faith*; This Expression has been so often us'd in a ridiculous sort of Writings, that it will sound mean to the generality of those that hear it.

A Star-light Evening, and a Morning Fair.——

[a] *Od.* 17, 550—463. [b] *Od.* 4, 227.

---Is

——Is a Line in *Dryden's Virgil*, [a] condemn'd by a very exact Critick, upon account of its being Low and Mean. 'Tis of the acquir'd kind. Any one, who has been at all converſant with the Poetry of a Belman, will certainly look upon it with ſomething of Contempt: Yet is there nothing Mean in it of itſelf; and a Critick in *France* might think it a good handſome Line. But the beſt Expreſſions degenerate, when us'd by the Populace, and applied to low things: the uſe, they make of them, infects them with a low abject Air.

Thus *Proverbial* Speeches, and all other Expreſſions very common among us, become unworthy of our Poetry. Foreign Proverbs are often great and emphatical to us; as many of ours may ſound great to Foreigners: yet at home, both, if vulgar, will be apt to appear mean; or at leaſt, unfit for Poetry. One Inſtance, or two will be ſufficient: in the *Tenth Odyſſey* we have this Line;

[b] With *broken hearts* my ſad companions ſtood.

And this in the 22*d*,

[c] —— *Dogs, Ye have had your Day.*——

[a] *Eſſay* on *Georg.* 1. Pref. p. 8. [b] V. 227.
[c] V. 41—35.

I ſhall not preſume to ſay, how far the *Odyſſey* or *Iliad* might be blameable for any of theſe Meanneſſes in the Days of *Homer* himſelf: it is the Priviledge of every dead Language, to be entirely free from them at preſent. We hear not the Proverbs, nor know the current Ridicule of thoſe Times. His Language is ſafe enough from the Vulgar now; And as to any Words, that might be vulgar enough then, to ſeem low, we are in an entire ignorance. This is a conſiderable Advantage which the Ancients have over every Living Writer; and for which, by the way, there ſhould be a large allowance made in any Compariſon between an Ancient and a Modern.

Thus any Meanneſs that is *acquir'd*, may be *loſt again*, or *worn off* by Time and Accidents. It is not ſo with Meanneſs in the Things themſelves. They have ſomething ſettled in them; and are deliver'd down to us thro' the Stream of Ages, unalter'd and the ſame. Perhaps, if we would take off the Veil, which Superſtition has flung over the Worſhippers of *Homer*, we might diſcern ſome traces of this in the Converſation of the *Suitors*; in the *Scene* at *Eumæus*'s Lodge; and in *Sicily*, when we are with the *Cyclops*. 'Tis true, the *Odyssey* is built upon an humbler Plan: *Homer* suits himself to his Design: and it may be very justly said (with Mr. *Pope*) [a] "*That where this Poem cannot support a Sublimity, it always preserves a Dignity, or at least a Propriety.* If these Points may fail in *Dignity*, they have always some *Propriety* in the Poem; either from the Speaker, or the Audience, or the Occasion.

To return to the Translation. Every Idea that has something aukward in it, has something mean, and ridiculous: The first Laugh in the *Iliad* is occasion'd by the aukward Behaviour, and odd Address of *Vulcan*; as the only Laugh in the *Æneid* is rais'd on the untoward figure, which *Menætes* makes in that Poem.

There seems to me to be something Mean and Aukward in this Image:

His *loose head* tottering as with wine opprest,
[b] Obliquely drops, and *nodding knocks* his breast.

Perhaps the *Sneezing-piece* in the 17*th* Book, (c) borders too much on the same Fault; or, if it be no Fault, on the same Disagreeableness.

---

[a] *Od.* Vol. 5. p. 237. 12°. [b] *Od.* 18. 282---239. [c] V. 625---541.

For

For the ſame Reaſon, all Deſcriptions that have any thing of the Nauſeous in them, might be avoided in Poetry, or at leaſt be but ſlightly touch'd in it: I cannot think 'tis any particular niceneſs or effeminacy in my Temper, which inclines me to wiſh, that the Colours had not been laid on ſo ſtrongly on ſome (*a*) Occaſions. The worſt Image I know of this kind is in the deſcription of the *Drunken Cyclops*: and what is ſurprizing to me, the very ſame Groſſneſs, on the ſame Occaſion, is kept up in (*b*) ſeveral of the beſt Poets that ever wrote.---Here You will forgive me, if I am ready to ſink under Authority, in a Point where my very Senſes almoſt contradict it. But when ſuch great Names, as *Homer*, *Virgil*, *Pope*, and *Addiſon* may be produced to defend one and the ſame Deſcription, what are we to think, *Antiphaus*? Can we ſay a thing is not offenſive, when we feel the contrary? or muſt we allow, that Nature ought to be juſtly and fully expreſs'd, even in the moſt nauſeous of Subjects?

It cannot be deny'd (anſwer'd *Antiphaus*, after having turn'd the Queſtion.

(*a*) See *Od.* 4, 543, and 548---10, 285. &c
(*b*) *Od.* 9, 443---373. *Æn.* 3, 632. *Addiſon's Miſc.* V. 1. Pag. 61. 12°.

for ſome time in his Mind) every Deſcription that is juſt, is *poetically good*; but then I fancy, 'tis as true, that a Deſcription poetically good, may be the more improper to be inſerted, on that very Account. This will be readily allow'd in all Caſes of Obſcenity: The *beſt Deſcription* in ſuch Points is certainly the moſt *improper*; and ſurely the ſame will hold in a great Meaſure of any Images directly nauſeous. We have, you ſay, the Examples of the greateſt Poets that ever wrote, againſt us: but if the reaſon of the thing be againſt them, no Authority whatever, nor any number of Examples, can be of the leaſt real Weight. I am delighted with the Correctneſs of a *Virgil* or an *Addiſon*; I admire *Pope*, and reverence *Homer*. But were there any one piece of Obſcenity in the Works of all theſe Great Men, wou'd ſuch a deſcription alter its Nature, and become amiable? 'Tis the ſame in other Caſes, as well as in Obſcenities: All things, that have ſomething in their nature Diſagreeable, will ſtill be Diſagreeable, where-ever we find 'em.

The Line you hint at in the *Drunken Cyclops* cannot but carry a very nauſeous Idea with it: and had Mr. *Pope* deviated from the Original, and dropt it in the

Engliſh,

English, I am perſwaded moſt people wou'd have look'd upon it, as a commendable Injury to his Author; I remember (*a*) a Paſſage (of this Nature, tho' leſs groſs than this) in the *Iliad*, which Mr. *Pope* has improv'd by concealing the Groſſneſs of it; and in the Note upon it, he ſays, *'tis unworthy of Homer; he does not ſee any Colour to ſoften the Meanneſs of it; it muſt ever have been too nauſeous to be deſcrib'd.*

What fine Criticks ſhould we make, ſays *Philypſus*, ſince we can be both ſo ready to wiſh a Tranſlator had err'd more frequently from his Copy?——But whatever thoſe ſevere Gentlemen may think, we ſhould certainly have a large Party on our ſide in the preſent Caſe. What would they ſay to another Principle? That it may be neceſſary to deviate from the *Words* of the Original, to preſerve the *Senſe* of it: And yet this may happen; As, for Inſtance, where our Notions of things are directly contrary to what was thought of them in *Homer's* Days.

Words are to be conſider'd, not as *Sounds*, but as they are *Significant*: and a ſtrict Tranſlator ſhould endeavour

(*a*) *Il.* 9, 612.

chiefly to give us the ſame Ideas which the Writer he repreſents, gave to his Readers. It is on this Account I ſhould take (*a*) *The Monarch of the Swains*, for Inſtance, to be a juſter Tranſlation of Συβώτης ὄρχαμος ἀνδρῶν, than the *Chief Swine-herd* would have been. In the preſent acceptation of things, a *literal Tranſlation* would have been a *Traveſty*: it would have made that ridiculous and mean, which was not mean or ridiculous in the Original.

Of old, *Uſeful* Employments were alſo *Honourable*. The chief Courtiers were Maſters of the Flocks and of the Herds: A Skill in Agriculture was reckon'd a very handſome part in the Character of a Monarch: *Homer* (*b*) places it upon a level with Military Science; and looks upon the Reputation it deſerves, as equal to the Glory acquir'd by Atchievements in War.

To preſerve ſomething of theſe (*c*) Primitive Notions of things, at leaſt not to ſink into thoſe very low Ideas, which we in the preſent world entertain of ſuch ſorts of Arts and Employments, a Tranſlator of *Homer* is oblig'd to vary the

(*a*) *Od.* 16, 35—36. (*b*) See Note on *Od.* 18, 412. (*c*) See *Od.* 4, 974. 14, 122. and 18, 412.

Ex-

Expreſſions in common uſe for the ſame things: Nothing wou'd be more ridiculous now, than to call a *Firſt Miniſter*, by the Name of a *Hog-herd*; or to ſay of *Kings*, that they overlook'd the *Dairy*.

There are ſome other Points, relating to the *Manners* of Antiquity, which may require ſome Alterations in the turn of expreſſing them. I have been too tedious already; Let me only mention one Particular of this kind, and I have done. The Heroes of Old, in rating each other, are very free with the mutual Terms of *Dogs*, *Cowards*, *Villains* &c. In the *Odyſſey* we have a Queen calling one of her Maids of Honour, *an Impudent Bitch*; and *Jupiter*, if I miſtake not, pays exactly the ſame Compliment to his Royal Conſort in the *Iliad*. I think no one can diſpute which is the better Tranſlation in the former Caſe, The *New*, which makes *Penelope* call her Servant (*a*) *a Loquacious Inſolent*; or the Literal of *Hobbes*:

Bold Bitch (ſaid ſhe) I know what deeds you've done.

This is equally a miſ-repreſentation of Fact, and ſhocking in its very ſound; It offends the Ear, and makes one ſtartle

(*a*) *Od.* 19, 110—91.

at

at the Behaviour of *Penelope*: A Reader ought to think that Lady well bred: This he cannot do, at least he will be prejudic'd not to do so, by hearing such Language now, however decent it might be thought in those Times.

I am oblig'd to you (says *Antiphaus*, perceiving that *Philypsus* stopt here) for the fair account you have given of these Lownesses in an *Epick* Poem: I know not whether your general rule of Meanness will hold in every Point, that might be mention'd; but in those you have produc'd, it seems to square very well. I imagine too, there is one Particular, of pretty large extent in this Question, not yet touch'd upon.——There may be several; but you have all that I have observ'd, says *Philypsus*——I doubt not (says *Antiphaus*) you have observ'd the same thing, and put it under some other Head; You must know, I wou'd rank all Thoughts which border on *Puerility*, all *cold Fancies*, all *forc'd Antitheses*, and any mere *turns*, and *sporting* upon words, under the Class of Meannesses in an *Epick* Poem.——As you have hinted such a Variety of Subjects, says *Philypsus*, will you not compleat the Favour, and afford some Instances too under these Heads?

—What

——What I can recollect (reply'd *Antiphaus*) is at your Service.

Does not there seem to you to be something *Affected* and *Cold* in this Thought, which I doubt not many will be apt to take for a pretty Clash in the Ideas.

Here ceas'd he; but indignant tears let fall;
(*a*) *Spoke* when he *Ceas'd*.——

Such is this Thought;

(*b*) And my tost limbs now *wearied* into *rest*.

Nothing is meaner than what is overwrought: I own 'tis in Poetry, as in Statuary; Figures that are to be set up at such a height must be something larger than the Life; but even then there are exact Rules of Proportion, and nothing is to appear too Vast to the Eye.

In giving ones Opinion of an exquisite Statue we may say, it *lives* or *speaks*: but when we go to refine on this, we grow affected and mean. Pardon me if I take this to be the Case in the last Line of this Couplet:

Alive each animated Frame appears;
(*c*) And *still to live, beyond the Power of Years*.

(*a*) *Od*. 24, 504--437. (*b*) *Od*. 10, 593--499.
(*c*) *Od*. 7, 123--94.

I was formerly pleas'd with the Inſcription under a *Saint Bruno* in *Italy*; but give it up now as carried too far; it tells us, as you may remember, (*a*) *That He is alive, and wou'd ſpeak, were it not for the Rules of Silence he had eſtabliſh'd.* A Man muſt underſtand the Hiſtory of the *Grand Chartreux* to take the meaning of this; and after all, it appears too forc'd and artificial.

A Fault of this kind is the more evident, when the Thoughts and Language look noble about it:

There terrible in arms *Ulyſſes* ſtood,
(*b*) And the dead Suitors *almoſt ſwam* in blood.

You know a late excellent (*c*) Philoſopher has endeavour'd to prove that no Action, which diſagrees with truth, can be good; and I ſhou'd not be new or ſingular in my Opinion, were I to aſſert the ſame of any point in Poetry. Every one knows, the Dialogues of one of the moſt (*d*) penetrating Criticks in the laſt Age, are wrote chiefly in this View. He aſſerts conſtantly, that no Thought can be good, which is not Poetically

(*a*) Egli è vivo, e parlerebbe, ſe non oſſervaſſe la ragola del Silentio (*b*) *Od.* 23, 47--51. (*c*) Mr. *Wollaſton*. (*d*) *Bouhours*.

true;

true; and I imagine this that he asserts, may be defended as easily in the *Fictions* of Poetry, as in any of the plainest Passages. But such an Enquiry wou'd take up more time, than Criticism deserves; and I mention it at present only as a Measure of such Thoughts as are *mean* from their being *false*, i. e. *really beneath what they pretend to be.*——This Rule, if just, wou'd be of particular service in this kind of Pursuits: I shall give you but one Instance; When *Circe* mentions *Ulysses*'s descent to the Infernal Shades, she adjoins this Reflection.

O Sons of woe! decreed by adverse Fates,
Alive to pass thro' hells eternal Gates!
All soon or late, are doom'd that path to tread;
(a) More *wretched* You, *twice number'd* with the Dead!

Do you not think this last Thought has something *Weak* and *Little* in it? according to your general Rule, it fails in its *Proportion*; That Proportion, I mean, which every Thought should bear to *Truth*.

If it fails in that, says *Philypsus*, I must allow it to be Mean by my own Rule; but I do not perceive in what respect that Sentiment is false.

(a) *Od.* 12, 32--22.

No!

No! ſays *Antiphaus*; I beg you would conſider the very Word on which the whole of the Reflection turns: It has plainly too Significations widely different. If their being *number'd with the Dead*, be taken in its ſtrongeſt Senſe, 'tis certain this did not happen twice to *Ulyſſes*, and his Companions; if in its weaker on this Occaſion, Their Calamity is put on a Level with ſomething much more terrible and calamitous than it ſelf.

Or thus: If this being *twice* number'd with the Dead be intended both in the ſame Senſe, the Sentence is directly falſe; if in very different unequal Senſes, 'tis fallacious and falſe in its Conſequence.

I beg pardon for putting on this grave face, and affecting ſuch an air of Demonſtration: but you muſt know this Thought is exactly the ſame in the Original, or (if any thing) rather more fallacious there than in the Tranſlation: in ſuch a Caſe all ones Gravity is ſcarce ſufficient; and the Superſtitious perhaps wou'd rather disbelieve a real Demonſtration, than allow of any Fault in *Homer*. I beg Pardon of them, for thus aſſuming the *Chair of Criticiſm* (as the nobleſt of (*a*) human Writers calls it) and am very wil-

(*a*) Lord *Bacon*. De *Augm*. *Scient*. Lib. 6. Cap. 4.

ling

ling to deſcend, and act in an humbler Sphere.

All ſporting upon Words may ſeem unbecoming of the *Epick* Muſe: I ſhall leave you to determine how far there may be any ſuſpicion of this in ſome particular Lines.

(*a*) *Thy laſt of Games unhappy has thou play'd* ——

——To me has ſome reſemblance to the rebellious Angels in *Milton*, where they run on in ſuch a vein of inſulting and punning. I know not how far the Original might help in leading a Tranſlator into the former Turn; but here is another Line which runs into it, without that wrong biaſs.

(*b*) They on the future *banquet feaſt* their eyes.

I ſhould think this yet more improper on any grave or affecting Circumſtance: Do you remember the Death of *Antinous* in the *Odyſſey*? 'Tis in the Inſtant of his lifting a Goblet of Wine to his Mouth:

Wretch that he was, of unprophetick Soul!
High in his hand he rear'd the Golden Bowl;
Ev'n then to drain it lengthen'd out his Breath,
(*c*)Chang'd to the deep, the bitter draught of Death.

(*a*) *Od.* 22, 32---27. (*b*) *Od.* 10, 205---180.
(*c*) *Od.* 22, 13---10.

I fear that ſome Points, which generally paſs for Elegancies, are of this kind. ——A Caſe, which touches all Readers of a little Taſte very much, is, (a) *when two very different Ideas are join'd to the ſame Verb:* This is very frequent in *Cowley*, and he has been often blamed for it; as in that Inſtance,

(b) Up roſe the *Sun* and *Saul*.

I know not how it is, there is ſomething agreeable in this management of Words, but it is very apt to injure the *Senſe*. A thinking (c) *French* Author lays down a Rule, which is very uſeful towards diſcovering Fallacies in Reaſoning; It is this: *To put the Definition inſtead of the Thing defin'd.* I have often try'd ſomething of this nature in Poetry; If we make the Experiment in the preſent Caſe, and inſert the *enlarg'd Meaning* inſtead of the *particular Words* uſed by the Poet, we ſhall generally find a Fallacy in this ſort of Verſe; or, at leaſt, a Lameneſs in the Senſe of it.

It will not be any great trouble to try this in one ſingle Point. The Poet,

(a) *Addiſon's Miſc.* Vol. 1. p. 239. 12°. (b) *Od.* 14, 454---410. (c) *Malbranche.* Search after Truth. V. 2. p. 74.

ſpeaking

ſpeaking of *Telemachus's* Voyage, uſes this Turn of Expreſſion:

To diſtant *Pylos* hapleſs is he gone,
(*a*) To ſeek his Father's fate, and find his own.

This ſounds very well: but what is the meaning of the word *Fate*, which is of ſuch double Service upon this Occaſion? Try it in your own Mind:

To diſtant Pylos hapleſs is he gone,
To ſeek (whether his Father be dead or not) *and find*
——What?

There's no need of trying it, ſays *Philypſus*; I allow it to be deficient upon the firſt hearing: But by the way, I wonder you let the *Antitheſis* in it eſcape ſo peaceably!

Indeed I am no great Friend to them (reply'd *Antiphaus*) eſpecially when they are multiplied upon us, as in this Line:

(*b*) *Duſt mounts* in *clouds*, and *ſweat deſcends* in [*dews*.

I do not fear my *Philypſus* ſhould miſtake me: it would be too ſcrupulous to diſcard every Antitheſis out of Poetry, as it ſeems affected to run into them very often. Some are of Force and Emphaſis,

(*a*) *Od.* 14, 209---180. (*b*) *Od.* 11, 740---599.

and ſome agreeable and engaging: Poſſibly, even *the Double Uſe of the ſame Word* is not abſolutely to be rejected. But however theſe Ornaments may obtain on ſome Occaſions, they ſeem generally too little and artificial for the more noble Parts of Poetry. They are of the *Ovidian* kind, rather than of *Homer*: and are more apt to hit the Taſte of School-boys, than of Men.

And now I have mention'd *Ovid*'s manner, give me leave to ſay that (in ſpite of his ſeveral Beauties, and that peculiar Eaſe and Addreſs with which he tells a Story) I fear his Writings are one great Reaſon of the trifling Manner keeping its ground ſo much in the preſent Age. *Ovid* is generally made uſe of to initiate our Youths in *Parnaſſus*: We look upon him as ſoon as ever we open our Eyes to Poetry: He is then, 'tis true, fit for our Taſte; but the misfortune is, he is too Agreeable: 'tis odds but this fondneſs grows up with us; and a falſe taſte of Wit, drawn from him, may influence our Writings many Years after we have flung him from our Boſom. The *Boyiſms* of *Ovid*, (as Dr. *Garth* calls 'em) are agreeable enough to infect us to old Age. Mr. *Dryden*, for Inſtance, was thus infected by 'em. *Ovid*, and

Cowley

Cowley our *English Ovid*, were his favourites at *Ten* Years old, and his Corrupters at *Seventy*.

As great Genius's, and more correct Writers, than Mr. *Dryden* may be touch'd with the same Infection; I will give you an Instance or two of this, with which a Person may be pleas'd, even while he condemns 'em.

(*a*) She to her present Lord laments him lost,
And views that object which she wants the most.

Again:

His arms he stretch'd; his arms the touch deceive:
(*b*) Nor in the fond embrace, embraces give.

Any one, the least acquainted with the Manner of the Poets, will readily perceive this to be of the *Ovidian* kind. It is pretty, and agreeable as *Ovid*: but to be so, it loses something from the Air of *Homer*; it sinks beneath that Simplicity and Nature, which is the distinguishing Character of his Writings.

Now you mention Mr. *Dryden*, and this sort of pretty Writing together, give me leave (says *Philypsus*) to commend one sort of *Turns*, which that Critick (*c*)

(*a*) *Od.* 19, 245---209. (*b*) *Od.* 11, 487---391.
(*c*) *Dryden's* Pref. to *Juvenal*, p. 84. 8º.

 judges

judges not only pretty, but really good and ſubſtantial: I will not defend all his Inſtances, but I would engage to do it were they all as good as that from (*a*) *Virgil.*——A very good Critick ſince has treated of this more diſtinctly. His Notions as I remember are, That a dextrous Turn upon Words, is *pretty*; The Turn upon the Thought, *ſubſtantial*; but the moſt *compleat* of all, is when the Turn of the Words and of the Thought concur: (*b*) *When both our Reaſon and our Ear are entertain'd with a noble Sentiment expreſs'd vigorouſly, and beautifully finiſh'd.* I ſhould be glad to know your Opinion, *Antiphaus*, how far a Perſon might admit theſe Turns, in *Heroick Poetry?*

As for the firſt (ſays *Antiphaus*) I believe one might venture to ſay, that it ſhould be rejected univerſally: I am ſo little vers'd in theſe Particulars, that I cannot readily ſay any thing as to the ſecond: the other (whether juſtly or not) takes one very much. I own, for my part, that I imagine them, not only beautiful, but uſeful: I remember an Inſtance of (*c*) one in *Virgil*, which fixes the Ima-

(*a*) Ignoſcenda quidem, ſcirent ſi ignoſcere manes.
(*b*) *Blackwall's Introd.* to the *Claſſicks*, p. 214.
(*c*) *Georg.* I. 404.

ges

ges very particularly on the Mind; and it is this which helps to touch us in those Lines of Mr. *Addison*, which strike every one who reads them:

The listning Soldier fixt in sorrow stands,
Loth to obey his Leaders just commands;
The Leader grieves, by generous pity sway'd
(a) To see his just commands so well obey'd.

If you ask my opinion in this Point, rude and unsettled as it is; I should think, that no *Turns* should obtain in an *Epick*, or any solemn Poem, except such as have more Strength, than Beauty: That in lesser Pieces, those may be allow'd which have more Beauty, than Strength: but that they can be justified in no Piece whatever; unless they have some share of Strength, as well as Beauty.

The great Art of them is to appear Unartful; as in these pretty Lines from Mr. *Philips's* Pastorals;

Fair is my Flock, nor yet uncomely I
If liquid Fountains flatter not; and why
Should liquid Fountains flatter us, yet shew
The bordering flowers less beauteous than they [grow?

As I take it; The Beauty of this Passage is in a greater degree, than its

(a) *Addison* Vol. 1. Pag. 76. 12°.

Strength;

Strength; and the natural Air of the Sentiments, is more exquiſite than either: The Turn of the Lines makes them obſerv'd by every Reader more than they would otherwiſe be; and yet that very Turn does not ſeem to be deſign'd, but rather to be the natural reſult of the Shepherd's Thoughts as he ſpeaks them.

If I have ſaid too much, *Philypſus*, you muſt blame your ſelf for it, who led me from my chief Deſign. I was juſt entering on the ſeveral Natural Pieces in the Poem before us.

Some fanciful Writers afford us nothing but Pictures and Deſcriptions: they continue Image after Image; and put one in Mind of thoſe *Americans*, who, when firſt they were diſcover'd, are ſaid to have us'd Painting inſtead of Writing.

Homer's Judgment will not allow him, in any of his Works, to be thus Perpetual in his Deſcriptions; and the deſign of the *Odyſſey* will not allow near the variety, which he has very juſtly employ'd in the *Iliad.* The *Odyſſey* is a Poetical Treatiſe of Morality: it does not admit of a profuſion of Colours: this is not to be look'd upon as a Defect: we might with the ſame Reaſon blame a

Book

Book of Maxims, or *Plato*'s Moral Dialogues, for not having all the Flouriſhes and Charms of Rhetorick.

And as the Plan of the *Odyſſey* in general excludes that great variety of Deſcription, which abounds in ſome Poems; the chief Scene, in the remaining Part of it, is ſo wholly Domeſtick, that it ſcarce allows room for any thing of that Nature. The Action now is confin'd; it lies all between either the Country-Houſe of *Eumæus*, and the Palace; or this latter, and the Gardens of *Laertes*. What a narrow Scene is this' for Deſcription? and yet theſe are the only *places* capable of any, if you except a two days Journey, and a ſhort Voyage in the 15*th*, neither of which could be enlarg'd upon without injuring the main Deſign. *Homer* was unacquainted with the modern Affluence of Painting, where-ever there may be any fine Object in the way: As theſe Opportunities offer only in an Epiſode, he paſſes them with the utmoſt diſpatch: we ſee his haſte in the very Lines, and indeed in every one of them diſtinctly:

With ſpeed the maſt they rear, with ſpeed un-[ſbind
The ſpacious ſheet, and ſtretch it to the wind:
Minerva calls; the ready gales obey
With rapid ſpeed to whirl them o'er the ſea;

Cruſus

Crunus they pass'd; next *Chalcis* roll'd away,——
The silver *Phea*'s glittering rills they lost.
(*a*) And skim'd along by *Eli*'s sacred coast.

It might be the indigence of his Subject this way, which induc'd *Homer* to repeat the view of Hell in the 24*th* Book; and the wanderings of *Ulysses* in the 23*d*. But nothing could make him run into Descriptions on that Occasion. We have the Names of Places repeated in Order; and tho' *Penelope* has the full Relation, the Reader is only tantaliz'd with hearing in general, that,

(*b*) He images the rills, and flow'ry vales.

These things, however they had been laid out, wou'd have been only Side-views. For in the main Scene, as it now lies in *Ithaca*, I think there are but four *Places* capable of Description. If I am not mistaken in this, it will give us great Reason to admire the Management of *Homer*; who, as he was too prudent to run out into any impertinent Descriptions; at that same time, has not omitted any one of those places, that might very well allow of a Description without wandring. We have distinct draughts

(*a*) *Od.* 15, 319.—296. (*b*) *Od.* 23, 336.

of

of *Laertes*'s Gardens, (*a*) *Eumæus*'s Lodge, of (*b*) the *Royal Palace*, and the *Road* between these and the Palace. These compleat the present Scene of the Poem; and any one by laying them together, may form an exact Picture of it in his Mind.

Some of these have been mention'd already on other Occasions; and the way from *Eumæus*'s House to the Metropolis deserves very well to be mention'd here: I dare say you will think part of it, the most delightful Road you ever travell'd in your Life:

Now pass'd the rugged Road, they journey down
The cavern'd way descending to the Town,
Where, from the rock with liquid lapse distills
A limpid fount; that spread in parting rills,
Its current thence to serve the city brings
An useful work; adorn'd by ancient Kings.
Neritus, *Ithacus*, *Polyctor* there
In sculptur'd Stone immortaliz'd their care;
In marble urns receiv'd it from above,
And shaded with a green surrounding grove;
Where silver Alders in high arches twin'd,
Drink the cool stream, and tremble to the wind.
Beneath, sequester'd to the Nymphs, is seen
A mossy Altar, deep embower'd in green;
Where constant Vows by travellers are made,
[*c*] And holy horrors solemnize the shade.

(*a*) *Od.* 14, V. 8 to 26. (*b*) *Od.* 17, 316 and 415.
(*c*) *Od.* 17, V. 230 to 245.

There

There is a ſort of melancholly Pleaſure hangs upon the Mind, where-ever we have a View of *Laertes* in his Retirement. The good Old Prince (*a*) Labours thorough Life; he (*b*) longs to lay down the Burthen: And when he is not ſo overcome with his Diſtreſs, as to (*c*) neglect his Employment in his Gardens, he ſeems buſy rather to (*d*) avoid Pain, than to enjoy Pleaſure. Thus is he engag'd, with ſomething of Diverſion, and much of Melancholly, when the Scene changes to his Gardens.

We have not a ſet Deſcription of theſe altogether; but it begins at this Point, and is carried on (*e*) ſucceſſively, till we may eaſily form an Idea of the whole.

Tho' *Homer* has not wander'd into any Deſcriptions of Places that lay out of this Scene of the Poem, he has here, and all along in the former part of it, brought in ſhort Draughts and Side-views of things by ſuch Arts, as are ſome of them neceſſary, and all very allowable in Poetry.

Such are all *deſcriptive Similies*: Wherein ſome Picture out of the Subject is bor-

(*a*) *Od.* 15, 151. (*b*) *Od.* 11, 226. (*c*) *Od.* 16, 155. (*d*) *Od.* 24, 285. (*e*) *Od.* 24, V. 237, 256, 268, and 395.

row'd

row'd to illuſtrate any Point that belongs to it. This affords us ſeveral occaſional Pieces, and ſome of them very natural: I have juſt dipt upon one of this ſort. 'Tis juſt after the Slaughter of the Suitors; They are yet gaſping, and *Ulyſſes* is ſurveying their Bodies, to ſee whether the Number be compleat:

So when by hollow ſhores the fiſher train
Sweep with their arching nets the hoary main,
And ſcarce the meſhy toils the copious draught [contain:
All naked of their Element and bare,
The fiſhes pant, and gaſp in thinner air;
(*a*) Wide o'er the ſands are ſpread the ſtiffening [prey.

It's a known Remark, that all Alluſions of this kind, drawn from calm Life (as Fiſhing, Hunting, and rural Affairs) have a peculiar Beauty: and 'tis as well known, that they acquire an additional Energy, when they are introduc'd amidſt any Confuſion, or to illuſtrate Images of Terror. *Virgil* (*b*) has imitated this ſort of Contraſt from a Similie in the *Iliad*; which affords frequent Inſtances of the ſame kind; nor are they wanting in the (*c*) Poem before us.

(*a*) *Od.* 22, 430---387. (*b*) Compare *Æn.* 2, 303. IA. Δ', 455. (*c*) See *Od.* 12, 300. and the Note there.

P 'The

The more concise and natural any Image, the stronger the Illustration. How do you approve of this, on a number of Females employ'd at the Loom?

——— Their busy fingers move
(a) Like Poplar-leaves, when *Zephyr* fans the grove.

When these occasional Images hit in several Points, they are the more descriptive of the things, which they are brought to Illustrate. *Homer* gives us an Idea of the Spirits in *Ades*, of their still Posture, their Motion, their Confusion, and the odd Noises they utter, all in one single Picture of this kind:

Trembling the Spectres glide, and plaintive vent
Thin, hollow Screams, along the deep descent.
As in the cavern of some rifted Den,
Where flock nocturnal Bats and Birds obscene;
Cluster'd they hang, till at some sudden shock,
They move, and murmurs run thro' all the rock:
So cow'ring fled the sable heaps of ghosts,
(b) And such a Scream fill'd all the dismal coasts.

It seems not improper to point out these distinct Likenesses; as the Translation has done in the present Case, more plainly than the Original; the same may be said of (c) some others.

(a) *Od.* 7, 135--106. (b) *Od.* 24, 14--9.
(c) See *Od.* 5, 420--330.

This

This is done ſometimes by inſiſting much on one Circumſtance, and (*a*) repeating it over and over.

Borrow'd Images appear with a particular Propriety and Grace, when they have ſome near Relation to the Scene, on which the Poem turns at the very Inſtant of applying 'em. Thus in the *Battle of Rivers*, in the (*b*) *Iliad*, every Similie is aquatick, and adapted to the Place. Thus if the Swiftneſs of a Deity paſſing o'er the *Land* is to be illuſtrated in this manner, *Homer* images it by the Swiftneſs of an *Eagle*: but when *Mercury* is flying over the *Sea*, by that of ſome (*c*) *Water-fowl*.

The Image of an Angler is us'd in the *Iliad*, of a perſon in the Field of Battle; in the (*d*) *Odyſſey*, of perſons at Sea; both on Occaſions which make that Image proper. But it ſeems more proper in the latter, from the Agreement of Place. In this, and all like Caſes, part of the Picture is nearer to us, and will be conceiv'd the more readily and clearly.

There may alſo be ſome propriety from any previous Relation between the

(*a*) As in Mr. *Pope's Iliad* 22, V. 257 to 262.
(*b*) Book, 21. (*c*) *Od.* 5, 64. (*d*) *Od.* 12, 300.

Person, and the *Thing* to which he is compar'd. Any faithless wavering Creature may be compar'd to the Sea; but it strikes one more, when *Venus* is said to be as (*a*) *Inconstant, as the Waves from whence she sprung.* Any rough Man may be compar'd to the Element, in another view; but there is a peculiar fitness in these Lines:

* A race of rugged Mariners are these
(*b*) Unpolish'd Men, and boist'rous as their Seas.

I remember, I us'd formerly to be mightily taken with a Similie in the (*c*) *Muscipula*; and I believe now, it was on this very Account. Ideas, which have been alreaded join'd on any other Occasion, will agree the more easily on a new one.

The Picture is less broken also, when the borrow'd Image is adapted to the present Circumstances: Where *Penelope* is represented as chast and beautiful, 'tis said she look'd (*d*) like *Diana* with all the Charms of *Venus*; when her Beauty is the chief Circumstance to be

(*a*) *Guarini's Pastor Fido.* Act. 4. Sc. 7. (*b*) *Od.* 7, 42. (*c*)—— Cui sæpe suis in montibus hircus Prolixam invidit barbam ——— De *Cambro-Brit.*
Thus *Virgil's*
Abietibus juvenes patriis & montibus æquos.
(*d*) *Od.* 17, 47---37.

insisted

insisted on, she is compar'd to (*a*) *Venus*, without any mention of *Diana*.

We may observe, by the way, that the Heathen Poets, in comparing a Person to any of their Deities, had a sure Method of giving their Readers a Picture of that Person. The Statues of their Deities were known by every one; and the Faces of each as well ascertain'd, as the Faces of the *Roman* Emperors (for instance) can be, by frequently conversing with their Medals; This I take to be one Reason, why this sort of Comparison is so very frequent in the Ancients: The Case is very different in any modern Composition; tho' we seem to be equally fond of the same Comparisons.

If it does not add to the Strength, at least it makes the Piece more agreeable, when these Images are unusual. Thus *Ulysses* in his Bed of Leaves, to a (*b*) Coal of Fire preserv'd in the Embers; and before in his raft at Sea, to an (*c*) heap of Thorns, driven by the Wind.

There may be a *Prettiness*, as well as a *Likeness* in these Images; I always us'd to be pleas'd with that Passage, where *Penelope* is compar'd to a (*d*) Nightingale;

(*a*) *Od.* 18, 229---192. (*b*) *Od.* 5, 630---488. (*c*) *Ibid.* 417. (*d*) *Od.* 19, 605---518.

tho' I am more pleas'd with the ſame Image in (*a*) *Virgil*; which, beſide its agreeableneſs, is perhaps the moſt compleat Inſtance, that can be given, of ſuch Similitudes as hit exactly in every Point. *Virgil* certainly excells *Homer* in theſe, as we may ſay that *Homer* excells him in the *Vague Similitude*; for both have their diſtinct Beauties.

'Tis the proper air of Poetry to be unconfin'd and free: The Muſe loves a flowing Dreſs: Her motions are ever Eaſy, and her very ornaments muſt be Natural. Such is the Muſe of *Homer*. And hence the Poet, in this ſort of Pictures, does not in the leaſt Scruple to take in ſeveral Circumſtances, that do not affect the main Reſemblance. When a Painter is copying a Piece, he muſt preſerve the Likeneſs; but he may vary in the Drapery, the Poſture, the Under-figures, and the Scene around 'em.

Thus in *Homer*'s *Philomel*, the main Likeneſs is very well taken: When the Poet has ſecur'd this, he touches upon the Hiſtory of *Itylus*; and launches out into Particulars, which are (*b*) ſo far from ſquaring with the Caſe of *Penelope*, that they have no manner of Relation to it.

(*a*) *Georg.* 4, 511. (*b*) *Od.* τ', 523.

Homer

Homer is almoſt ſingular in another ſort of Similie, the Reverſe of the former: when the Principal Figures have in themſelves no Likeneſs, but agree in ſome one Circumſtance of Action. Theſe are very frequent in the *Iliad* and *Odyſſey*: and I cannot ſay, whether it be from a true Judgment, or a ſcrupulous Niceneſs, that later Writers endeavour to imitate them but very rarely.

Perhaps this is blameable; and ſo may be that ſtringing of ſeveral Similies together, which we ſometimes meet with in *Homer*. I do not mean when ſeveral things are choſen to illuſtrate the (*a*) *ſame Point* more fully: but when Similies on *different* things follow too cloſe on the Neck of one another. In the 2*d Iliad*, (*b*) we have one of theſe ſtrings which takes up thirty Lines; And tho' they are all excellently well choſen, and have one common Point of Union between them all, yet they may ſeem ſomething faulty, as they are too numerous for the Place in which they ſtand, and too much crouded on one another.

Now I have digreſs'd ſo far on two or three Vices in ancient Similies; I ſhall juſt mention one or two of a later

(*a*) See Ιλ. ξ, 394. (*b*)—β, 453 to 483.

Date

Date. Such is the *continued* Similie, which is very liable to the great Fault of mixt Metaphors, when a Writer, to lengthen a *comparison*, carries it beyond the *Likeness*. I remember one of Mr. *Dryden*'s in a (*a*) Dedication, that begins very well. "The Greatness of Birth "shews a Nobleman with advantage; "but if he degenerates, *the least Spot is* "*visible on Ermine*.——This does not seem to be continued so happily, as it is begun. "To preserve this Whiteness in "its Original Purity, You (my Lord) "have, *like that Ermine, forsaken that* "*common tract of Business, which is not* "*always clean.*

The Art of extracting Similies out of a thing directly contrary to your purpose, is I think wholly Modern. Every one knows an Instance of this in that famous Doctor, who to illustrate the *Danger* of the *Church*, compares it to one of the *Prophets, who was encompass'd with Horsemen and Chariots of Fire*——for his defence.

Nothing is so opposite to the Design of this Beauty in Poetry, as to labour after a vast Number of Likenesses in any the minutest Points; and to multiply

(*a*) Before his Translation of the *Georgicks*.

them,

them, rather to ſhew how far the Poets Wit can carry the Reſemblance, than to ſtrengthen the Image of the things deſcrib'd. This deſcends even to playing upon Words; nay ſometime to particularize ſeveral Points in which they are *unlike*, as well as thoſe in which they *agree*. This is the *Cowlean* Similitude: and I could produce [*a*] monſtrous Inſtances of it from a very fine Writer, where he endeavours only to imitate *Cowley* at a Diſtance. 'Tis the ſame Perſon who has introduced Similies into his *Proſe*, in a manner unknown to the Ancients: but he who would blame any of his Writings of *this kind*, muſt blame them, as Mr. *Locke* does Eloquence, with the Tenderneſs of a Lover.

It is not difficult to judge of any Similie, Ancient or Modern. Their [*b*] chief Deſign is to make things clear: Obſcurity and Confuſion is their great Fault: Poetry may go much farther in them than Proſe; but, even in Poetry, none can be good, which do not give us

---

[*a*] See a *Pindarick Ode* on *Cowley*, in *Dryden's Miſc.* (Vol. 4) particularly the whole third *Stanza*.

[*b*] Ad inferendam rebus lucem *repertæ ſunt* Similitudines.——Præcipuè cuſtodiendum, ne id quod Similitudinis gratià adſcivimus, aut obſcurum ſit aut ignotum. *Quintil. Inſtit*. Lib. 8. Cap. 3.

either

either more diſtinct, larger Notions of the thing, or at leaſt of ſome Circumſtance of the thing, to be deſcrib'd.

I long to add ſeveral things on this Head; but I have wander'd too far already from our chief Deſign: it is time now to conſider a higher Claſs of Deſcriptions and Images (which we touch'd upon when we were talking over the former Books of the *Odyſſey*) that Poetical power of expreſſing the *Paſſions*, and even *Ideas* yet in the Minds of Men.

I am not angry with You, *Philypſus*, for preventing much of what might have been offer'd here, when you were conſidering the Starts and Turns, which our Paſſions occaſion in the various manners of Speaking. I know not how ſuch a Notion would appear to the World; but you have thoroughly perſwaded me, that all the Figures of Speech, of the [a] Nobler Order, are view'd in a truer Light, when we look upon them, as naturally Expreſſive of what we feel within us; than when we conſider them, only as the Arts and Machineries of Writing.

It was on this Occaſion you went thorough the moſt paſſionate Scenes in

---

[a] Figures either belong to the *Diction*, or the *Sentiment*: the latter is what is here intended.

the

the *Odyſſey*; for ſuch are the ſeveral Enterviews in which *Ulyſſes* makes himſelf known to his [*a*] Friends, his [*b*] Son, his [*c*] Father, and his [*d*] Conſort. *Penelope's* [*e*] Speech at that juncture is excellent; and indeed all her Speeches in general are of the *Pathetick* kind, and (under this view) afford us the moſt beautiful Paſſages in the whole Poem.

To the many things that have been ſaid on the *Double Paſſions* (as you were pleas'd to let me call them) give me leave to add one particular Caſe more: what I mean, is *Diſſimulation*. We have frequent Deſcriptions of this in the *Odyſſey*: Every Inſtance of it (if paſſionate at all) will fall under this Conſideration; and that in the higheſt Degree, as the Paſſion *aſſum'd*, and the *real*, are direct Oppoſites. Every one, who only pretends to *Courage*, is certainly affected with *Fear*; and when we put on a falſe Gayety, the *Heart* is as dull and oppreſs'd, as the *Countenance* is enliven'd.

Could we look into the Breaſt of one who affects a Livelineſs, when his Thoughts are really Gloomy; we ſhould ſee his Spirits in ſuch contrary Emotions,

---

[*a*] Book, 21. [*b*] B. 16. [*c*] B. 24. [*d*] B. 23. [*e*] Od 23, 215.

as

as are defcrib'd in the Suitors, under thofe unaccountable mixt fits of Mirth and Heavinefs.——

(a) *Pallas* clouds with intellectual gloom
The Suitors Souls, infenfate of their doom;
A Mirthful phrenzy feiz'd the fated croud,
The Roofs refound with caufelefs laughter loud---
Then down each cheek the tears fpontaneous flow.

Such is that (b) *Smile* of *Penelope*, which has fomething very uneafy in it: She feems all the while to ftruggle with her Tears. 'Tis like a tranfient Gleam of Light, when the Heavens are overcaft: all around is Gloomy; and the Light itfelf is Dim and Waterifh.

This perhaps is an Inftance not of the affected, but the natural Kind. 'Tis true, one Paffion fometimes ufurps the Effect of another: Without tumbling over *Des-Cartes* for a Solution of the matter, we know, that an Excefs of *Joy* often breaks out into *Tears*; and that *Rage* may vent itfelf in a *Smile*: Thefe indeed are contrary Appearances; but 'tis very different in all Points of Diffimulation. The Mixture then has fomething peculiar in it. Contrary to the natural Blending of fuch Emotions, this

(a) *Od.* 20, 419. (b) *Od.* 18, 194---162.

has

has always an Air forc'd and artificial. The Soul was not made to be a Counterfeit: every time we wou'd teach her theſe new Arts, we fling her off her Biaſs, and give her an unnatural Motion. There will ever be ſomething aukward in the Paſſions of the moſt profound Diſſemblers.

Only view *Ulyſſes*, when he is ſtruck to the Soul with the Affection and Tears of his *Penelope*, and at the ſame time reſolv'd to conceal thoſe his Emotions from her, as much as poſſible:

[a] Withering at heart to ſee the weeping fair
His eyes look ſtern, and caſt a gloomy ſtare;
Of horn the ſtiff relentleſs balls appear,
Or globes of iron fixt in either Sphere;
Firm wiſdom interdicts the ſoft'ning tear.

Even *Ulyſſes*, that *Ulyſſes* who is ſo [b] Celebrated among the Ancients for his Command over his Paſſions, does not appear without ſomething forc'd and unnatural in his Looks, amidſt all his Diſſimulation. He can command his Tears; he can command his Tongue; but ſtill his very Features would betray him.

I know not what to ſay to one thing: That *Homer* makes Diſſimulation one of

[a] *Od.* 19, 247. [b] See Note, *ibid.*

the greateſt Excellencies of his Hero. The Heathen ſyſtem of Morality was incompleat enough to bear with this proceeding: and even Chriſtians of the greateſt Name have border'd much on the ſame Notions. One of our Ancient Writers, who was as capable as any of them to do it, has (*a*) launch'd out into a long defence of *uſeful Frauds*; and *Father Paul*, to mention one not inferior among the Moderns, reckons Diſſimulation (*b*) expreſsly among the *Vertues* of *Pope Clement* the *Seventh*. I do not mention this as any Argument for the thing; but to extenuate the Proceeding of *Homer*: 'Tis no wonder that he ſhould miſtake a counterfeit Virtue in the Dark, which ſuch great Men could not diſtinguiſh in the Light.

But whatever Colour Diſſimulation may bear in the Schemes of Morality, it is certainly a great Excellence to paint

---

(*a*) See *Chryſoſtom.* Tom. 6. pag. 5. Ed. *Savil.* ΘΑΡΣΕΙ, ἔφλω ἐγὼ &c.

(*b*) Where the Hiſtorian ſays that *Pope* died "Con allegrezza non mediocre della corte: la "quale ben ammirava le *vertu* di quello, che "erano una gravita naturale, et eſſemplare parſi- "monia, & *diſſimulatione*; odiava però maggior- "mente l' avariatia, durezza, & crudelta. *Hiſt.* del *Concilio Trid.* p. 68.

Diſſi-

Diſſimulation well in Poetry. The pretended Paſſion muſt appear moſt ſtrongly, and yet the real Paſſion muſt appear under it. It muſt be like the Drapery in Pictures, which ſhews the turn of the Limbs, at the ſame time that it hides them; and in particular, puts one in Mind of that Veil in *Homer*, *which ſeems and only ſeems* to ſhade the Face of *Penelope*.

There is nothing more difficult in Poetry, than to expreſs juſtly Ideas in the Minds of Perſons whom we deſcribe. But tho' this be the leaſt obvious, 'tis perhaps the moſt agreeable of all Studies. The Poet muſt ſearch carefully into the Nature of Man, and the Working of his Thoughts in general; He muſt know what Emotions are natural on each Accident of Life; and on every ſingle Occaſion is to conſider, not only the Circumſtances of Actions, but alſo the Temper, the Education, and the very *make* of the Perſon concern'd in them. Theſe will alter Men's Views of the very ſame Point; When *Neſtor* talks of Atchievements in War, he will dwell chiefly upon the Prudence and Experience of a General; *Hector* will mention the great effects of Strength and Courage; *Tydeus* muſt place the whole on a bold daring Spirit, without taking the Body into the

Account; while *Polypheme*, on the contrary, must speak of nothing but the Advantage of a vast Size and superior Strength.

A Man's Notions of Excellence are form'd generally from some advanc'd Powers of his own. Each Man is apt to make himself the Measure of all the Species; and his Species the Standard of all Perfection. All Beings above him must be exactly like the superior Moyety of his own Being, and all below him must be purely of the Inferior. The Vulgar of Mankind form their Heaven hereafter out of those things which have pleas'd them most in Life; and the very Notions of the Deity in mostMen take a Turn from their own Complexions. The God of proud *tyrannical* Minds is a Being, that delights only in the *Glory of being Terrible*; as with the soft and pitiful, The Deity is *all Mercy:* the Gods of *Epicurus* were mere pleasurable Intelligences; and the Deities of the *Irroquois* are *Mighty Hunters.* Commend me to that Philosopher who said, that *were his Horse to give us his Notion in this Case; A Broad Chest and a Flowing Mane would certainly be the Principal things in it.*

One cannot easily apprehend how general an effect this has in the Actings of our

our Minds. I know not that it is yet designedly manag'd in any System of Philosophy, (for Mr. *Locke's Association* of *Ideas* seems to be something very distinct from it) and as it wants a Name, give me leave to call it for the present, The *Assimilation of Ideas.*

If you would save me from a Fit of Philosophizing, be so good as to reach that Volume of the *Odyssey* just by you, That I may read you a Passage which took with me particularly, on this Account. 'Tis where *Ulysses* has acquainted the *Cyclops* with his real Name and Character: this is part of the Monster's Answer;

Oh Heavens! oh Faith of ancient Prophecies!
This, *Telemus Eurymides* foretold:———
Long since he menac'd such was Heavens command,
And nam'd *Ulysses* as the destin'd hand.
I deem'd some Godlike Giant to behold,
Or lofty Hero, haughty brave and bold;
Not this weak Pigmy wretch, of mean Design,
[a] Who not by Strength subdu'd me, but by Wine.

Even the Excellence of those things, with which we converse chiefly, is apt to influence our Thoughts in the same manner. Hence the Eastern Writers Image the Height and Stateliness of any

---

[a] *Od.* 9, 604--516.

illuſtrious Perſon, by *Cedars* : *Homer*, by the (*a*) *Delian-Palm-tree* ; and *Virgil*, by what a *Britiſh* Reader will think the moſt Noble, *a* (*b*) *large Lofty Oak*.

There's a Paſſage which, I remember, I was mightily pleas'd with formerly, in reading *Cervantes*, without ſeeing any Reaſon for it at that Time ; tho' I now imagine, that which took me in it comes under this View. Speaking of *Don Quixot*, the firſt time that Adventurer came in ſight of the Ocean, he expreſſes his Sentiments on this Occaſion in the following manner, *He ſaw the Sea, which he had never ſeen before ; and thought it much bigger than the River at* Salamanca.

This Turn of Thought is not ſo commonly obſerv'd perhaps as it might eaſily be in Life. There are other occaſional *Traces* in the Mind, which are known and obvious : Things that are common in ſome Degree to all Men ; and ſuch are all thoſe Apprehenſions which follow from any *Maſter-Paſſion*. One might expatiate here very Agreeeably on each of them ; but I am ever apt to be too Tedious ; and will therefore confine my ſelf to one ſingle Paſſion, that of *Fear*.

(*a*) *Od.* ζ', 163—6, 193. (*b*) *Æn.* 9, 682 and 12, 700.

We

We may ſee in the Deſcriptions of the Poets, how this Paſſion acts on the Soul through all its different Degrees, from a *Wavering* and *Irreſolution* of Mind, to the Exceſs of *Confuſion* and *Deſpair.*

When a Coward (as moſt Cowards are Vain-glorious) undertakes any Enterprize of Difficulty, the Moment he is engag'd in it, his Mind turns all upon the Danger of the Undertaking. He immediately wiſhes himſelf fairly out of it; His Body begins to tremble, and his Thoughts are all confus'd and irreſolute. Thus it is with *Dolon.* That Wretch engages under the Covert of the Night, to ſteal to the Camp of the *Greeks*, and diſcover their Motions. Before he is got half way, The firſt tread of Men that he hears, *He hoped in his Mind* (ſays (*a*) *Homer*) *that 'twas a Meſſenger from* Hector *to recall him.*

The whole Book, where we have this Image, is nothing but one Picture of Fear in different Poſtures; The apprehenſions of diſtant Danger are very naturally expreſs'd in the *Grecian* Guard;

——— Cautious of ſurprize,
Each Voice, each Motion draw their ears and eyes;
(*b*) Each Step of paſſing feet increas'd th'affright.

(*a*) Ιλ. κ', 355. (*b*) *Il.* 10, 221---189.

This

This Deſcription ſeems to have been improv'd beyond the Original from [a] *Virgil's Achemænides*.

Any near Danger has more viſible Effects; The Motions of a Perſon, thus affected, are [b] broken and diſorder'd; his Colour comes and goes: His Eyes are [c] diſturb'd; he cannot bear to look [d] full on the Face of his Enemy: he approaches faintly, and winks even when he ſtrikes.

Fear has another ſtrange Property of *Magnifying* our Ideas of the Danger. When we are poſſeſs'd with it, we are apt, like *Soſia* in the Play, to take every Shadow for a Man, and every Man for a Giant. If the Danger be preſent, we think it greater than it is; and to its real Terrors, add a Thouſand that are only imaginary. Thus the Suitors view

---

[a] ——Vaſtos a rupe Cyclopas [*Æn.* 3, 648.
Proſpicio, ſonitumq; pedum, vocemq; tremiſco.

[b] ——Ex oculis ſe turbidus abſtulit. *Æ.* 11, 814.
———————— Tum pectore ſenſus
Vertuntur varii. Rutulos aſpectat & urbem,
Cunctaturq; metu, telumq; *inſtare tremiſcit*. 12, 916.

[c] Tum primum noſtri Cacum videre timentem
Turbatumque oculis.——————— 8, 223.

(d) ————'Ουκ ἐτάλασσας
Στήμεναι ἄντα, κατ' ὄσσε ἰδὼν δηΐων ἐν ἀϋτῇ,
'Ουδ' ἰθὺς μαχέσασθαι.————Ιλ. ρ', 169.

Ulyſſes,

Ulysses, when he is ready to revenge himſelf upon them: their Fears (*a*) aggravate every Fierceneſs of his Actions; they look upon him as more than human, as an incens'd deſtructive Deity.

If I miſtake not, there's a certain great Writer who calls Fear, *A natural Inebriation of the Mind*: it ſhews every thing Double: I know not what the *Mythologiſts* may teach; But this, in my Opinion, might account for the Multiplicity of *Cerberus*'s Heads, and all the Hands of *Briareus*.

There is ſomething very Expreſſive in a Thought of *Virgil*'s, if we might take it under this View:

——— Se Turni media inter millia vidit,
(*b*) *Hinc acies*, atque, *hinc acies* aſtare Latinas.

This ſpreading of any Danger in our Ideas may widen ſo far as to poſſeſs the whole Mind. Then it is, that it takes away all (*c*) Power of Action, even (*d*) of Flight; it fixes (*e*) the Eye entirely

---

(*a*) *Od.* 24, 201 to 208. (*b*) *Æn.* 9, 550.
(*c*) *Od.* 12, 245. (*d*) *Od.* 18, 284.
(*e*) ——— Subitus tremor occupat artus;
Diriguere oculi: tot Erinnys ſibilat hydris,
Tantaque ſe facies *aperit*. ——— *Æn.* 7, 448.

in

in one horrid Stare: and even (*a*) ſhuts up all the Senſes, to any other Object, but that of its Terror and Amazement; It is this Exceſs of Fear which, in any eminent Danger, makes a Perſon (*b*) think it impoſſible that he ſhould Eſcape; and it remains ſo Strong and Lively, that after he is got perfectly out of Danger, he can ſcarce perſwade himſelf, but that he is ſtill in the midſt of it——

——— With tim'rous Awe,
From the dire Scene th' exempted two withdraw,
Scarce ſure of life, look round, and trembling move
(*c*) To the bright altars of Protector *Jove*.

All theſe are Points which lie in common between Painting and Poetry; I wou'd willingly touch upon one thing more under the ſame View: I mean, thoſe pieces in Poetry which anſwer Copying in Painting; and each of which is really *the Picture of a Picture*.

You will give me leave by *Picture* here to underſtand any Artificial Images

---

(*a*) Ὣς ἔφατ', οὐδ' ἐσάκουσε πολύτλας δῖος Ὀδυσσεὺς, Ἀλλὰ παρήϊξεν &c. ——— Ιλ. θ', 98. See Note on *Odyſſey* 10, 295. (*b*) This ſort of Idea is ſtrongly expreſs'd in the *Odyſſey*.

Gods! ſhould the ſtern *Ulyſſes* riſe in might,
Thoſe gates would *ſeem too narrow* for thy Flight.

(*c*) *Od.* 22, 417—284. [18, 427—6, 385.

of

of things; from Embroidery, Embossing, or any other Method of expressing Nature by Likenesses of Art: And indeed 'tis of this kind, that all the Pictures spoken of in *Homer* are; and, I believe, all in *Virgil*. At least, what we call Painting now, was not the Painting of the *Homerick* Ages.

It is to the Honour of the Art (in this general Sense) that the Poets, when they are copying from Painting, generally exceed themselves. I believe there is not a more masterly Piece in all *Virgil's* Works, than his Copy of *Troilus*; Thus the same Hand in the Images of *Æneas's Shield*: As in that of *Achilles*, *Homer* has all the Life and Expression that Poetry is capable of.

In both of these, the Poets use a way of speaking in relation to Picture, which is very Strong and Emphatical; and which may shew the high Notions they entertain'd of this Art: They do not say, that theImages *seem* to perform such Actions; but talk of 'em as *real Life*: They say directly, that they Move, and Act, and Speak. The Criticks, who have blam'd some Boldnesses of this kind, shew only their own (*a*) Coldness, and

(*a*) See *Pope* and *Dacier* on the Shield of *Achilles*, *Il.* Book 18.

want

want of Taste. 'Tis a Figure as just as it is daring: it animates the Description; and where the Poet is (*a*) more cautious, he is less lively on that very Account.

My want of Skill, in this Noble Art, is the same disadvantage in viewing these *Poetical Pictures*, as want of a proper Light would be to the *Real*; but with all this Disadvantage, they seem extremely Beautiful: And I cannot resist the Temptation of setting one or two of 'em before you.

The Design on the *Shields* affords such a variety of Images exquisitely well wrought, and dispos'd so justly, that it would be perfectly Gothick and Barbarous to take them to Pieces. Ignorant as I am; The (*b*) young *Romulus*, and *Remus*, and (*c*) the *Genius* of the *Nile*, strike me particularly in the one; and in the other, The (*d*) *Ambuscade* and *Engagement*, the (*e*) still rural *Prospect*;

(*a*) Thus where *Europa* is said
——— Terras spectare relictas
Et comites clamare suas, tactumque vereri
Assilientis aquæ, timidasque reducere plantas:
One should forget it was only in *Picture*, did not the Poet take so much pains to inform us of it;
Ipsa *videbatur* terras &c ———
Verum taurum, freta vera *putaras*. Met. 6, 107.

(*b*) See *Æn.* 8, 634. (*c*) *Ibid.* 711. (*d*) See *Pope's Il.* 18, 595 to 626. (*e*) *Ibid.* 677.

and

and (*a*) the *Dance*, conſider'd as a Poetical Piece of Painting.

To what Perfection muſt Embroidery have arriv'd in *Homer*'s Days, if its Works could equal his Deſcriptions of them? How full of Life is (*b*) that Figure in *Ulyſſes*'s Robes? And, I ſuppoſe, the *Ceſtus* of *Venus* was of the ſame Nature, in which was——

——Ev'ry art, and ev'ry charm,
To win the wiſeſt, and the coldeſt warm:
Fond Love, the gentle vow, the gay deſire,
The kind deceit, the ſtill-reviving fire,
Perſwaſive ſpeech, and more perſwaſive ſighs,
(*c*) Silence that ſpoke, and eloquence of eyes.

Hercules's Belt, and the Deſcription of it in the *Odyſſey*, is the Reverſe of this. The Belt it ſelf perhaps was of a different Make, anſwerable to the Shield of *Achilles*; which, by the way, may intimate ſomething of an Art, that is now loſt, which (if you will allow me in a mere Conjecture of my own) ſeems to have been a ſort of *Moſaick-work of different Metals*; (*d*) Braſs, Stannum, Silver &c, intermixt with Gold; (*e*) all varied, and (*f*) ſhaded, ſo as to expreſs the diffe-

(*a*) *Il.* 18, 683 (*b*) *Od.* 19. 258---2[illegible] (*c*) *Il.* 14, 252---127. (*d*) See [illegible], 475 (*e*) *Ibid* 480. (*f*) *Ibid.* 549

R rent

rent Properties and Actions of the things describ'd: But whatever the materials were, the Workmanship certainly excell'd them greatly. Any one, to be convinc'd of this, need only turn his Eyes on the *Hercules* in *Ades*, where

Gloomy as night he stands, in act to throw
The aerial arrow from the twanging Bow.
Around his breast a wond'rous Zone is roll'd,
Where woodland Monsters grin in fretted Gold;
There sullen Lions sternly seem to roar,
The Bear to growl, to foam the tusky Boar:
There War and Havock and Destruction stood;
(a)And vengeful Murther, red with human blood.

These are all Copies: And I have done, if you will give me leave only to set *Virgil*'s *Troilus* before you; which is certainly as fine a Piece as any drawn by that great Hand:

——— *Amissis* Troilus *armis*
Infelix Puer, atque impar congressus Achilli,
Fertur equis, curruque hæret resupinus inani,
Lora tenens tamen: huic cervixq; comæq; trahuntur
(b) Per terram, & versa pulvis inscribitur hasta.

How beautiful does this look in the Poem and in the Picture? Yes, the Painter and the Poet have one and the same *Art*; or rather one and the same *Power of Creating.*

(a) *Od.* 11, 756---608. (b) *Æn.* 1, 482.

Aut

Aut utramque credes esse pictam:
Aut utramque credes esse veram.

I am extremely oblig'd to you (says *Philypsus*) for so various a View of these Beauties. Believe me, I have scarce known for some time, whether I was not got into some strange Picture-Gallery, where one meets every Moment with new Subjects of Admiration and Delight. The Misfortune is, You have only led me thorough by the hand; and given me a transient View of them: when I could have dwelt Hours upon admiring each by itself. 'Tis just like some Travelling Enjoyment of this kind; when we have been forc'd to run over whole Apartments furnish'd with Pieces by the greatest Masters, too numerous to be observ'd particularly; You have delighted me in haste; and I know not how it is, I find my self pleas'd and dissatisfied at the same time.

I am sure, says *Antiphaus*, I have dealt with you, like the *Connoisseurs*, which a Traveller often meets with in places, where there are the best Collections: Were you left to your Yelf, you would enjoy a thousand Beauties in them; but I must be plaguing you all the while with pointing out the most particular; tho', after all I know only where they ſtand, who they were drawn by, and what they repreſent.

But we forget, *Philypſus*, that we are at preſent half Travellers in earneſt: We are from home; and you ſee the Sun is juſt ſetting——No,——interrupted *Philypſus*, We have half an Hour good, at leaſt; And if you have any thing farther on this head, I beg you would favour me with it:——As you pleaſe, ſays *Antiphaus*.——You know, we have hitherto been viewing thoſe Points in which Poetry and Painting agree; there is one Method behind, which Poetry has of impreſſing its Images, peculiar to itſelf.——The Poet can imitate the Colours of the Painter; but the Painter can never imitate the Sounds of Poetry: You may *ſee* the Hero fall in Picture; but in the Poem you *ſee* him fall, and *hear* the Clang of his Arms.

Yes, *Philypſus*, there is a natural fitneſs in Sounds. Every Paſſion has its diſtinct Voice; each Action its proper Turn; and every Motion a particular Sound that may correſpond to it.

Only obſerve the difference in the Sound of theſe Lines; 'tis as ſenſible as that of the real Sounds, which they deſcribe:

describe: Compare this Couplet, of Mr. *Pope*,

(*a*) Trembling the spectres glide, and plaintive [vent
Thin hollow Screams along the deep descent.

With this of the same hand,

——— The string let fly,
(*b*) Twang'd short and sharp, like the shrill Swal-[low's cry.

Thus we might (*c*) compare in reading *Virgil* several Descriptions of Rivers: There we have the full course of the *Po*, and the windings of the *Tiber*, the (*d*) largeness of *Benacus*, the (*e*) slowness of the *Mincio*, the (*f*) murmuring of a Brook, and the broken (*g*) course of a River incumber'd with Men and Arms; in a word, every variety of streams that can be conceiv'd, all imag'd in the various Numbers and Cadence of his Verse.

In Poetry, the Bow *twangs*; the Arrow (*h*) *whizzes* thro' the Air; and (*i*)

(*a*) *Od.* 24, 6. (*b*) *Od.* 21, 449---411.
(*c*) *Fluviorum rex Eridanus.* *Georg.* 1, 482.
Saxosumque sonans Hypanis. *Georg.* 4, 370.
Or these ——— *Fluvio Tiberinus amœno*
Verticibus rapidis, & multa flavus arena
In mare prorumpit. *Æn.* 7, 32 ——— Fragosus
Dat sonitum saxis & torto vortice torrens *Æ.* 7, 567.
(*d*) *Georg.* 2, 160. (*e*) *Georg.* 3, 14. (*f*) *Georg.* 1, 109. (*g*) *Æn.* 1, 103. (*h*) *Od.* 21, 461. (*i*) *Il.* 1, 64.

the Quiver *rattles* on the Shoulder of the Warrior; Even the particular difference of the ſame ſort of Actions, is to be diſtinguiſh'd in the ſound of the Verſe; and the Javelin, that (*a*) *flies impetuous* from *Ulyſſes*, *languiſhes* in the hand of the Suitors. This very Circumſtance, as I take it, is beautifully deſcrib'd by the Tranſlator of *Vida*, among ſeveral other (*b*) excellent Images of the ſame Kind.

We do not only meet with a great Variety of theſe ſignificant Numbers in the *Odyſſey*; but are inſtructed too in the *Methods* of rendering our Numbers proper and ſignificant. Here we are taught how the Poet roughens his Verſe to imitate the Subject he is to expreſs. Thus the Note tells us that his Deſcription of the Sea abounds (*c*) "with the "harſheſt Letter our Language affords. "It is clog'd with Monoſyllables, that "the Concourſe of the rough Syllables, "might be more quick and cloſe in the "pronunciation, and the moſt open and "ſounding Vowel occur in every word, On the contrary, a gentle flowing Stream runs as eaſy and ſmoothly in the

(*a*) *Od.* 22, 292. (*b*) See *Pitt's Vida*, p. 108. &c. (*c*) See Note on *Od.* 12, 283.

those

Defcription: We then hear (*a*) "nothing "of thofe rough Confonants; Inftead of "them we meet with feveral Liquids, "and thofe Liquids are foften'd with a "multitude of Vowels.

What a violent and ftrong Motion does *Homer* give to *Sifiphus*'s Stone in its fall?

(*b*) αὖτις ἔπειτα πέδονδε κυλίνδετο λᾶας ἀναιδής.

Whence this Rapidity and Violence in the Numbers? (*c*) If we obferve it we find that "There is not one Monofylla- "ble in the Line, and but two Diffylla- "bles; Ten of the Syllables are fhort, "and not one Spondee in it, except one "that cou'd not be avoided in the clofe (which perhaps too may be of Service towards imaging the ftopping of its Courfe at laft) "There is no Hiatus or "Gap between word and word, no "Vowels left open to retard the Celerity "of it:" and yet, tho' the Motion be carried on with fuch a vehemence, one feems to fee the *bounding* of the Stone, as well as the *Impetuofity* of its Defcent.

I fhould think (tho' the Notes do not mention any thing of it) that the Tran-

(*a*) See Note on *Od.* 14, 1. (*b*) Οδ. λ', 597.
(*c*) See Note on *Od.* 11, 736.

flator

ſlator expreſſes this double Image in the Engliſh; when he makes the Stone

(a) —— Reſulting with a bound, [ground.
Thunder impetuous down, and ſmoak along the

At leaſt, In both we may ſay of the Verſification, as of the Stone it deſcribes;

Ipſa ſuis viribus ruit.

The oppoſites to theſe expreſs a Slowneſs and Difficulty of Motion; When a Hero ſtrains

—— Some rock's huge weight to throw,
(b) The line too labours, and the words move ſlow.

Thus is *Siſyphus* deſcrib'd in the former Picture;

With many a weary ſtep, and many a groan,
(c) Up the high hill he heaves a huge round ſtone.

Never was a Tranſlator more juſt to his Original; The Obſervation which has been made on the *Greek*, theſe Lines anſwer, will hit equally with the (d) *Engliſh* "The Verſes are clog'd with long "Syllables, and with Vowels open upon "one another; the very Words are

(a) *Od.* 11, 738. (b) Mr. *Pope's* Art of Criticiſm. (c) *Od.* 11, 736---594. (d) See Note on *Od.* 11, 736.

"heavy

" heavy, and as it were make reſiſtance " in the pronunciation.

In the ſame manner *Virgil* and *Homer* deſcribe the Labour of the Giants, when they endeavour to ſcale Heaven. (*a*) *Virgil*, cheifly by the openneſs of his Vowels: *Homer*, by the reſiſtance of his Syllables, and the pauſes of his Lines; and his Tranſlator, by ſlow Syllables, burthen'd with ſeveral Eliſions, cloſe upon one another.

The Numbers are thus minutely adapted to the Motions deſcrib'd by theſe great Maſters; And we need not wonder if they obſerve like Rules in Points of greater concern; Such are all Occaſions where they ſpeak the Language of the Paſſions: or endeavour to touch the Soul of the Reader either with Pleaſure or Pain.

(*a*) Ter ſunt *conati* imponere *Pelio* Oſſam
Scilicet, atq; Oſſæ frondoſum involvere Olympum.
Georg. 1, 282 Sec. Ed. *Ruæi.*

———Ἀθανάτοισιν ἀπειλήτην, ἐν Ὀλύμπῳ
Φυλόπιδα στήσειν πολυάϊκος πολέμοιο· [Ὄσσῃ
Ὄσσαν ἐπ' Οὐλύμπῳ μέμασαν θέμεν, αὐτὰρ ἐπ'
Πήλιον εἰνοσίφυλλον, ἵν' οὐρανὸς ἄμβατος εἴη.
Ὀδ. λ, 315.

Heav'd on *Olympus* tott'ring *Oſſa* ſtood;
On *Oſſa*, *Pelion* nods. ——— *Od.* 11, 388.

When

When *Homer* deſcribes any terrible Object, (*b*) "He rejects the more flowing "and harmonious Vowels, and makes "Choice of ſuch Mutes, and Conſonants "as load the Syllables: Then long weighty Sounds, and Words of many Syllables are proper; and often a deſign'd harſhneſs, unuſual pauſes, and a broken ſtructure in the verſe.

But the Lyre muſt be new tuned, when the Subject is agreeable or delightful. The Poet then ſoftens every Line (*b*) "with Vowels, and the moſt "flowing Semi-vowels: he rejects harſh "Sounds, and the Colliſion of rough "Words: The Tone of the Verſe muſt be neither ſerious, nor majeſtick; but rather qualified by as great a Frequency of ſhort Syllables, as can well be admitted, without rendring the Lines Weak and Effeminate: The Cadence is ſoft and gene his Words deſcend like a kind refr ſhing Shower; or like the Snow that melts in falling.

The *joyous Verſification* admits of more ſprightly Notes, and a greater Mixture (*c*) of Energy and Vigour: ſometimes ſhe riſes even to breakes, and pauſes:

(*a*) See Note on *Od.* 6, 153. (*b*) See Note on *Od.* 6, 193 [Mr. *Pope's* Ode on Muſick,
(*c*) Exulting in Triumph now riſe the bold Notes.

but

but they muſt be always, like thoſe in Muſick, pauſes of Delight: and the Verſe muſe ſpring on again, when it recovers itſelf, without loſing any thing of its Exultation and Vivacity. ——— Unleſs ſome (*a*) afflicting Theme breaks in, and turns our Thoughts away, to diſmal Scenes, where ſighs and melancholly Reign: The Muſe, compaſſionate, ſpeaks all in Tears, and moves with the ſame (*b*) ſlow Melancholly Air.

It is ſcarce to be imagin'd, *Philypſus*, how great the Powers of Sounds are, when adapted to the Subject and the Paſſion. For my part, I ſhould think that our very *Bodies* are diſpos'd to receive them; that this Frame of ours is like an Inſtrument ready tun'd; and when the proper Key is touch'd, our Nerves tremble and anſwer it with a

(*a*) As *Virgil* from the glories of *Rome*, to the death of *Marcellus*. *Æn.* 6.

(*b*) Quantos ille virum magnam Mavortis ad urbem
Campus aget gemitus! vel quæ, Tiberine, videbis
Funera, cum tumulum *præterlabere* recentem.
Æn. 6, 874.

This *Delay* alſo fixes the melancholly on ones Mind: and for the ſame reaſon *Repetition* ſeems to be particularly uſeful on theſe ſubjects:

——— Ut vultum vidit morientis & *ora*,
Ora modis, *Anchiſiades*, pallentia miris;
Ingemuit miſerans graviter. ——— *Æn.* 10, 823.

Kind

Kind of Musical Sympathy. How far this may reach in others, I know not; but as for my particular Make, 'tis strangely susceptible of such Impressions. After a Period set to Melancholy, I have been surpriz'd to find my Eyes full of Tears: There are some exquisite Lines which I can never read without a certain *Shivering* thorough my Blood, that I cannot express to you: I have felt my Spirits Burn within me, upon hearing a Point of War, well wrote; and have been almost ready to start from my Seat at the Poetical Sound of a Trumpet.

This Energy of Sounds, and the great and various Emotions they are capable of raising in our Breasts, may serve partly to excuse those Criticks, who are very particular in laying down Rules, as to this part of Versification; The Ancients, as well as Moderns, have left us whole Treatises upon it: and those who have wrote in a more general way, are very diffusive, when they come to this Part of their Subject. They speak to every the least Circumstance; and Readers, who have never thought over this Point, would be surpriz'd to find the great *Cicero* very industriously *settling Quantities*, and *measuring Words* fit for such and such a Period. They would wonder,

wonder, whence he is so peremptory for *Iambicks* on this Occasion; and on another, so great a Partizan for *Tribrachs*, and *Dactils*.

Why, seriously, says *Philypsus*, I have often thought him quite tedious on these particulars: The Orator, even the Critick, seem'd to be lost sometimes, and nothing but a mere Pedant appear in their room. I admire the force of Numbers (continu'd he) as much as any one; but when I have been reading the Rules at large in the Criticks, I could not help thinking them too minute and trifling. If a Man must be taken up thus in weighing Syllables and ranging of Vowels, what Elegance of Language can we expect, or what Life in his Compositions?

What you say (answer'd *Antiphaus*) is what, I believe, most Men think on this Occasion: and were a Poet always to be studying his Rules, such an Objection would be very powerful: But it is with this, which is only the Mechanism of Verse, as it is in the Mechanism of Writing. We must learn to draw the Figure of the Letters, and study how to form the particular Turn of each, before a Man can write down a whole Sentence; By use this knowledge grows familiar; We then write by a (*a*) sort of Instinct; and our Pen runs over each Letter, without our considering, distinctly at each which way we shall direct it. 'Tis much the same in these Arts of Versification. When we have learn't the force of Letters, and the Powers of Sound; when we know what Syllables are proper to express such a Motion, and what run of Verse hits such particular Images, Use makes the Mind ready in applying what is proper; and the Thought is as nimble in suggesting Words of a suitable Sound, as the Hand is in Motions proper to set down those words on our Paper.

But it will be half a life, perhaps, before the Poet can come to this Readiness ——I do not say it is to be acquir'd immediately, answer'd *Antiphaus*, but acquir'd in some Measure it must be, by any one who desires to be a true Poet: In the mean time, a Man may indulge his Vigour, he may compose his Lines with full Spirit, and set them to Musick afterwards; Let a Man write with Flame, if he will but correct at Leisure.

(*a*) See *Quintil. Instit.* Lib. 10. Cap. 7. Est igitur usus quidam irrationalis &c. Or Mr *Lock's Essay*. Lib. 2. Cap, 9. Sect. 9, and 10.

Besides:

Besides: this is not so difficult to be attain'd, as one wou'd imagine. The fitness of Sounds to things is natural: *Invention* itself will go some way in the Work; and where there is naturally (What we call) a *Good Ear*, Nature will do the Business almost without the help of Art. I do not speak this in a declamatory way, Good *Philypsus*; I imagine Fact and Experience will go a great way in proving what I say. A Man, who thinks vehemently, will speak swiftly; and when we are on a grave Point, our Words will of themselves be in a great Measure slow and weighty. This is yet plainer from the *Invention* of Languages; How many single Words are there in every Tongue, that have been originally cast in a proper Mould, and on the first Heat carried off the Images of things impress'd upon them? I was saying too, that the posture of the Mind at the time of Composing, will assist the turn of the Composition; And is this more absurd in particular Cases, than that the Temper of a People in general should affect their Language in the same manner? Yet has it been often observ'd that the Dispositions of a People are perceivable in that Turn of Words they chiefly delight in. Thus the *French*

Tongue is brisk and voluble: The *Germans* talk in vaſt Syllables and perpetual Conſonants: *Engliſh* is neither too ſoft, nor too rough: tho' our *Northerly* Situation inclines us rather to the latter: And, as the *Spaniard* is the moſt haughty of all Nations, their Language is the moſt Grand; it prides itſelf in firm Syllables, in a frequency of the fulleſt Vowel, and the moſt ſonorous Terminations of its Words.

Nature certainly forms us within for fit Sounds: We ſee every Day that even Brutes can expreſs their Paſſions by the *Tone* of their Voice; and is not an Intelligent Being as well qualified by Nature to adapt Sounds to his Sentiments?

Indeed they are thus adapted already in a Multitude of Inſtances; Our Language abounds with ſuch words; and in many Caſes we need only utter our Sentiments in the moſt common Expreſſions, to ſpeak with this Significance. What was it that led the firſt Inventors into this frequency of ſuch words? Was it Art, or the Natural Reſemblance, and their Obviouſneſs upon that Account? 'Tis in this Light we muſt underſtand our Maſter Critick, where he calls

calls Nature (*a*) "The great Original "and Mistress of propriety in the pre- "sent Point: It is she that leads us to "imitate things by Sound; and to ex- "press what we conceive, by Words "that are turn'd according to those "strong Likenesses, which we form in "our Minds.

'Tis plain the Use of Words is arbitrary: we might if we had a fancy for it, call any thing by any Name: Yet there is something from within, that has influenc'd all Nations so far, as to lead them to descriptive Sounds, in their giving Names to things; and that more frequently than one would readily imagine. What Nature has done in single Words the Poet carries on in Composition; Almost all the particular Names of Sounds themselves, for instance, are naturally significant in most Languages; as with us, the *Roaring* of Waves, the *Whistling* of Winds &c. Of such Words, assisted by a proper structure of Quantities, and a significant Cadence of Verse, the Poet makes an Hurricane by Land, or a Storm at Sea. Nature first presided in establishing those proper sounds, and still directs in the Assemblage of them.

(*a*) *Dion. Hal.* Περὶ Συνθέσεως, &c.

Hence it is that this Point takes ſuch a Compaſs in the Doctrine of the Criticks. Some of them, no doubt, carry the Matter too far, when they would require this Natural Significance of Sounds, to be kept up in every thing we write. Such was *Voſſius*. It would make you ſmile to hear ſome of his Fancies: He talks as if every Language, like that of his Favourites the *Chineſe*, ſhould be nothing but Muſick: He would have our very Actions all Tuned: A Soldier can't run the Gauntlet, but he muſt be (*a*) ſlaſh'd *in Time*; and his very (*b*) Barber muſt Shave him in a juſt proportion of *Dactils* and *Spondees*.

Hermogenes is perhaps more trifling, tho' in a graver manner: He queſtions *whether this ſort of Sounds be not preferable to the Sentiments in a Poem.* This is to oppoſe two Things, that are in the ſtricteſt Amity and Concord. Theſe

(*a*) The Ancients (ſays he) us'd Muſick in every thing; *Adeo quod ipſæ quoque plagæ ad numeros harmonicos ſontibus ingerebantur.* De Viribus Ryhmi. p. 47. (*b*) Non ſemel recordor me in ejuſmodi incidiſſe manus, qui quorumvis etiam canticorum motus ſuis imitarentur *pectinibus*; ita ut nonnunquam Iambos vel Trochæos, alias Dactylos vel Anapæſtos, nonnunquam Amphibraches aut Pæonas quàm ſcitiſſimè exprimerent; unde *haud mediocris oriebatur delectatio.* ib. p 62.

Sounds

Sounds do not, like the Modern, pretend to rival the Senſe; their whole Buſineſs is to make the Sentiments more ſtrongly perceiv'd, and more effective on the Mind.

I have heard it frequently objected to thoſe Gentlemen, the Criticks, that they find out ſeveral Beauties of this Kind in the Works of *Homer*, which he, never ſo much as dream't of in compoſing 'em. In many Caſes this may be true; and in many the Lines may be juſtly commended, and really ſignificant, tho' that particularBeauty might not be deſign'd in compoſing them: But thoſe, who can perſwade themſelves, that *Homer* never deſign'd any ſuch thing in his Writings, I ſhould think, might ſoon bring themſelves to believe (what has been ſo frequently produc'd as an inſtance of Abſurdity) that his Poems might be made by chance.

The Notes of Muſick in a good Compoſition are fitted to the Subject: And a good Copy of Verſes wrote for Muſick will be fitted for Notes. I cannot once doubt, that the firſt Stanza in Mr. *Pope*'s Ode for St. *Cæcilia*'s Day has a *deſign'd* Harmony all thorough it. 'Tis juſt the ſame Caſe with *Homer*'s Poems:

They

They were all made for Musick; and have been all sang to the Lyre.

As for my part, says *Philypsus*, I find Musick enough in them, even now, without the Lyrist. Neither have I any quarrel with the Criticks for giving me pleasure, and pointing out Beauties of this kind, whether design'd by *Homer* or not. But I wonder at one thing: while they speak of the Defect in this point perpetually, I never yet heard them speak of any Excess in it: 'Tis certain, that the greater Number of Poets err in neglecting the significant Turn of their Verses: but is there no erring too by an Affectation of it?

I thank you, (answer'd *Antiphaus*) for putting me in mind of this particular. Undoubtedly there may be faults on both sides: Even in the Poem before us I imagine, this is sometimes carried too far, and sometimes us'd improperly: The Infirmness of a Couplet, mention'd on another Occasion, agrees with the thing describ'd, and may perhaps be blameable on that very Account.

(a) His loose head tottering as with wine opprest
Obliquely drops, and nodding knocks his breast.

(a) *Od.* 18, 282--239.

Terrible

Terrible Images have ſomething engaging; and the Mind takes a ſecret Pleaſure even in *Melanchelly: Diſagreeable* (*a*) objects alone are the worſe for being well deſcrib'd: A Poet is to reject, as well as to chuſe; 'Tis want of Art to ſet every thing in a ſtrong Light: and there are many Objects, which if they muſt have a place at all, require at leaſt to be flung into Shades.

If this be true, there are ſome few Images of this ſort, which I think are drawn too ſtrongly, or too laviſhly:

(*b*) Down dropt he groaning ———
(*c*) He ſaid: chill horrors ſhook my ſhiv'ring Soul.
(*d*) They curſe their cumbrous pride's unweildy [weight.
(*e*) There wallowing warm &c.

To me the Screaming of the Ghoſts, as deſcrib'd at the end of the *Eleventh Odyſſey*, is rather *diſagreeable* than *dreadful*:

Swarms of Spectres roſe from deepeſt Hell,
With bloodleſs viſage and with hideous Yell,
They ſcream, they ſhriek; ſad groans and diſmal [ſounds
(*f*) Stun my ſcar'd Ears, and pierce hells utmoſt [bounds.

(*a*) *Longinus* condemns a Paſſage in *Heſiod* on this very Account: de *Subl.* Cap. 9. (*b*) *Od.* 14, 473---425. (*c*) *Od.* 4, 725---538. (*d*) *Od.* 1, 214---165. (*e*) *Od.* 4, 547---405. (*f*) *Od.* 11, 782---632.

I leave this to your judgment; for it is very difficult, in these Cases, to discern the *True* from the *Faulty*: A *harshness* of Sounds is often proper and significant; but when and how far, is a knot that I will not pretend to untye.

I beg leave to repeat a Passage from the *Iliad*, in which some of the Lines may be strain'd too much, under this notion of rendering them significant:

First march the heavy Mules, securely slow,
O'er hills, o'er dales, o'er crags, o'er rocks they go:
Jumping, high o'er the shrubs, of the rough ground,
Rattle the clatt'ring cars, and the shockt axles bound.
But when arriv'd at *Ida*'s spreading woods
(Fair *Ida*, water'd with descending floods)
Loud sounds the Axe, redoubling strokes on strokes;
On all sides round the Forest hurls her Oakes
Headlong. Deep-echoing groan the thickets brown;
(*a*) Then rustling, crackling, crushing, thunder down.

This last Verse in particular may be an Instance of employing descriptive Sounds too thick upon one another; but this, if it be a fault, is such an one as in the present state of Poetry, requires an unusual Eminence in the Writer, to be capable of committing it.

'Tis much more frequent among our Poets to neglect the Sentiments in their Versification; to give up the significant

(*a*) *Il.* 23, 147--120.

Structure

Structure of Words, for mere harmony and softness of Verse; and even to make use of Numbers contrary to the Image or Passion they are describing; tho' to describe Actions of Rapidity, for instance, in slow solemn Measures, is as absurd, as for an Actor to scold, or rant, with the tone and steadiness of a Philosopher.

We have not time, *Philypsus*, otherwise I should have ventur'd on some farther Faults of our Versification: but I must not now run out into Complaints on the frequent *Consonants* and frequent *Elisions*, multiplied so much in our Verses, tho' both ought to be particularly guarded against, in a Language naturally overladen with them:——On the neglect of *Measure*, and taking all Syllables whether long or short to be of Equal Time: and the Lameness and Inequality from hence in Verses of the same kind: ——The discord of the *Emphasis* or Accent, and of the *Pauses*:——the repeated *Cadence*, and continued *Likeness* of Sound. I need only mention some other Identities of Sound, as all middle and double Rhimes, and all that are alike for two Couplets together. And methinks, *Philypsus*, as all these likenesses of Sound would be given up at the first word, unless there be some particular Reason for

for retaining that fashionable jingle at the close of our Verses, we may even reckon that as bad as the rest. I should have said something on this: but 'tis no great matter; since it stands condemn'd over and over by the greatest Criticks among the Modern. For my part, I'le talk no more of it, that we may go in Humour to our Claret.——I begin to wish my self in your Parlour. The Evening shuts in apace. Come, good *Philypsus*, let us be going, I beseech You.

FINIS.

9780371817490

SD - #0015 - 110222 - C0 - 229/152/23 - PB - 9780371817490 - Gloss Lamination